VERSIONS OF THE PAST

Versions of the Past

THE HISTORICAL IMAGINATION
IN AMERICAN FICTION

Harry B. Henderson III

New York   Oxford University Press   1974

042630

For Andy

FOREWORD

A persisting view of American literature is that it lacks a sense of history. D. H. Lawrence set the tone and theme of much later criticism; in the 1920's he portrayed the classic American writers as running away from themselves, fleeing the essential realities of "place," inventing ingenious but duplicitous myths of escape. Critics since have fashioned a truly massive engine of interpretation based on the supposed anti-historical streak in the native literary imagination.

Certainly against the detailed social features of European literature American fiction does seem eccentric, enormously rich in invention as if to compensate for a thinness in detail. If it takes a lot of history to produce a little literature, as Henry James observed regarding Hawthorne, and if history had so far deposited only a meager crust here, how can the writer be blamed for searching out alternatives to the novel of social and historical association? And at a deeper level, if the whole culture was geared to think of itself as "new," to take its bearings from a "break" with Europe, if the past was seen as all that America was not, then writers could hardly be expected to think differently. Even the image of the past seemed to be removed from the process of history, stripped of specific associations, transformed into idea, into a state of consciousness. It is telling that in his famous work on the historical novel, Georg Lukács mentions only one American, Cooper, and then only briefly.

Of course to deny history, to hate it, curse it, wish it away—all these are attitudes toward history; they contain implicit assumptions about the connection between past and present, about the passage of time, whether it is continuous or discontinuous, linear or cyclical, and about whether man can affect the direction. It is impossible to avoid having an attitude toward history. Kenneth Burke, making this point, showed that in order to see such attitudes in literature you first have to see the literature itself as historical, as occurring within a context, a process, a set of circumstances that gives the writer something to think about and some leading terms to use in his thinking.

The importance of Harry Henderson's book is that it recognizes historical thinking in American fiction where it had not been seen before. He writes that "a significant tradition of historical fiction in America has gone almost unnoticed." What has gone unnoticed is not just the few attempts to write historical novels on the model of Walter Scott, but, much more significantly, the many instances of a complex and imaginative thinking about history, about a real and definite past, in many of the classics of American literature. Thus Henderson treats works like *Satanstoe*, *The Scarlet Letter*, *Billy Budd*, *A Connecticut Yankee in King Arthur's Court*, *The Grandissimes*, *The Red Badge of Courage*, *The Financier*, *Absalom! Absalom!*, *The Sot-Weed Factor*, *The Invisible Man*, and *Armies of the Night* "as though they belonged in significant respects to the same literary category." They are all deliberate responses to a specific history, and to the writer's sense of pressure, of dilemma, in the present. They all, in some measure, look to the past for evidence of typical human behavior and for an explanation of the present. Henderson's book compels us to reconsider the view that American writing has been deficient in a sense of history.

We are fortunate to have this book, particularly at this time, when interest in a social and historical approach to literature is growing. Henderson gives us some genuinely new readings of books that had seemed already fixed in the canon with canonical interpretations. His discussions of Hawthorne, Melville, Mark Twain and Stephen Crane will need to be taken into account; these writers appear here in a fresh light.

Moreover, Henderson reaches his interpretations through a method that equally deserves our attention. The study of literature from a historical point of view has floundered in the past generation on what seemed an inescapable dilemma. We have been used to thinking of literature as an "intrinsic" activity, independent of connections between the artist and his society, thus calling for an "intrinsic" criticism. In a changed atmosphere, affected by the reintroduction of Marxist ideas into Anglo-American criticism, this idea is being questioned. But the dilemma remains: if the relations between a text and the social experience of writer and reader are in fact necessary rather than contingent, how can criticism do justice to both the text and its context? How to locate the connections, to situate the work? How, in short, can criticism become historical without violating the aesthetic integrity of the text?

It should be said that the dilemma has vexed Anglo-American critics more than it has Continental critics, who are accustomed to thinking of literature as a form of consciousness among other forms rather than as a discrete structure of words. Henderson profits from his reading of such critics as Lukács, Lucien Goldmann, and the American Kenneth Burke. And from them he learns that the dualism of "extrinsic" and "intrinsic" might be overcome by the recognition (which comes ultimately from Hegel) that history is itself a form of consciousness, an "imaginative ordering." That is, instead of placing the literary work in a measurable relation to an "outside" reality, Henderson identifies the historical imagination by focusing on what the writer himself conceived history to be, on how he orders events, and what assumptions guide his ordering.

The book opens with an enlightening analysis of the major nineteenth-century historians, from Motley and Bancroft to Henry and Brooks Adams, in order to reconstruct two major frames of reference (or, in Burke's terminology, "frames of acceptance"), the "progressive" and the "holist." These are, in Henderson's words, "interlocking constellations of assumptions"; they hold together ideas regarding the nature of historical time and the possibilities of action, as well as ideas regarding the basis of social cohesion. They are abstract models, something like Max Weber's "ideal types," and Henderson uses them as tools of analysis, as convenient devices for describing key elements in a writer's thinking about history.

At the same time, the frames have a wide currency in the culture, and so their appearance within the conceptual apparatus of a writer links him to a body of thought in his society. Henderson has impressive abilities as an intellectual historian, but the instinct of the literary critic prevails, and he scrupulously avoids imposing the structure of the frames upon specific texts; in his discussions the frames dissolve into literary detail. He writes that the frames "should not be considered static patterns of ideas and responses. The balance of elements from the two frames is not determined in a vacuum but rather by the creative needs of the writer as he shapes his work."

The "progressive" frame holds that society moves steadily forward toward the fulfillment of ideals like freedom and justice; heroic action consists in furthering these ends. The "holist" frame denies that such ideals, which it sees as extra-historical, can play a decisive role in history; it credits culture, manners, the specificities of time and place, as elements resisting change. Along with members of their culture, writers tended to perceive the historical situations which provide themes for their fiction from within these frames, or to combine elements of each. The frames mediate the way Cooper represents the Anti-Rent agitation, how Hawthorne responds to the reform movements of his day, how Melville deals with social unrest and rebellion, how Stephen Crane translates the Civil War into a parable of naturalism, while remaining outside the structures of either frame.

The most impressive sections of the book are, I find, the chapters on Hawthorne and Melville. Henderson reverses the typical approach which sees *The Scarlet Letter* and *Billy Budd* as mythic works by showing that the authors confront critical issues in the history of their society, issues concerning freedom, authority, the continuity of tradition, and the consequences of defiance. He shows that in these works the authors engage the frame of acceptance themselves, are alive to inadequacies in each, and test their own assumptions against the pressure of complex experience. Unlike *A Connecticut Yankee*, which Henderson sees as collapsing in the face of Mark Twain's inability to modify his progressive outlook, the historical works of Hawthorne and Melville contain their contradictions and conclude in ambiguity rather than neat resolutions.

A summary does not convey the high degree of interest Henderson generates in his analyses. The book is written with authority, ranges widely in American and European literature, and will be recognized, I am certain, as opening a new direction. It poses large and challenging questions. What are the sources of the two cardinal frames? How do we account for their hold upon the literary imagination and for their persistence? Can we find a similar set of mediations in the fiction of contemporary life, as in, say, the "realism" of Howells, Frederic, Fuller? Has the long poem in America been the vehicle of corresponding historical thinking, and does the difference in mode result in differences in conception? Interest in questions of this sort, questions about literary genres and their social origins, is strong at present, and Henderson's book makes a valuable contribution.

The book was barely completed when Harry Henderson died in an automobile accident in 1972. Although final revisions were left to other hands, the text remains faithful to the scope and subtlety of his thought, and to the wit, the personal warmth, and the mature seriousness that marked his teaching and conversation. Henderson wrote as he spoke, with quiet, unassuming reasonableness, and with understated but unmistakable conviction. The tone of the book is modest, but that should not mislead readers. The argument breaks decisively with formulations that have prevented the social and historical elements in American literature from being recognized. Henderson attempts a correction of vision. His book makes us realize again how much he is missed.

Alan Trachtenberg

Cambridge, England
January 1974

A Note About the Author and This Book

Harry Henderson did not live past 30. A stranger in a hurry turned him into an anonymous accident statistic. This book was his first major scholarly work, the fruit of ten years of thought and study.

His absorbing interest in American history and literature unified his entire life, beginning in the first grade with his writing of a history of the United States and continuing through his work as a scholar, teacher, and political activist with the American Independent Movement in New Haven. The last thing that happened to him while a member of the Yale faculty was his arrest on a picket line in support of striking service employees at Yale. Intellectually he had an affinity for the ironists and Marxists—among them Kenneth Burke, George Lukács, Karl Mannheim, Thorstein Veblen, Henry Adams, and especially Herman Melville—and to contemporary "tough guy" writers, Nelson Algren, Dashiell Hammett, and Norman Mailer. He contributed regularly to AIM's paper, *Modern Times*, while teaching and sharing in the care of his infant son Andrew.

When Harry died he had nearly completed the manuscript of this book. The major portion was finished virtually as it appears. The last two chapters, dealing with twentieth-century American writers, had been roughly drafted and loosely assembled with connecting passages in note form. Harry's father and I spent weekends for a year revising the final chapters and polishing the entire text, aided by consultations with Norman Holmes Pearson, Alan Trachtenberg, Oxford University Press editors James Raimes and Stephanie Golden, and especially Harry's friend, Peter O'Connell. But it is Harry's father, a writer, and I, a Russian scholar, who must take responsibility for any errors.

Elizabeth Henderson

New Haven, Conn.
May 1974

PREFACE

THE historical novel, as a genre, has never won the place it deserves in literary history and critical esteem because it possesses two salient faults in the eyes of most students of literature: impurity and vulgarity. The meaning of what some have called the "non-literary" impurity of the historical novel is the subject of this study. The vulgarity of the genre—the steady popularity of the historical novel over a century and a half, punctuated by fads when the historical novel has been the dominant middle-brow reading entertainment—perhaps has been a worse barrier to critical understanding.[1] Aristotle defined tragedy through an examination of the finest specimens of that dramatic form which his civilization had produced. The historical novel has been interpreted with astonishing consistency by a normative method, which takes the most mediocre, rather than the best, as the most representative. Alternatively, it has been glossed as "the novel as written by Scott," a formula which is not of much aid when one is attempting to consider writers who may justly be said to have a genius of their own: Tolstoy, Dickens, Flaubert, and Manzoni are some of the most obvious nineteenth-century masters. And yet the vulgarity of the genre is also a source of vigor, for the popularity of the historical novel has tempted the art of a significant number of major novelists, from the early nineteenth century to the present time.

This has been especially true in America, where in the nineteenth century virtually every major novelist (with the partial exception of James) wrote historical fiction. What are the consequences for critical understanding of grouping for study the historical fiction of major writers, of analyzing the genre in terms of the great and near-great rather than the best-selling mean? I propose to concentrate on the historical novels of such writers as Cooper, Hawthorne, Melville, Twain, Crane, and Faulkner in this study; to treat *Satanstoe, The Scarlet Letter, Billy Budd, A Connecticut Yankee in King Arthur's Court, The Red Badge of Courage* and *Absalom! Absalom!* as though they belonged in significant respects to the same literary category.

I have selected these books and essentially defined the form of the historical novel for this book in the most obvious and least controversial way possible. All these works, as well as most of the other novels treated, are "set" in the unexperienced past, in the world that existed before the author was born. While this is restrictive, it is not my intention to propose a prescriptive, universal definition of the form of the historical novel. Similarly I shall not attempt to discuss the metamorphosis of the American historical imagination in poetry and drama. However, since my concern is with the historical imagination of major novelists, I have also examined some novels of contemporary social change that place a specifically historical perspective on events that the author has lived through. These novels of "contemporary history" lack the particular characteristic, which I shall discuss in the Introduction, of creating a "whole" imaginative world which belongs to the novel of the past. Yet their inclusion is justified by the new twentieth-century emphasis, first apparent in Henry Adams' *Democracy*, on history evolving through the present and shaping the future. Among such novels are *U.S.A.*, in which John Dos Passos' "newsreel" technique highlights the rise to dominance of modern industrial conglomerates; *Invisible Man*, in which Ralph Ellison attempts to find in black American history guidelines for contemporary black struggles; and *Armies of the Night,* in which Norman Mailer frankly presents "the novel as history" and "history as a novel."

Most of this effort to explore the historical imagination in American novels is concerned with the nineteenth century, since historical themes were more central to the development of the American culture at that time than in the years since the advent of naturalism at the turn of the century. Indeed, only Faulkner, in the twentieth century, has brilliantly demonstrated a new depth and significance in historical imagination.

I have carried out this study because the normative definition of the historical novel has produced, for the most part, critical approaches which are well adapted only to pedestrian fiction. Ernest Leisy's splendidly complete survey *The American Historical Novel* (1950) treats these novels as merely "fictionalized" history and categorizes them according to the events they are supposed to portray.[2] The essays in David Levin's *In Defense of Historical Literature* (1967), though much more selective in focusing on major figures only, maintain the same essential attitude towards the relationship of history and "creative" literature as does Leisy.[3] For both, history is first of all a body of "knowledge" acquired by a more or less scientific method. The historian—as Levin discusses him in his earlier book, *History as Romantic Art* (1959), presents this supposedly objective knowledge dressed in the language and forms of his imagination, or of the imagination of the "age." [4] The hierarchy is clear: historical knowledge precedes rhetorical art. This positivistic conception of history, I would submit, is inadequate for the appreciation of great works of the historical imagination, whether novels, plays, verse, or "objective" scientific history. The only thorough theoretical study of the genre, Georg Lukács' formidable *The Historical Novel* (1937), owes much of its excellence precisely to its author's central concern with the problematical nature of the perception of historical reality.[5] My hope in this study is to create an appreciation of the self-awareness and complexity of the historical imagination of American writers.

In dealing with a topic as seemingly eccentric as this one, I am particularly grateful for the interest and encouragement of the advisors and critics I have had, and particularly aware of intellectual debts which I cannot begin to acknowledge. This book owes its completion as well as much of its inspiration to its sponsor as a doctoral thesis, R. W. B. Lewis, who has helped me generously at every stage. The germ of the idea for the approach to history and literature undertaken here has grown from a seminar taught by Ralph Ellison at the University of Chicago some years ago. Professor Walter P. Metzger of Columbia University gave me direction in the historical and biographical research on Melville. I have benefitted greatly from the valuable suggestions of Norman Holmes Pearson and A. N. Kaul during the writing of the original version of the book, and Richard Blau, Richard O. Boyer, and Jay Leyda were kind enough to read and criticize all or parts of the whole manuscript before the final rewriting.

New Haven, Conn.   H.B.H. III
January, 1971

Notes

1. Cf. James D. Hart, *The Popular Book: A History of America's Literary Taste* (Berkeley and Los Angeles: University of California Press, 1961), especially chapters V, XI, and XIV.
2. Ernest E. Leisy, *The American Historical Novel* (Norman: University of Oklahoma Press, 1950).
3. David Levin, *In Defense of Historical Literature* (New York: Hill and Wang, 1967).
4. David Levin, *History as Romantic Art* (New York: Harbinger, 1963).
5. Georg Lukács, *The Historical Novel* (Boston: Beacon, 1963), first published in the U.S.S.R. in 1937.

CONTENTS

VERSIONS OF THE PAST

Chapter One

INTRODUCTION: THE AMERICAN
HISTORICAL IMAGINATION

HE development of a significant tradition of historical fiction in America has gone almost unnoticed by scholars and critics, and yet the reasons for this neglect are not difficult to discover. Initially, American writers felt that the nation had no history, no sense of the past comparable to that of European nations. Seventeenth- and eighteenth-century American writers saw the Past as something that existed only abroad, and if anything, America seemed to represent a decisive break with the Past. This idea has persisted down to the present day, for in addition to sharing the conventional disdain for the historical novel as a low, mixed form, students of American culture have seen a special implausibility in the notion that the American historical imagination could produce and sustain a native literature of vigorous artistic growth. And it must be admitted that American literature has not been remarkable for an assured presentation of complex social relationships. Almost sixty years after Henry James complained of the inorganic relationship of Hawthorne's work to the thinly textured society of the older writer's day, Lionel Trilling could protest that as yet "we do not have the novel that touches significantly on society, on manners." [1] And Richard Chase could cite this same weakness of social perception among American writers as the cause

for what he defined as the true form of the American novel: no
novel at all, but a romance with distinctive elements of idyll and
melodrama.[2] Without a strong imaginative grasp of the intricacy
of their contemporary society, how much more deficient must
American writers have been when confronting society in the perspective of time?

Many of the masters of American literature seem to give evidence not only of an impoverished consciousness of society, but of
a profound inability to respond creatively to the idea of historical
continuity. The apprehension of history was especially problematical in nineteenth-century America, where the sense—perhaps one
should say the belief in the sense—of a schism with the past was
exceptionally powerful. Henry Nash Smith and R. W. B. Lewis
have exposed the attraction for American writers of the belief in
the possibility of a new start. Indeed, the prevailing Edenic metaphor of nineteenth-century American literature—featuring the society's innocence, its freedom from the corrupt societal forms of
Europe, its opportunity to develop its own way—expressed an intellectual repudiation of the emotional grip and power of the
Past. This inevitably complicated the stance of American writers
towards the very notion of history.

In what is in a sense the first archetypal American historical
novel, *Letters from an American Farmer* (1782), Crèvecoeur saw
the Past invading idyllic America, betraying the New World to
history. The *Letters* have been in part misunderstood because of
a failure to read the work as a formal whole—an epistolary romance of ideas. The varying personae of the author, which include
the simple husbandman, the educated and affluent patron, and
the Russian visitor, proclaim the intended artifice of the work, as
do the classical parables of the Farmer's anecdotes. The ideas—
about the nature of man and his place in the ecology of the world,
the role of self-interest in political economy, the consciousness of
history—are the chief "characters," acting out the episodic tragedy of the New World.

The *Letters* are usually read for the pastoral charm and physiocratic democracy of the early letters, which appear in such seemingly bizarre contrast to the dark tone of the later epistles. The central metaphor of the first eight letters is the figure of man as a plant, and the central image is of his culture—whether in Pennsylvania or the whaling towns of Nantucket and Martha's Vineyard —growing to resemble the natural environment upon which it thrives. The pastoral tradition exemplified here, which has been so fully traced by Leo Marx, can exist as a literary convention only in the face of a "civilized" counter-society, a standard of sophistication which the rustic implicitly rejects.[3] Crèvecoeur introduces "civilization" in his portrait of Charleston in the famous Letter IX, the "gay capital" where the "chosen race eat, drink, and live happy, while the unfortunate one grubs up the ground, raises indigo, or husks the rice, exposed to a sun full as scorching as their native one, without the support of good food, without the cordials of any cheering liquor." [4] In contrast to the pastoral ecology, which had relied on man's self-interest to bring about the good of the community, Crèvecoeur now finds that there is no innate propensity of man's nature, guided by his interest and unhampered by ancient institutions, to be benevolent. "Is there, then," he asks, "no superintending power who conducts the moral operations of the world, as well as the physical?" [5] If man is not an intrinsic part of *natural* history, how can he come to terms with the known history of the race?

The history of the earth! Doth it present anything but crimes of the most heinous nature, committed from one end of the world to the other? We observe avarice, rapine, and murder, equally prevailing in all parts. History perpetually tells us of millions of people abandoned to the caprice of the maddest princes, and of whole nations devoted to the blind fury of tyrants. Countries destroyed, nations alternately buried in ruins by other nations, some parts of the world beautifully cultivated, returned again into their pristine state, the fruits of ages of industry, the toil of thousands in a short time destroyed by a few!

. . . We certainly are not that class of beings which we vainly think ourselves to be; man, an animal of prey, seems to have rapine and the love of bloodshed implanted in his heart, nay, to hold it the most honourable occupation in society; we never speak of a hero of mathematics, a hero of knowledge or humanity, no, this illustrious appellation is reserved for the most successful butchers of the world.[6]

The ninth letter concludes with the "farmer's" harangue on history and the stark description of the execution by slow torture of a rebellious slave. The pastoral turns to tragedy as the protagonist —not merely a man but the ideal of a society "better" than that of Europe—is pursued by the Nemesis of History. The Serpent has entered the Garden through the offices of Man's cherished self-interest. Significantly, Crèvecoeur's tenth letter describes two snakes fighting insensately to the death. In this new awareness of history, the pastoral charm of nature is stripped away and only brutal struggle remains.

The last letter, "Distresses of a Frontier Man," appears to be the product of a radically different order of imagination from the other letters, but is, in fact, the fulfillment of Crèvecoeur's dark intuition of the fate of American society. In this letter the belief that a benevolent self-interest would exempt America from the fate of the Old World is dissolved. The New World cannot escape history, and selfish warfare on the frontier *is* History for Crèvecoeur. The plan of the Farmer to flee to the wilderness to escape the holocaust is prophetic of the fate of the notion of history itself. The nineteenth-century American would never be able simply to accept history as the extension of the present into the past.

History invades not only the reality of the American writer, but also his imagination. Thoreau reflected this urgent intrusion of the past most tellingly in *A Week on the Concord and Merrimack Rivers* (1849), in which he constantly relates the geographical places he visits in his travel narrative to the early Indian and frontier history of the region. This theme reaches a climax on the penultimate day of the trip when Thoreau relates the turn-of-the-eighteenth-century tale of two women and a boy escaping from Indians after having murdered ten of their captors. Midway through the tale, Thoreau adroitly adopts the present tense:

Early this morning this deed was performed, and now, perchance, these tired women and this boy, their clothes stained with blood, and their minds racked with alternate resolution and fear, are making a hasty meal of parched corn and moose-meat, while their canoe glides under these pine roots whose stumps are still standing on the bank. They are thinking of the dead whom they have left behind on that solitary isle far up the stream, and of the relentless living warriors who are in pursuit. Every withered leaf which the winter has left seems to know their story, and in its rustling to repeat it and betray them. An Indian lurks behind every rock and pine, and their nerves cannot bear the tapping of a woodpecker. . . . On either side, the primeval forest stretches away uninterrupted to Canada, or to the "South Sea"; to the white man a drear and howling wilderness, but to the Indian a home, adapted to his nature, and cheerful as the smile of the Great Spirit.

While we loiter here this autumn evening, looking for a spot retired enough, where we shall quietly rest to-night, they thus, in that chilly March evening, one hundred and forty-two years before us, with wind and current favoring, have already glided out of sight, not to camp, as we shall, at night, but while two sleep one will manage the canoe, and the swift stream bear them onward to the settlements, it may be, even to old John Lovewell's house on Salmon Brook to-night.[7]

The mixture of tenses suggests a complete imaginative merging of historical past and perceiving present. Notice especially Thoreau's description of how "their canoe glides under these pine roots whose stumps are still standing on the bank." Yet Thoreau does not point the superficial moral of the comparative brevity of the American historical experience. Rather he maintains that despite the imaginative immediacy of the episode, it comes to us from a primordial period. "From this September afternoon, and from between these now cultivated shores, those times seemed more remote than the dark ages." [8] On looking at a brightly illuminated picture of Concord of the later eighteenth century, he finds "that I had not thought the sun shone in those days, or that men lived in broad daylight then." He concludes: "The age of the world is great enough for our imaginations." [9] He might also have said, the age of the New World.

The immediacy of experience of the past expressed by Thoreau is one of the central problems of the aesthetics of historical fiction. As one examines the performances of novelists as "historians," one cannot simply seek their "sources" as though they compiled their works in what R. G. Collingwood called "scissors and paste" fashion.[10] Rather, one must start from the assumption that all true history involves an imaginative ordering of materials in an attempt at the recreation of experience. Claude Lévi-Strauss has suggested one possible explanation of the way this experience is recreated in his comparison of history with myth:

On the one hand, a myth always refers to events alleged to have taken place long ago. But what gives the myth an operational value is that the specific pattern described is timeless; it explains the present and the past as well as the future. This can be made clear through a comparison between myth and what appears to have largely replaced it in modern societies, namely, politics. When the historian refers to the French Revolution, it is always as a sequence of past happenings, a non-reversible series of events the remote consequences of which may still be felt at present. But to the French politician, as well as to his followers, the French Revolution is both a sequence belonging to the past—as to the historian—and a timeless pattern which can be detected in the contemporary French social structure and which provides a clue for its interpretation, a lead from which to infer future developments.[11]

The essential, unexceptionable definition of myth maintains that it is a traditional, communal story. The Indian tales of *A Week on the Concord and Merrimack* are this kind of traditional history, yet they are not merely local, but national in their communal resonance, and belong to the national legend of expansion into the wilderness as surely as do Filson's *Narrative* of Boone, the novels of Cooper, and the works of Parkman. So too with the traditional apprehension of such other national properties as Puritan society, the American Revolution, the Plantation South, the Civil War: the novels of Hawthorne, Melville, Crane, and Faulkner project the personal vision of the author in a context of communal post-knowledge. History becomes the modern myth, a collection of traditional tales which are timebound yet possess contemporary relevance and emotional force. This gives historical fiction its special qualities.

But unlike the writers of Europe, who had a vast array of national, regional, and institutional mythology and a rich literary tradition to draw upon, the nineteenth-century American writers who attempted the imaginative use of the American past were confronted with special problems. One was the belief, exemplified by Crèvecoeur, that America was the New World. Another was the rapidity of change and growth of the society. Moreover, the vast wilderness of the West, the democratic ideals that guided the formation of the Republic and its institutions, the continuing mass migrations from diverse European cultures, all contributed to the psychological need to formulate unifying myths characteristic of the new nation. In this period writers selected and shaped those elements of history that created a usable past for America.

A study of historical fiction which concentrates on major writers should have as its aim above all the enhanced appreciation and sharpened judgment of the individual works for their own sakes. There is no inevitability about any particular critical approach to this literary phenomenon which stands at the juncture of history and art. Yet there are, I believe, varying degrees of appropriateness among the approaches which have been so far advanced. The foremost of these views historical fiction as the literary representation of a philosophy or quasi-philosophy. At its simplest level, the philosophical critic might analyze Cooper, for example, as a Romantic, and discuss the evidence of "Romantic" concepts in his work. Roy Harvey Pearce offers a history-of-ideas variation of the philosophical approach in his *Savagism and Civilization*, in which he is much more analytic about the "ideas" that writers like Cooper express than the critic who starts from a literary-historical category, but inevitably presents a more disembodied and one-sided impression of the work of art.[12]

These "philosophical" approaches share the unspoken assumption that the genuinely creative artist expresses himself in terms of his *Zeitgeist* but does not himself reflect deeply on the "ideas" he has adopted. A rather different "philosophical" approach is exemplified in two excellent books on Twain, Roger B. Salomon's *Twain and the Image of History* and Henry Nash Smith's *Mark Twain's Fable of Progress*, both of which maintain cogently that Twain held uneasily but consciously to an ideology of progress and that his intellectual doubts of this dominant theory are evidenced in his work.[13]

I have several reservations about these "philosophical" methods, notwithstanding their comparative fertility in this otherwise neglected field. First of all, it is difficult to gain much insight from them into writers whose thought cannot be easily reduced to a popular ideology. What of the ambiguous Hawthorne, Melville, Faulkner? Secondly, there is a loss of proportion when we *start* from, say, Twain the thinker rather than Twain the artist. Novelists—perhaps especially American novelists—are not necessarily to be proposed as profound philosophers because their novels contain profound insights into the human condition. Finally and most seriously, the "philosophical" approach tends to perpetuate the attitude referred to earlier which would see the novel only as the rhetorical expression of a group of ideas, ignoring the role of artistic medium in meaning.

The most formidable counterpart to the critical approach to historical fiction through "ideas" is the historistic method. Essentially, this method attempts to appreciate and judge a given work of historical fiction in terms of its "treatment" of "real" history. The chief criterion for judgment is the critic's own understanding of what that true history was and the excellence he accords the work of art depends to a considerable degree on its conformity to the critic's vision of "real" history. David Levin has presented the case for this criterion most fully in "Historical Fact in Fiction and Drama: The Salem Witchcraft Trials," which maintains that "in criticism and in fiction and drama there is no necessary conflict between an appreciation of the most complex historical facts and the achievement of artistic excellence." [14] This attitude is by no means the exclusive prerogative of literary specialists. There has recently been a heated public controversy as to whether William Styron's *The Confessions of Nat Turner* provides an "accurate" picture of Turner and of slavery.[15] The furor reflects an integral aspect of the art of the historical novel, for both artist and audience assume that such novels are indeed a form of "history" and should be so judged.

The historical method, like the philosophical approach, is clearly useful and necessary as a preliminary guide to understanding the art of historical fiction. It implies that it is possible for the critic to rationalize historically the artistic creation. In other words, he may "translate" the characters, events, and structure of the novel into conventional "history" as a means of uncovering the author's attitudes and social vision. For example, in discussing Cooper's *The Spy*, one may begin by investigating the *historical* role of the land ("The Neutral Ground"), of the opposing sides, of the Great Man (Washington), of the Spy (or suspected renegade), and the significance of Cooper's presentation of the American Revolution predominantly in terms of masked identities and shifting loyalties. Having generalized from the particular historical "types," one can then begin to discuss Cooper's attitudes towards revolution in general and the American Revolution in particular.

Another aspect of this method concerns techniques of historical investigation and exposition, the historiographical strategies and tactics of the historical novelist.[16] This is necessary for the appreciation of, say, the meaning of the shifting narrative points of view in *Absalom, Absalom!* An understanding of the historical methodology is especially important, however, when writers have imperfect control of their materials and mix their historical modes, creating philosophical "ambiguities" which are actually inevitable from the clash of techniques. For example, in discussing Twain's *Connecticut Yankee,* it is important to distinguish his use of the "literary" medieval figures of Malory and/or Tennyson from his Whiggish interpretation of the role of the Church in the Middle Ages. Similarly, it is helpful to recognize the effect Twain creates by compressing more than a thousand years of European history into one "age" and to attempt to analyze in turn the effect of this compression on Twain's historical analogies with the United States of his time. This type of discrimination among historical modes must precede discussion of meaning in the novel as a whole.

Obviously, one must transcend the narrowly historistic if one is to place the emphasis where it belongs: on the artist's, not the critic's, imaginative concept of the past. This is one of the merits of Lukács' generic approach to the historical novel; the best chapters of his book are devoted to Scott's creation of the "classical form of the historical novel" and to the formal and imaginative differences between the historical novel and the historical drama. Lukács' emphasis on the common roots of the novel and history in epic gives his analysis a very strong theoretical foundation and points the way for further study.[17] Lukács had the certainty of a unified aesthetic, the product of his comprehensive theory of literary realism and his conviction that the Marxist interpretation of history of the 1930's permitted him an unusual grasp of the essence of historical reality. Though these certitudes are less accessible today, Lukács clearly showed the desirability of a critical approach which emphasizes the common traits of history and the novel as a basis for criticism of the historical novel.

Perhaps the strongest element shared by the historical novel and conventional history is an informing social vision, a vision which projects fairly explicitly an image of social structures and the relations among them. This is not necessarily true of all novels, or even all nineteenth-century realist novels. The conception and creation of a fictional "world" in the past involves many of the problems one associates with utopian fiction—indeed, as has often been remarked, the historical novel is an inverted utopian novel.[18] In both, the illusion of a "whole" society must be created, either in the past, in the future, or "elsewhere." Thus the historical past may figure in the novel as an escape, a Golden Age, or a point in time from which some vision of the "future" (time-present for the author) is projected. In terms of literary modes, these might be the settings for, respectively, romance, "epic," and satire. Because he tries to give an illusion of a "whole" society, the author of an historical novel presents a total image of the culture, delineating social roles and social structure in a way that makes them unusually accessible to analysis. In other words, the skeleton of the writer's social imagination is laid bare because of the necessary explicitness of the historical novel's total representation. On the other hand, the historical novel, unlike many utopian novels, forces the novelist to grapple with the question of social *change*. Even in the novel of utopian "escape"—for example, *Satanstoe* or *The Europeans*—the author must also project the *process* of social transformation.

The "wholeness" of the social imagination common to both historians and historical novelists in their representation of the past suggests the approach which in this study complements the philosophic and historistic methods. It is possible to detect consistent structures informing the images of the historical past here examined, structures that are quite unlike philosophies and ideologies reared upon one or two unshakeable assumptions. Instead, these structures appear as interlocking constellations of assumptions about history and society, which lack hierarchical order among them, but which are mutually reinforcing. Though seemingly alogical in their composition, the structures are self-contained systems, each being the schematic blueprint for a complete representational theory of society. Awareness of these structures, I believe, may permit analysis of the historical novel to go beyond examining the historical "content" of works and to come closer to the true unity of the artistic creation. I more fully elucidate the details of these structures in the following chapter, which considers the great nineteenth-century historians. However, I will mention the two dominant structures here.

The first structure I have called the "progressive" frame, the immediate intellectual descendant of the Puritan and other historians of the seventeenth century as well as of the Enlightenment. Briefly, the leading concepts imbedded in this structure are the eternally constant nature of man and the idea of history as consisting of measurable change on an absolute scale. By the nineteenth century that scale might only incidentally be divine, but it was always absolute and Ideal: the eschatological goal had simply ceased to be Judgment Day and had become the full realization of the Idea of Liberty.

The other structure is here called the "holist" frame. Its lineage is uncertain, but Vico may be called its spiritual father, and it appears, at least philosophically, to be a demonstrably "newer" attitude towards society and history than the progressive.[19] It is characterized by a relativistic view of time-bound man and by a belief that historical change is not measurable except *in terms of the period under consideration*. Instead of the unity of all times and places, the holist frame emphasizes clear cultural boundaries among cultures separated by space *or* time. During the nineteenth century, neither frame enjoyed exclusive ascendancy, for there were parallel currents which complemented each. For example, in the later nineteenth century historicism appealed to the holist imagination, just as the related hope for a "scientific" history had progressive, positivist roots. The balance of the two frames in the nineteenth-century American historical imagination permitted them to reach a kind of classical definition and exposition. One of the fascinations of the American historical imagination in this period is the extent to which the narrative histories and historical fiction reveal both structures responding to the currents and tensions of the age. In part this phenomenon is due to the new historical consciousness which swept the West after the French Revolution, and especially in the wake of Scott's achievement. The historical imagination acquired a centrality in nineteenth-century America which it had not had during the Ages of Reason and of Common Sense.

This study is not primarily concerned with these imaginative structures from the viewpoint of the philosophy of history but wishes to assess their function in historical art. Though, as I shall try to show, the imaginations of the novelists and historians are not so independent of these structures that they can freely manipulate them, the structures do not exert their influence upon disarmed and unaware imaginations. These structures—systematic configurations of attitudes and conventions regarding the representation of historical reality—are largely conscious. In fact, I believe it is safe to say that one or both imaginative frames were present in the minds of at least all educated adults of the period 1820–95 and continue to be so today.[20] Yet the ability to transcend the limiting forms of philosophies, ideologies, and structures is the mark of the truly creative artist, and the structural approach here advanced is meant to be suggestive, not definitive. It is enough for my purposes if these structures, common to both history and historical fiction, may offer a new and fruitful approach to "historical" novels that are also great novels.

Chapter Two

THE ROMANTIC HISTORIANS:
THE STRUCTURES OF THE
HISTORICAL IMAGINATION

SURELY one of the most persuasive arguments advanced by those who resist the notion that, for example, *The Red Badge of Courage* is an historical novel is that the book seems to contain so little "history." Implicit in such an attitude is the assumption that there is agreement among all readers and novelists on what "history" is. Actually the question posed not long ago by E. H. Carr, "What is history?", is now—and was in the nineteenth century—the subject of lively disagreements among both the philosophers and the practitioners of historical writing.[1] My principal concern here is with the latter, and more particularly with the great American historians of the nineteenth century, Bancroft, Prescott, Motley, Parkman, and Adams. The great literary historians offer a peculiarly appropriate introduction to the concepts of "history" which were immediately available to our major historical novelists. In the first place, they belong to the same cultural milieu as the novelists, and their intuitive ways of imagining the past come from the same intellectual stock as the ways of the "imaginative" writers. Secondly (with the partial exception of Adams), these historians practiced various modes of *narrative* history, as opposed to historical writing which is concerned with, and takes its form from, a "problem." These historians imagine the past in a form susceptible of narrative treatment, and are thus performing an imaginative and philosophical act almost directly parallel to that of the novelists.

The narrative historian and the historical novelists share a comparative indifference to the philosophy of history *per se*. Instead of examining a "theory of history" which guided these historians, this chapter will attempt to explore the theories of social representation implicit in their work. It is not unusual, of course, for a very fine historian to be only a pedestrian social theorist, for, like the novelists, their *forte* is in the doing. Yet these writers did evolve artistically "serviceable" theories, or imaginative social structures, designed for narrative representation, in their writings. It will be helpful, I believe, to see those structures embodied clearly in the works of the historians before moving on to their more complex and even contradictory appearance in the art of the novelists.

In approaching the Romantic historians (leaving Adams out of consideration for the moment) with an eye to the forms of their social imaginations, one can discern two distinct and fully developed techniques and traditions, represented by Bancroft and Motley on the one hand, and Prescott and Parkman on the other. The denomination of these two traditions, once identified, is a rather vexing problem. The Bancroft-Motley approach could be called "Whig," "progressive," "Idealist," "liberal," or "Germanic," according to taste and purpose. For the purposes of this book it shall be called "progressive," and I shall strive to limit the meaning of that label to the historian's ruling belief that the historical treatment of a subject should be constantly informed by the notion of historical progress and improvement in human affairs. As I have indicated, this is not a discrete "idea of progress" for progressive writers but is the salient characteristic of a whole structure—interlocked congeries of ideas and forms of representation. The Prescott-Parkman approach has no conventional labels that I am aware of. The two historians have usually been treated in their "belletristic" aspects or, when their approach to social representation has been appraised, whether by their contemporaries or by ours, it has been dismissed with allusions to Whig interpretations, the Great Man theory, racism, romanticism, and a general want of seriousness. In terms of social representation the distinguishing mark of both historians seems to be a holist treatment of society. Prescott and Parkman were less interested in selecting those social institutions which might most clearly illustrate the theme of Progress than they were in creating an illusion of a whole civilization or culture, in which each institution or characteristic of a society might be seen as integral to the total culture. In this form of representation, manners weigh equally with morals, and may in fact bear moral significance. We might call this approach to social description "functionalist" since it shares many characteristics with that modern school of sociology, including an affinity for a more or less static treatment of society. *Gestalt*, with its emphasis on the forms and configurations of the object under examination (here a past society) and the way in which the forms affect each other in perception, is an especially apt description of the social imagination of Prescott and Parkman, but, like "functionalism," the word carries too many distracting overtones.[2] The designation "holistic" will serve here as a convenient, if not entirely satisfactory, substitute for these terms.

I frankly propose to look at the nineteenth-century American masters of narrative history as exemplary figures, and for this reason no doubt some violence is done in this cursory examination to the subtlety of the dialectic of progressivism and holism in their works. Yet I believe the Romantic historians may in the main be seen as representative of one or the other of these two structures which I hope to anatomize here so that they will be more easily recognizable in the fiction.

George Bancroft (1800–91) is by far the most influential of the nineteenth-century "progressive" historians. His *History of the*

United States from Its Discovery is probably the classic exhibit of the Whig interpretation of history in American historical literature. Yet while he is certainly guilty of the "pathetic fallacy" which Herbert Butterfield has distinguished as the besetting sin of historians who tend to judge the past by particular standards of the present, Bancroft's approach is more than a "trick of organization" or a means of simplifying historical narrative.[3] For Bancroft subscribed fully to the idea of progress, and at least one function of his history was to be the didactic one of demonstrating the evolution of liberty by a process both natural and Providential. The junction of the two is important, for although Bancroft was an heir of the Enlightenment and was influenced strongly by German transcendentalism, he was also the rightful heir of the Puritan historians of the seventeenth century.[4] The last-mentioned influence can be detected not only in the mysterious workings of Providence alluded to throughout the *History*, but also in Bancroft's tendency to see history as a constant war between two forces for the soul of the world. The differences from the Puritan historians are as striking as the similarities. The goal of historical development was not the Judgment Day but the emergence of natural beauty (a concept which the Puritan Winthrop, for example, specifically anathemized), and Bancroft was dialectical enough to allow a place in his epic of progressive development for the Devil's party of conservatism. At moments Bancroft could veer towards a functionalist explanation of historical conflict:

. . . if behind every party there lies what an English poet has called an "eternal thought," and if the generating cause of every party, past or present or hereafter possible, is a force which never disappears, which in its proper proportion is essential to the well-being of society, and which turns into poison only in its excess. It may take a diversity of names as it comes into flower respectively among savages or the civilized, in empires, or in republics; yet every party has its origin in human nature and the necessities of life in a community.[5]

Yet for Bancroft all dialectic reduces to one, the same in every society. This is only possible, of course, when "progress" in all societies is in the same direction. The goal, or "natural liberty," is a compound of two concepts; the first, a beneficent Nature, and the second a liberty so defined by the historical record of its emergence that it could not degenerate into intellectual license. For Bancroft the idea of Nature not only explained the natural laws which were working for Progress everywhere, but connected the myth of the Garden with Democracy in a way which clearly foreshadows Turner. On Connecticut's settlement he wrote:

The laws of honest justice were the basis of their commonwealth, and therefore its foundations were lasting. These humble emigrants invented an admirable system; for they were near to Nature, listened willingly to her voice, and easily copied her forms. No ancient usages, no hereditary differences of rank, no established interests, impeded the application of the principles of justice. Freedom springs spontaneously into life; the artificial distinctions of society require centuries to ripen.[6]

Bancroft is quite definite in distinguishing the concept of liberty from the atheist ideal of the *philosophes*, however, and claims the failure of the French Revolution to be the result of French scepticism which "professed to receive no truth but through the senses, denied the moral government of the world, and derided the possibility of disinterested goodness." [7] The truth must be Divine for only in this way does it acquire its quality of inevitability.

The significance of this school of progressive history for the historical novel lies especially in Bancroft's selection of certain institutions which for him best represent society at any given time and in his depiction of the range of human motivation in history. Bancroft almost exclusively concentrates on those institutions through which he can reveal the evolution of natural liberty most clearly, that is, church and state. Bancroft is not limited to political history, but even his excursions into ecclesiastical, military, and diplomatic history are attempts to treat the development of a civilization at the highest level of abstraction, using the highly formalized social structures of the church, diplomacy, and warfare. This urge goes beyond the traditional approach to history as "past politics," because his philosophical didacticism is also evident in his portrayal of the individual in history. This is important for the purposes of this study, because the subject of the historical novel is precisely the individual in history.

The question of the individual in history is indissolubly linked with that of the hero, or Great Man in history. This whole subject has become so clouded and overladen with emotional and moral overtones that the critic's first responsibility must be to endeavor to limit the connotations of these terms rather than to amplify their resonance.[8] I shall merely consider the extent to which the Great Man is portrayed as an effective or causative agent in history, and, along with this classic philosophical problem, a question which is more relevant to historical *narrative*, namely, to what degree the Great Man is rendered by the historian as a complex, "personalized" individual. One can hardly do better than to look first at Washington, the dominating figure of Bancroft's history of the American Revolution.

Bancroft's Washington in many ways displays the qualities of a superman, since he seems to be almost a different order of being from the rest of mankind, to be in fact an incarnate tool of History. The passivity of the conception is very important; Bancroft's hero appears chiefly as an instrument of historical forces (here the rising American people), just as do the actors in a Puritan history like Edward Johnson's *Wonderworking Providence of Zion's Saviour*. But Washington is more than a focus for natural laws. He is a truly representative man without personal idiosyncracies and without an individual fate. Washington

never drew to himself admiration for the possession of any one quality in excess, never made in council any one suggestion that was sublime

but impracticable, never in action took to himself the praise or the
blame of undertakings astonishing in conception, but beyond his
means of execution. . . . his qualities were so faultlessly proportioned
that his whole country rather claimed him as its choicest representative, the most complete expression of all its attainments and aspirations. He studied his country and conformed to it. His countrymen felt
that he was the best type of America, and rejoiced in it, and were
proud of it. They lived in his life, and made his success and his praise
their own. . . . he was the life and moderator and stay of the most
momentous revolution in human affairs, its moving impulse and its
restraining power. Combining the centripetal and the centrifugal forces
in their utmost strength and in perfect relations, with creative grandeur
of instinct he held ruin in check, and renewed and perfected the institutions of his country.[9]

Washington's appearance, in patriotic rhetoric, as a national
apotheosis was not unusual then or later in the nineteenth century. More important is the passivity of his role as receptor, of his
apparent existence in a world in which great currents and forces
move, forces capable of creating a nondescript superman. The
impersonal language of physics toward the end of this passage
reveals the extent to which Bancroft's Great Man is an imposing
cipher. It is not only the stolid Washington whose portrait lacks
individual definition. Even the comparatively colorful and brilliant
Jefferson was "specially fitted" for writing the Declaration of Independence by "the sympathetic character of his nature, by which
he was able with instinctive perception to read the soul of the
nation, and, having collected its best thoughts and noblest feelings, to give them out in clear and bold words, mixed with so little
of himself, that his country, as it went along with him, found
nothing but what it recognised as its own." [10] The Great Man of
Bancroft's progressive history seems to be marked chiefly by a
kind of "negative capability" which leaves him always open to
the voice of the people and the workings of natural law.

John Lothrop Motley (1814–77) is probably the most distinguished of Bancroft's literary successors. Motley attended Ban-

croft's Round Hill School, was educated in Germany like his pred-
ecessor, and enjoyed a career which resembled Bancroft's in many
other respects, including diplomatic service. His *The Rise of the
Dutch Republic* exhibits all the characteristics of the progressive
school with some interesting variations of Motley's own, for Motley's history is less "philosophical" than Bancroft's, and more
unashamedly "literary" in its intentions. His basic credo as an
historian is also more direct and less transcendental than Bancroft's. In *Historic Progress and American Democracy* Motley refers to "the law governing all bodies political as inexorably as
Kepler's law controls the motions of the planets. The law is Progress: the result Democracy." [11] This is an article of faith for
Motley, one which does not need constant demonstration, and
which may, for artistic reasons, be ignored in the interest of con-
vincing narrative. Motley's justification of his faith, though poignantly understandable in the wake of the Civil War, is strikingly
naive philosophically:

Unless we hold fast to the fact, that in human as in physical history,
Nature is ever patiently producing her effects through long lapses of
time, by causes which have been in operation since the beginning, History is but another word for despair. But history is never hysterical,
never proceeds by catastrophes and cataclysms; and it is only by remembering this that we can comprehend its higher meaning.[12]

The Rise of the Dutch Republic brings some elements into
play which were only latent in Bancroft's work. Although Progress
is still portrayed as the result of the struggle of an heroic people
with autocracy, the conflict here has cultural and "racial" overtones, since the theme of the history is the Dutch battle for independence from Spain. These overtones are never developed into a
full-blown culture-war, however, and Motley uses the notions of
"race" and "nation" as costume dressing and a half-conscious appeal to the baser instincts of his readers. That is, it grows out of
the rhetoric rather than the philosophy of his history. It does have

this overall significance, however, that when Motley sketches the history of the Dutch from their early "freedom" in the Frisian swamps (a germ theory like English Whig belief in an Anglo-Saxon democracy in the Golden Age) on to their conflict with the Spanish, we realize that he is writing the history of a folk (*Volk*), not that of the "masses." His ideal, like that of Bancroft, is an independent and united nation, not the indefinite "rise" of the People, no matter how "democratic" that phenomenon might be. Motley is progressive, but he is quite clear that progress can take care of itself. In the establishment of the Republic, he judiciously notes, the leaders struggled for "historical" freedoms and opposed the more inflammatory "theoretical" ones. In emphasizing the analogy of the Dutch experience with the American, he remarks of the Dutch Declaration of Independence that like "the actors in our own great national drama, these Netherland patriots were struggling to sustain, not to overthrow; unlike them, they claimed no theoretical freedom for humanity—promulgated no doctrine of popular sovereignty: they insisted merely on the fulfillment of actual contracts, signed, sealed, and sworn to by many successive sovereigns." [13] As a supreme statement of salutary passivity, Motley later adds, "Without a direct intention on the part of the people or its leaders to establish a republic, the republic established itself." [14] It is a history of natural laws rather than human wills; it is a world which is poor in opportunities for tragedy.

The proof of this remark may be found in the dominating Great Man of *The Rise of the Dutch Republic*, William the Silent. Motley's choice of heroes is noteworthy, because there already existed a literary tradition celebrating rival figures in the revolt, chiefly through Goethe's *Egmont* and Schiller's *Don Carlos*. Motley debunks the latter figure mercilessly and convincingly, but he has noticeably more difficulty with Egmont, a brilliantly romantic character beside the colorless William, and one whose blindness and betrayal makes him kin to Parkman's La Salle and Prescott's

Pizarro. William has the suffering, enduring character, as David Levin has pointed out, of a Byronic hero, and the silent, seeming passivity of a Taoist ruler.[15] William's "representative" character is apparent throughout the history, for he is always Man realizing the Idea of Progress rather than a man realizing his own ideas.

Motley deviates more strongly from Bancroft in his villains than in his heroes. Bancroft's history, in fact, had few villains, properly speaking, but for Motley the tensions inherent in an historical dialectic built around a party of Right and a party of Wrong disintegrated into melodrama.[16] Thus William is pitted against Philip II and a succession of royal governors treated in vigorous and occasionally lurid fashion. As Pieter Geyl has recently pointed out, this Good/Evil bifurcation is not justified by the facts of Netherlands history.[17] Yet though it might not be "good" or "accurate" history, Motley attempted to defend his melodramatic technique on the grounds that history must appeal to the emotions as well as to the intellect. This belief underlay his justification of excruciatingly detailed descriptions of massacre, rape, and torture committed by the Spanish for their *impression* on the reader.[18] That the impression they make on the modern reader is of an appeal to righteous prurience may explain the immense popularity of these volumes in the nineteenth century. Richard Chase's intuition of the tendency of the classic American novel to find its form in melodrama or idyll may find additional confirmation in the American progressive historians—with Bancroft closer to idyll than Motley.[19] A melodramatic polarization of values is certainly one of the imaginative consequences of the progressive version of history, and this is as true for Motley as it was to be later for Twain.

William Hickling Prescott (1796–1859), the slightly older contemporary of Bancroft, is the best early representative of the historical tradition that ran parallel to that of the progressives. He stands today head and shoulders above his peers of that day in Hispanic studies, Ticknor and Irving, and his sequence of works on the rise and incipient decline of the Spanish Empire (*Ferdinand and Isabella, The Conquest of Mexico, The Conquest of Peru*, and *Philip II*) also retain a wider reading public today than those of either of his "progressive" contemporaries. Yet while Prescott is seemingly the most accessible of all Romantic historians if approached via that classic form of smiling denigration—that is, reading him as "literature"—one discovers that the type of historical and social imagination exemplified in these works is not entirely susceptible of purely formal analysis, despite the many attempts which have been made to do so. The problem is that the meaning of the image of society in Prescott's works has never been examined fully except by critics who found in him only an "aristocratic" or "drum-and-trumpet" historian. The problem of Prescott is not answered satisfactorily through the avenues of the philosophy of history or traditional literary analysis. Nor does the distinction of "history" from rhetoric remain as viable as it was to Michael Kraus, who described Prescott's technique thus: "The scientific method was to be followed in accumulating materials, but the writing of the historical narrative belonged in the field of belles lettres." [20] Rather one must seek the matrix of Prescott's creation in the structure of a social imagination which could fulfill the demands of history and art. The formulas of Prescott's historical imagination took their basis from a structural conception of the society of the past which was strikingly different from that of the progressives.

The difference between the two basic styles may be seen most clearly, perhaps, by examining the Introductory Book of *The Conquest of Mexico*—an extended interpretation of pre-Columbian Mexican civilization—and comparing it with the opening chapters of *The Rise of the Dutch Republic*. In both cases there is an attempt to evoke an image of a civilization on the eve of a cultural and military confrontation with sixteenth-century Spain, yet the resemblance of the two prologues ends with their similar formal function. Motley's aim is to create a sense of racial homogeneity and love of freedom extending back through Teutonic conflict with the Roman Empire to the prehistory of the wandering tribes of Northern Europe.

Prescott, while not ignoring the vertical slice through time, is less concerned with constant "genetic" qualities of the Aztecs and their predecessors than with giving the reader "a just idea of the true nature and extent of the civilization to which the Mexicans attained." [21] The depiction of this horizontal slice of time in the Introduction and Appendix, which Prescott claims "cost me as much labor, and nearly as much time, as the remainder of the history," remains an extremely ambitious attempt to apply archaeological and ethnological methods in defining the domain of the Aztecs as a *whole* civilization. [22] In this pursuit, Prescott investigates pre-Aztec history, the climate and products, the institutions of state, the military, laws, mythology, religion, writing, science, domestic arts, manners, administration, and recent history.

Perhaps most significant is Prescott's use of the "comparative civilizations" technique to fill in gaps in the picture of Mexican civilization and to order the whole. This technique, which, as we shall see, led to heavy attacks from the nascent science of ethnology after Prescott's death, was also used by Prescott in *The Conquest of Peru*. Prescott's purpose in both cases is not only to fix these civilizations on a scale of "progress," but to invoke the concept of "civilization" itself, with all its institutions, social, domestic, and intellectual, and to give the narrative of the conquest the dramatic structure of a clash between two complete cultures. The completeness of the cultures is worth emphasizing, since the progressives had tended to describe nations and civilizations purely in terms of political and religious ideas, structures, and institutions, and to attempt to show how this institutional complex was informed by the characteristics of a racial or genetic "nation." For Prescott, all aspects of a civilization are, at least theoretically, historiographically equal, and there is no greater weight given to the institutions of church and state, which for a progressive should most clearly show the evolution of the Idea of Liberty.

In this sense of wholeness which he tries to evoke, Prescott's *History* is reminiscent of modern gestalt psychology, which emphasizes that the perception of reality (here the historian's perception of a past society) is the perception of a total image. Each part of this image is necessary and the image cannot simply be resolved into its parts. Thus early Mexican civilization is a complete entity (as is sixteenth-century Spanish civilization), and the historian, while not refusing his "philosophic" duty to moralize, abstracts ideas at his peril from the civilization and period he is describing. Also, like the structural functionalism of much modern-day sociology, Prescott seems to express the view that each institution of a civilization has a necessary function in the whole, though he does not necessarily endorse the health of the resultant. Whether one approaches Prescott through Vico or through Scott, the dominant impulse of his social imagination is clear: man makes his society, and his society is most rewardingly apprehended in its full cultural complexity.

The consequences of this *Gestalt* or holist image of society for the portrayal of the individual in history are equally complex. The proliferation of institutions and the resulting density of Prescott's historical world—and this is true for his Spain as well as the New World—tends to limit the individual, or at least to define his scope more narrowly. Unlike the Great Man of the progressive historians, who may incarnate an Idea, the Great Man of Prescott's history is much more likely, insofar as he incarnates anything, to incarnate a type, a sociological rather than a philosophical concept. Paradoxically, Prescott's tremendous interest in individuals and his tendency to construct his histories as much as possible around dominant figures have tended to foster a belief that Prescott subscribed to a Carlylean theory of Great Men. Actually, the figures he chose as subjects come much closer to the Carlylean Noted Man, or Emerson's "talented man"—that is, an outstanding but purely representative social type.[23] As a causal agent on the grand scale, his role is nearly nil, and he is governed by congeries of definable forces plus a vague but serviceable Spirit of the Age. Here, for example, is a concise statement of the causes of the conquest of Mexico and Peru:

For the inhabitants of Mexico and Peru, the appearance of Europeans in America was *accidental* in the sense that it did not follow from the social development of these countries. But the passion for navigation which possessed West Europeans at the end of the Middle Ages was not accidental; nor was the fact that the European forces easily overcame the resistance of the natives. The consequences of the conquest of Mexico and Peru by Europeans were also not accidental, in the last analysis, these consequences were determined by the resultant of two forces: the economic position of the conquered countries on the one hand, the economic position of the conquerors on the other.[24]

The words are not Prescott's, but those of the Russian Marxist, Plekhanov; change the words "economic position" to "cultural position" in the last lines and they stand as a fair description of the causal framework of Prescott's *Mexico* and *Peru*, always remembering that "accidental" means "susceptible of alteration by individual action." Yet an historical figure may also be freed by the historian's close fit of cultural and historical circumstance, as in the philosophical paradox that "necessity creates freedom." In Prescott's portrait of Isabella, there is a full recognition of the possibilities for freedom offered by a complete historical role:

If there be any being on earth that may be permitted to remind us of the Deity himself, it is the ruler of a mighty empire, who employs the high powers intrusted to him exclusively for the benefit of his people; who, endowed with intellectual gifts corresponding with his station, in an age of comparative barbarism, endeavors to impart to his land the light of civilization which illumines his own bosom, and to create from the elements of discord the beautiful fabric of social order. Such was Isabella; and such the age in which she lived. And fortunate was it for Spain that her sceptre, at this crisis, was swayed by a sovereign possessed of sufficient wisdom to devise, and energy to execute, the most salutary schemes of reform, and thus to infuse a new principle of vitality into a government fast sinking into premature decrepitude.[25]

At the same time that he invokes this image of benevolent potency, Prescott absolves Isabella of genuine guilt in the establishment of the Inquisition and the expulsion of the Jews, just as he absolves Cortez of blood-guilt in the massacres perpetrated in the New World, appealing in both instances to the effects of the Spirit of the Age and warning against moral anachronism. Thus in effect Prescott denies the kind of extra-cultural moral force here imputed to Isabella. This concept of role-playing distinctively separates the historical individual of Prescott from that of the progressives. Motley, for example, cheerfully admits that William the Silent could not comprehend the real nature of the rebellion he led and yet makes William's moral credit and virtue shine the brighter for the "progressive" results he had not aimed at. Prescott, on his side, creates the figure of the individual in terms of a Spirit of the Age, a *Zeitgeist* which both limits and frees him. It limits him in terms of moral insight and ability to transcend his historical consciousness and situation. It frees him to plan and to act in a full, committed, and strenuous but uncomplicated manner within the historical definition of his role. Thus Isabella is not condemned to be "bad" as a ruthless conqueror, but is judged on her performance in her role. Not only does this conception of historical role envision the hero as an historical agent rather than an historical instrument of progress, but the notion of a defined social and cultural role elevates manners—in the broadest sense—to a high position as evidence upon which to base historical judgment.[26]

The contemporary attacks on Prescott are perhaps the best indication of how antipathetic Prescott's holist view of society was to the progressive imagination. The most weighty and significant assaults were launched, from completely different metaphysical standpoints, by Theodore Parker and Lewis Henry Morgan. Parker, the prominent transcendentalist theologian, delivered a two-part assault on Prescott, entitled "Prescott as an Historian" and "Prescott's *Conquest of Mexico*," in the *Massachusetts Quarterly*. Parker's critique is written from a resolutely progressive orientation, and demands that history be "philosophic"—that is, be "philosophy teaching by experience." More rigorous than Bancroft and Motley, Parker exemplifies perfectly the progressive search for a controlling Idea in the writing of history. He resents the *literary* motive behind Prescott's portraiture, and finds that Prescott shirks his duty in not condemning the iniquities of Isabella and Cortez. Parker sees as the worst and governing fault of the histories Prescott's failure to attempt to write of the past in the light of the most enlightened moral standards of his own day. In Parker's own words, "The book lacks philosophy to a degree exceeding belief." [27]

The criticism of Lewis Henry Morgan and such disciples as A. F. A. Bandelier took Prescott, along with other representatives of the "romantic school of archaeology," to task from the standpoint of the new science of ethnology. Morgan, whose early work on the Iroquois had led him on to major investigations of consanguinity in the social organization of all Indians of the Americas, challenged Prescott and his successors for being over-credulous of the early Spanish authorities. According to Morgan, the Spanish had been guilty of "unavoidable self-deception" because they had looked at Mexican civilization through their own feudal stereotypes. In "Montezuma's Dinner," an article published in the *North American Review* in 1876, he charges the Spanish with the "grossest perversion of obvious facts" which allowed them to "fabricate the Aztec monarchy out of a democratic organization." [28] Rather than trust such authorities, Morgan *deduces* the organization of the Aztecs from general laws applicable to all tribes of the "Red Race," and from the exact stage the Aztecs are presumed to have reached on the evolutionary path from Savagery to Civilization, namely Middle Barbarism. Although Morgan himself has been called into question by later authorities, and Prescott's reliance on the Spanish writers largely vindicated, the ethnological critique is instructive in assessing the latent propensities of both holists and progressives. Morgan's adherence to an iron law of evolution and progress, his claim that one can intuit the whole of a culture from a few vital racial and institutional details which reveal its "stage," places him clearly in the progressive tradition.[29]

Prescott's preference for a "comparative civilizations" method which would allow him to see Mexico as a *civilization*, with European and Oriental analogues, rather than a sub-civilized "culture," whatever its scientific validity, has an obvious artistic purpose. In Prescott's fictive historical world, all figures are defined by their social "role," so that Montezuma and Guatemozin must be either "civilized" or "inexplicable." The latter alternative, needless to say, would have been a severe handicap to *The Conquest of Mexico*. Prescott wished to project before his readers "a certain ideal of manhood, a little medieval, but nevertheless good." [30] This ideal could appear in different kinds of civilized contexts, but neither savages nor barbarians of the "Middle Status" could possibly fulfill it. The Aztecs and the Incas were *perforce* "civilized." Prescott's successor in the holist tradition was not to find so easy an answer to this troublesome problem.

Francis Parkman (1823–93) inherited the historical image of society as a functional whole in an era in which the positivist assumptions of the new social sciences were undermining the Romantic medievalism of Prescott. It is a significant coincidence that Parkman's *Conspiracy of Pontiac* was published in the same year (1851) as Morgan's *League of the Ho-De-No-Sau-Nee*; the "scientific" assumptions about the nature of society with which Parkman had to deal were far more potentially constraining than those which had confronted Bancroft, Motley, and Prescott. Parkman's decision to write "the history of the American Forest" as

France and England in the New World is intimately bound up with this change. Parkman had wanted to write a full history of the Indians in their conflict with the invaders from Europe, but was discouraged by his own researches into Indian life, as recorded in his journals and *The Oregon Trail*.[31] In this book, Parkman observes and judges the Indians according to a cultural scale of progress. While he does try to give some picture of Indian customs, religion, and organization, he is, as he wrote to Morgan, no ethnologist, and rather than use the special tools of a recognized science (as Prescott used the tools of the historian in *Mexico* and *Peru* and as Parkman himself used them on New France) Parkman makes, or deliberately appears to make, instant, impressionistic judgments from an "understood" position—that of Brahmin culture.[32]

In his own historical work focusing on Indians, *The Conspiracy of Pontiac*, it is clear that though Parkman could *conceive* of North American Indian life as a *Gestalt*, he had difficulty in dramatizing it as a cultural entity. Parkman's view of the Indian includes an analysis of Indian culture (more than a little tinged with racialism) that seems to preclude the idea of progress as a universal law of human nature. Of Pontiac himself he observes that

not he alone, but many of the most notable men who have arisen among the Indians, have been opponents of civilization, and staunch advocates of primitive barbarism. Red Jacket and Tecumseh would gladly have brought back their people to the rude simplicity of their original condition. There is nothing progressive in the rigid, inflexible nature of an Indian. He will not open his mind to the idea of improvement; and nearly every change that has been forced upon him has been a change for the worse.[33]

Like Prescott, Parkman revels in the complexities and varieties of societies and history, but this very quality of apartness in the North American Indian handicapped him. The right of conquest between two civilized nations, however, which so perplexed Pres-

cott, no longer applies when totally alien cultures are pitted
against each other. The Indians cannot be reclaimed; the alternatives are either extinction of the race or to leave "the western
world to eternal barbarism." [34] The results of this central cultural
attitude are manifest throughout the book, for though Parkman's
ostensible subject is the Anger of the Indians at Bay, with all the
epic intimations of that theme, and though his ostensible hero is
Pontiac, the Indian leader does not dominate the history, and
the reader's attention is directed more to the reactions of the
British-Americans than to the actions of the Indians. Parkman,
instead of attempting to enter into the councils of the Indians,
expends his powers on an estimate of the role of the frontier in
provincial politics. Parkman's problem is that the Indian was
actually beyond his powers of characterization because he could
not be placed in the context of a fully articulated social and cultural role. Pontiac remains a shadowy, unrealized figure, the "Sa-
tan" of a "forest paradise." [35]

Parkman found his true subject in a different culture clash,
that of the French and English for imperial dominion. Yet his
subject for most of the seven volumes of his history is really the
French alone, who offer all the cultural features that the holist
historian seeks. The French in America represented a high standard of civilization in a semi-independent social entity: New
France. The institutions could be studied and the health of the
social organism assessed by conventional means. Social roles were
highly sophisticated and represented a clear value system. Finally,
New France had the obvious dramatic interest—for the holist
imagination—of a civilization on the verge of its fall. This is the
condition of Prescott's Mexico and Peru and even—from the
perspective of the nineteenth century—his Spain, the start of
whose decline he traces in *Philip II*. It is the condition of Parkman's Indians and French, and, as I shall try to show, the predominant condition described by Cooper in a number of cultural
groups and societies. The major key of the "rise" of nations,

whether the Dutch Republic or the United States, is peculiarly within the progressive range of tones.[36]

Parkman's most complete examination of the *Gestalt* of New France appears in *The Old Regime in Canada* (1874), in which he anatomizes the colony's ecclesiastical, administrative, economic, and social history, touching on everything from diplomacy to local customs, dress, and mores. This extended essay, reminiscent of Prescott's chapters on the Aztecs, illuminates another facet of the holist imagination. Though apparently seeking the principle of vitality in a given civilization—the homeostatic balance which is achieved by all the institutions and mores acting upon one another—both Prescott and Parkman were also consciously acting as social pathologists. Just as "superstition" and human sacrifice were the corrupting diseases of the Aztecs, "absolutism" is the malady of New France, and in both cases the diagnostic helps the historian to explain and indirectly to justify the downfall of the civilization. This literary phenomenon has led some critics to maintain that Parkman was too enamored of the Idea of Progress, but this is, I think, a real distortion of his emphasis, for Parkman was palpably more concerned with explaining historical "decline" than in celebrating evolutionary "rise." [37] Parkman's image of New France shows the chronic conflict of the elements of social dissolution (represented by the somewhat anarchic *coureurs du bois*) with royal plans for a settled and stable peasantry.[38] Parkman diagnoses this acute condition through the syndrome of effects which accompany the *joined* forces of Absolutism and License. It is easy to imagine a progressive interpretation of the same conflict as one of Tradition *versus* Liberty.

The individual in Parkman's history is, as with Prescott, eminently a representative social type who would be incomprehensible if removed from his milieu. The Jesuit explorers, Frontenac, La Salle, Montcalm, and Wolfe are all nearly completely defined by their cultural roles. Again as with Prescott, this definition releases artistic resources to the author which are denied to the pro-

gressive historians, whose portraits of historical figures tend to be
as unpersonalized as the Ideas the progressive Great Men represent. That is, the portraits of Prescott and Parkman can be specifically biographical and idiosyncratic. In almost direct proportion
as their characters are freed of a significantly causal role in history,
they are freed to pursue destinies which are personal and a fate
that is private. Howard Doughty has astutely and persuasively
indicated how Parkman created in La Salle a tragic hero comparable to those of Melville, and one may recognize how far that
achievement is made possible by the fact that La Salle represents
a cultural type and is playing a cultural role which is in turn
closely linked with Parkman's estimate of the function of the
aristocracy in seventeenth-century France. The most characteristic chapter of Parkman's masterpiece, "The Hardihood of La
Salle," has for its central theme the impact of the raw American
wilderness on the epitome of the French chivalry, giving a broad
cultural significance to La Salle's purely personal transcendence.

It may be convenient at this point to review the characteristics
of the holist and progressive frames as they reveal themselves in
the work of the great Romantic American historians. The progressive imagination sees humanity advancing on an absolute, measurable scale of eternal standards or moral values such as Liberty,
Equality, or material well-being. The holist imagination emphasizes the unbridgeable barriers which separate eras, and which
render all comparative judgments across time subjective and relative. In the progressive imagination values are eternal and humanity is universal. In the holist imagination both values and "human
nature" itself are formed by culture. For the progressive, ideas
have extreme, transcendent importance. For the holist, it is manners and mores which are significant. The progressive sees society
as essentially composed of two forces, from whose clash comes
change. The holist sees society as a seamless web of relationships.
The natural subject of progressive narrative is revolution and/or
the rise of nation states. The holist imagination is drawn to the

clash of disparate cultures, and the decline and fall of civilization. The progressive tends to believe that reason conforms to science and so emphasizes historical "laws." The holist tends to believe man's reason is non-scientific and to search for the causes of historical events in the contingencies of the cultural matrix.

My description of these two structures emphasizes their unchanging and exclusive nature, as it must, in the interests of revealing their internal consistency. Yet these structures seldom appear in their pristine form in a given narrative, because they are always transformed by the social and artistic vision of the author, who adulterates his dominant frame with elements of its structural opposite in order to respond more fully to his sense of reality. As should be obvious, the two frames have very different social functions. Despite the fact that progressives like Bancroft and Motley were staunch defenders of social stability, it is clear that the progressive frame itself may be understood as a means of organizing the imaginative and emotional resources of people to accept and advance social change. In like manner, the holist frame is a means not only to organize narrative, but also to organize and promote a deep appreciation of social stability.

The function of the progressive frame is to celebrate the status quo by dramatizing its creation. At the same time, covertly during the nineteenth century, overtly since the penetration of Marxian ideas, the progressive frame prepares one to see the status quo upset. The holist frame functions by absolving the past from ethical and historical judgment at the same time that it alienates one from contemplating the possibility of change in the present. Both structures functionally order and reinforce social attitudes. Thus they determine the social function of historical narrative and of the historical novel just as they control the literary form of the work. The social function of these frames cannot be understood if the structures are conceived of as static patterns of ideas and responses. The social function of the progressive and holist frames is not finally determined in a vacuum, but rather in the crucible of the artistic process, in which the writer's creative imagination and the needs of his own historical imagination meet to shape the finished work of art.

⤳ Literary Theory and Practice of the Romantic Historians

Investigation of the role of the individual in history—the creation of character in historical narrative—leads quite naturally to the question of whether these Romantic historians ever approximate novelistic technique. The study of the histories themselves is rewarding in this regard, but the body of fiction and fiction criticism left by the Romantic historians also should be considered. The world-view of a writer is not bound by the particular genre in which he writes, but is certain to affect both literary taste and historical imagination.

George Bancroft offers little light here, for although he was extremely avid as a translator, critic, and student of literature in his younger days, even issuing a volume of his own verse in 1823, he neither wrote nor criticized prose fiction. Happily, however, Motley provides one with a reply to the question of what an historical romance composed in accordance with progressive historical structures might be like. His answer is *Merrymount: A Romance of the Massachusetts Colony*, published in 1848 with a preface in which he swears that despite the similarity of theme and title, he had not read Hawthorne's "May-Pole of Merrymount" either before or after writing his romance.[39] Motley's deference to the older writer is just, for to read *Merrymount* is to measure Hawthorne's achievement. Though an inferior romance, *Merrymount* succeeds in keeping before the reader Motley's true subject: the contention of ideas, men, and life styles for the New World. Puritan virtue triumphs over Renaissance vice, but in a manner more suited to a progressive trimmer like Motley than to a hot Calvinist. Of New England Puritanism, despite his reser-

vations about its intolerant spirit, he can only exclaim with mid-
Victorian enthusiasm:

It was a great movement, not a military, nor a philanthropic, nor a
democratic movement, but a religious, perhaps a fanatical movement,
but the movers were in earnest, and the result was an empire. The
iron character of these early founders left an impression upon their
wilderness-world, which has not yet been effaced; and the character
of their institutions, containing much that is admirable, mingled with
many objectionable features, has diffused an influence, upon the
whole, healthy and conservative, throughout the length and breadth
of the continent.[40]

The main lines of Motley's aesthetic and rhetoric of fiction
emerge clearly from *Merrymount*. Historical fiction should be
accurate in details, colorful in characters, and should present an
historical conflict in the form of a melodramatic struggle of Good
and Evil. Yet, although history may instruct, fiction need only
amuse. In an essay on Balzac published at about the time *Merrymount* was composed, Motley attacked the new school of "moralistic" fiction—Dickens, Sand, Sue—and praised Balzac for being
"an artist, not a mechanic." [41] On the direction of fiction in America, where pseudo-Dickensian novels were abounding in the 1840's,
he is specific:

Neither are we quite converted to the philosophy of the moderns, nor
do we quite understand that broad, genial, and universal sympathy so
much commended of late, and which seems to sympathize only with
the degraded. We think it odd that the new school should find so
much favor in our own land. In the countries of the older world, where
the *prolétaire* is starving, and the Pariah writhing like a worm in the
dust, and both are crushed into insignificance by privileged heels,
we can understand this movement, this literary and social tendency;
but in a country where there are neither Brahmins nor Pariahs, no
castes and no classes, no top and no bottom . . . we don't see, we
confess, so much danger to the elevated position of the people. If

there is any body in this country but the people, we should be glad
to be introduced to him.[42]

In other words, the new school of sentimental social conscience
is un-American. In part this is the Adamic attitude, but one should
note that the Adamic attitude is not always or even typically
joined with progressive social views. The insistence on America's
fresh start, here somewhat chauvinistic, includes an insistence
upon the absence of contradictions between democratic ideals
and reality, a proclamation that the classless society is not only
desirable, but already exists. The holist school, of course, would
insist upon class distinctions as both socially and artistically desirable. For the progressives, history was to be portrayed through
melodrama and the boldest painting of rights and wrongs—
though Bancroft would more often emphasize the positive and
Motley the negative side of the matter. Fiction is for amusement,
and though like history it has its rules for engaging the sympathies it need not bear the burden of moral instruction. A final
division of rhetoric is made for political discourse, which is concerned with the arts of justice, moderation, and compromise. The
school of Dickens crosses these boundaries and makes political
life a subject for melodrama—and herein lies its danger for social
stability.

Prescott, who wrote a much larger body of literary criticism
than Parkman, provides an interesting holist comparison with
Motley's progressive genre theory. Like Bancroft and Motley, he
recognized romance as having generic demands of its own, and in
an essay on Brockden Brown he adumbrates them:

We had none of the buoyant, stirring associations of a Romantic age;
none of the chivalrous pageantry, the feudal and border story, or
Robin Hood adventure; none of the dim, shadowy superstitions, and
the traditional legends, which had gathered like moss around every
stone, hill and valley of the olden countries. Every thing here wore a
spick-and-span new aspect, and lay in the broad, garish sunshine of

every-day life. . . . It required the eye of genius to detect the rich stores of romantic and poetic interest that lay beneath the crust of society.[43]

The tone here is very familiar, for it is precisely the lack of this "feudal" past that Cooper and Hawthorne are to decry as inhibiting their fiction. For Prescott, these associations were the life and breath of historical art also, and the advantage of fifteenth- and sixteenth-century Spain as a literary subject for Prescott lay largely in his ability to claim that characters like Cortez conceived of themselves "romantically." Yet while Prescott agrees with Motley in finding Romantic fiction and history unified in *tone*, he describes their generic differences in very different terms. Prescott distinguishes them on the philosophic grounds of the relationship of the genre to reality rather than by approaching this distinction through social function (moral instruction *versus* amusement). In his early (1827) essay, "Novel-Writing," Prescott employs the classic Aristotelian distinction between history and poetry:

History has to do with the outward appearances of things; with actors in masquerade. How often may even an eyewitness be deceived! De Retz has somewhere remarked on the impertinence of writers "who in the seclusion of their closets, pretend to suggest the motives of conduct, which he, who was the focus of intrigue, was altogether unable to explain." On the other hand, fiction has no concern with actions of individuals, but with passions in the abstract, with the moral constitution of man, a subject, from obvious reasons, much less liable to misconception. In a word, history represents events as they are, and men as they appear; while fiction represents events as they appear probable, and men as they are.[44]

Especially noteworthy is Prescott's emphasis not on the greater philosophic truth of fiction (as in Aristotle) but rather the profound unreliability of history, which he sees as a bewildering sequence of "appearances" by "actors in masquerade." The aesthetic and philosophic position implied here goes far towards explaining the importance of role-playing in the holist treatment of the individual in history. In this connection Parkman's well-known criticism of Cooper is relevant, because Parkman, while criticizing more from a standpoint of "realism" than "romanticism," sees the novel as being in the same province as history insofar as it must be accurate and reveal reality without instruction in philosophic or moral "truths." [45]

↜ Coda: Henry and Brooks Adams

Of the great line of nineteenth-century Harvard-educated historians, Henry (1838–1918) and Brooks (1848–1927) Adams represent a break with the previous traditions that is more than generational. Only fifteen years younger than his distant cousin Parkman and a friend of both Bancroft and Motley, Henry Adams exhibits a temper which is recognizably "modern" to the reader of today (as does Brooks), as distinguished from the Romantic mode of his predecessors. Yet the break the Adamses' work signalizes is a transitional, not a revolutionary one. Concentrating on Henry, one can see that the corpus of his work represents as much an attempt to resolve the tension between the holist and progressive traditions in a synthesis as it is to make a new departure in the name of "scientific" history.

The interest in a scientific history itself clearly establishes Adams as a true, though critical, descendant of the progressive tradition. Like the progressives, Adams believed that serious history must reveal historical laws operating through time, even though he came to reject the premises upon which Bancroft and Motley had founded their "laws." This dominant trait of Henry Adams' imagination, the belief that only such a revelation of temporal development can redeem history from antiquarianism, a belief that was shared unreservedly by Brooks, is in its way an extension of progressive history.[46] Coupled with Henry Adams' concept of law and conflict as being the essence of historical understanding went the belief that power was history's true subject and institutions the correct object of historical examination. It is worth noting that *The Old Regime* is the only one of Parkman's books of which the younger historian could wholly approve.

The distance separating Adams from the optimistic tradition of Bancroft and Motley, however, is ironically indicated by Adams himself in the chapter of *The Education of Henry Adams* entitled "The Perfection of Human Society." The phrase was Motley's, and the perfection alluded to was encompassed by "the London dinner and the English country house." This was the flaw of the Idealist progressives from Hegel through Bancroft to Motley: progress stopped with the *status quo*. In common with most nineteenth-century evolutionary thought, the evolutionary progressives did not care to confront the question of how one evolves beyond the perfect society. In addition, Adams felt convinced that the progressive historians had simply imposed their *a priori* pattern on history—"falsification" was the blunt word he used for it—out of a facile optimism. In his later historical speculations, Adams took the subject of progressive historical law seriously, scientifically, and with a vengeance.

A less complex version of this shift may be seen in the work of Brooks Adams, especially in *The Emancipation of Massachusetts* (1887) and *The Law of Civilization and Decay* (1896). The first of these books is written from an avowedly progressive point of view. As an attack on the Puritan "theocracy" it has many of the overtones of the "liberal" attack on the Puritans which was to reach its high mark in the 1920's. Brooks Adams, however, concentrates far more on the institutions than on the allegedly Hebraic ideas of the controlling "priest-caste." Instead of merely condemning the "oppressors," or depicting them melodramatically *à la* Motley, Adams seeks to explain the institutional *necessity* of their actions. On the one hand this is much more methodologically precise, and is consistent with Adams' generally much more rigorous conception of historical law than that which informs the histories of Bancroft and Motley. On the other, Adams is borrowing slightly from the conception of functional necessity given institutions by the holists. That is, he recognizes that the temptation for a member of a particular caste or cultural institution to act in a culturally determined way is overwhelming.

His most significant innovation in progressive thought is his explanation of Progress not as the rise of the idea of Liberty in Idealist fashion, but as the result of a pseudo-biological Darwinist evolution based on the trait of mental flexibility and adaptability. This trait, according to Adams, is not only identical with "liberty" but a sign of evolutionary advancement.[47] The historical dialectic thus becomes more deterministic; there is no free emergence of mind or openendedness. This has definite consequences for the depiction of the individual in history, of which I shall speak in a moment.

Henry Adams, less dogmatic and more elusive than his brother, tempered his condemnation of "antiquarianism" with a social imagination which could be fully as holist as that of Prescott and Parkman. Even the famous Adams theme of failure indicates his temperamental sympathy with the elegiac tones so characteristic of the holist vision. Instead of tracing the decline and complete fall of a society, like Prescott and Parkman, Adams preferred to inspect the peak of success for the seeds of disaster: thirteenth-century France in *Mont-Saint-Michel and Chartres*, the republican America of Jefferson in his *History* and the biographies, and the imperial America of the *Education* and the late essays. Adams' use of the extended cultural overview, as in "The United States in 1800" (the first six chapters of the *History*) was probably borrowed from the most durable Whig-progressive historian of all, Macaulay, whose chapters on "England in 1688" may well have served Adams as a model. Yet Adams' introductory chapters to the *History* are nonetheless a holist excursion into social history and are in large part detachable from the progressive (or anti-progres-

sive) movement of the *History* itself. They contain a broad cultural, economic, and social panorama which is finally no more than
a backdrop to the activities of the political leaders and diplomats.
The holist cast of Adams' thought is seen most clearly not in the
History—which is best understood in the present context as a
profound revision of progressive history—but in *Mont-Saint-
Michel and Chartres*.

Mont-Saint-Michel and Chartres, relating as it does to the
whole question of late nineteenth-century medievalism, may be
seen in part as an extended reaction to industrialism, Darwinism,
and Progress. Today there is really no realm of the historical
imagination comparable to this aesthetic pseudo-feudalism, whose
characteristic figure is William Morris, with his combination of
revolutionary realism, utopianism, and "medieval" aesthetics. Pre-
Raphaelite theories of color and design are part of the basic frame
of reference of Adams' masterpiece, and the revolution in taste
seems to be one of the positive forces helping Adams' admiration,
for once, to overcome his irony. The central theme of the work,
as Adams conceived of it, was the search for cultural unity at a
time when for him the entire question of unity had become extremely problematical. The message constantly iterated by the
Education is that all natural and historical phenomena are radically discontinuous. This lesson was fatal for the hope, which
Adams had tried to fulfill in the *History*, of discovering "whether,
by the severest process of stating, with the least possible comment,
such facts as seemed sure, in such order as seemed rigorously consequent, he could fix for a familiar moment a necessary sequence
of human movement." [48]

The result was a turn from an evolutionary-progressive, "rigorously" consequential view to one based on the physical sciences,
non-evolutionary, radically discontinuous and catastrophic, in
which the central problem is to discover the basis for any kind
of consequentiality in the universe. The aestheticism of much of
Mont-Saint-Michel and Chartres is in large measure an expression

of this fragmentation of the imagination, of an increasing awareness of oppositions in human history that are not dialectical, but
polar. Thus for Adams, the problem of the book was to discover
the unity of the age in one force, quite a different procedure from
looking for the thrust of the drive for progressive change; a search
for the Spirit of the Age, not the Spirit of Freedom. Prescott and
Parkman too were at pains to remind the reader of the gap existing between the times they are describing and time-present, a
psychic distance which usually cannot be measured by merely
chronological means.

The book closest in temper to *Mont-Saint-Michel and Chartres*
is not properly history at all: William James' *The Varieties of
Religious Experience,* in which an equally modern, almost equally
skeptical mind approaches the same subject, "medieval" faith and
taste, with the same scientific and humane attitude, accepting this
faith as a genuine and positive phenomenon worthy of disinterested explanation. This helps to explain why *Mont-Saint-Michel
and Chartres* is *almost* a classic expression of the holist approach
to history. It focuses on the expressions of a civilization in art,
architecture, literature, religious emotion, theology, and to a limited extent politics and life style. The break from the traditional
holist approach appears in the author's explicit search for unity
in this pattern; the pattern is not enough by itself. This unity
may seem to be superimposed, but it is the *unity* he desires to
show the reader, not the civilization alone (which would be antiquarianism). At least this is true so long as Adams is performing
as an historian, and is not in his other and enormously successful
role of dilettante tourist in which he is not describing a whole
civilization but merely appreciating its artifacts.[49] It is important
to remember that Henry Adams' works of the historical imagination *per se* were not preoccupied with the *concept* of a progressive
or anti-progressive law in history, and that he never tried, like
Brooks, to write a history in order to "illustrate" a law. Henry was
more concerned with the kind of law involved in the perception

of the past, the laws of the historical imagination itself; in the *History* and in *Mont-Saint-Michel and Chartres* it is the documents, literary, political, and architectural which command attention. This self-reflexive awareness of the historical imagination makes *Mont-Saint-Michel and Chartres* appear as the connecting link between *The Scarlet Letter* and *Absalom, Absalom!* In all three the true subject of history is the contemplation of the past.

The implications for the novel of the Adams brothers' transformation of the two older traditions of "literary" historiography are most apparent in their handling of the individual in history. Henry Adams expressed his distaste for the role-playing men of action who dominated the pages of Prescott and Parkman. The popular acceptance of history purely as story and of men in history as role-players was precisely what provoked his vehement declaration:

Since Gibbon, the spectacle was almost a scandal. History had lost even the sense of shame. It was a hundred years behind the experimental sciences. For all serious purpose, it was less instructive than Walter Scott and Alexandre Dumas.[50]

Yet neither were Adams' historical figures to be modeled on the "representative men" of the progressives. The obvious candidate for such portrayal in Adams' *History* was Thomas Jefferson. Jefferson's role in the *History* is *self*-defined, not socially defined, as Adams makes clear in his elaborate exegesis of the inaugural address in which Thomas Jefferson declares his intended course of action as President. Against this self-definition Adams sets the course of Jefferson's behavior. Jefferson fails to live up to his self-definition because of a crucial inability to master the national energies, the very forces that in the hands of Bancroft or Motley would have appeared to have been mysteriously channeled through him. Jefferson is at the mercy of history, passive and strangely evasive. The *History* is not deterministic, yet Adams gives one a sense of defining man's place in an increasingly naturalistic order.

Brooks Adams was less resistant to determinism, especially in *The Law of Civilization and Decay*. There he accepts a concept of typology (starting from his two basic types of "imaginative" and "economic" man) which goes far beyond the social roles of the holist tradition. The characters of Prescott and Parkman are at least aware of the limits of their roles and this almost tragic apprehension of the gap between reality and the restricted consciousness of the role is accessible to the historian for dramatic purposes. Brooks Adams defines his characters through types which are determined by historical relation to a specific environment, very basic human drives (fear and greed), race, energy, and the vaguest and most menacing kind of impersonal forces, like "acceleration." [51] At least part of the road to Crane's Henry Fleming, the hero of *The Red Badge of Courage*, is clear. The characteristic of mental flexibility that for earlier progressive historians had meant access to an idea or to the force of the people as the prime movers in human affairs, and that Brooks Adams had initially called "free variation," has now disappeared. In the new law there is to be no flexibility in human responses.

The more subtle and humane historical imagination of Henry Adams reveals the force of this typology still more tellingly. He is intensely interested in individuals, but as supreme social types, not as beings who have a symbolic value and are proper objects for worship. The mythical qualities of historical figures like the Virgin or George Washington have a value quite independent of the figures themselves. The typology of his later work is inevitably reductive, though not so much so as Brooks'. One need only remember his anti-Darwinian version of Grant as an atavism, his description of Theodore Roosevelt as "pure act," his description of the caveman aspect of St. Francis and the modern aspect of St. Thomas. Henry Adams' historical individuals retain much of their representative character as summations of historical forces, but become stock figures of historical taxonomy rather than historical melodrama. To be sure, this constant evolutionary reference by Adams is largely ironic, but irony is one of Adams' main strategies for replacing the old dispensation in historical laws with a new one. Adams is a critical heir of both frames of the historical imagination, his characters incapable of tragedy yet doomed to live without well-founded hope. The naturalist's solution appears in history as in art at the turn of the century. The concluding description of the Gothic cathedral in *Mont-Saint-Michel and Charters* could—barring style—be Dreiser:

The delight of its aspirations is flung up to the sky. The pathos of its self-distrust and anguish of doubt is buried in the earth as its last secret. You can read out of it whatever else pleases your youth and confidence; to me, this is all.[52]

Chapter Three

COOPER: THE RANGE OF THE
AMERICAN HISTORICAL NOVEL

'I' has become almost traditional to compare Cooper and Parkman as artists of the American forest and as interpreters of the American Indian. Cooper has more in common with Parkman than subject matter, however, for his vision of the American past is a function of the same social imagination as governs *The Conquest of Mexico* and *La Salle and the Discovery of the Great West*. Evidence of the holist imagination at work is most palpable in that feature of Cooper's novels which critics have held in least esteem, namely the conventional lovers whose sole purpose—beyond their "sentimental interest"—seems to be to assure the continuity of the race and unbroken possession of the wealth to which Cooper's heroes are inevitably heir. Further evidence appears in the occasionally snappish attribution of moral worth to what his more fastidious day did not shrink from calling deportment, as well as Cooper's incessantly repeated defenses and redefinitions of the "gentleman." Although the holist may be a relativist among cultures, within a given civilization the sanctity of the role becomes a moral absolute, not to be tampered with. Yet Cooper's positive values as a novelist, as well as his crankiness, must also be attributed to the holist frame. One of his real strengths, for example, is his appreciation of the mores and institutions that bind society together, even though his admiration for the means of social stability sometimes made him more inventive than accurate as regards the society of the red man, and unfortunately partisan (in defense of, for example, Episcopalianism and the rights of private property) as regards the society of the white man. The most important feature of Cooper's holism is his attempt to render the dimensions of man within or on the margins of society. These dimensions may seem rather constricted to most modern readers, since most of Cooper's characters appear so narrowly confined within their social definition—as gentlemen, savages, or boors—as scarcely to exist except as the representation of a social type. Yet Natty Bumppo and the other great characters of Cooper's fiction are also products of the holist mode, and are great in much the same way as Cortez and La Salle are great. Self-sufficient and alone within the social definition of his role, the holist hero is almost inevitably the protagonist of an adventure story. This psychologically limiting conception of character could not satisfy the novelist as it could the historian, however, and so Cooper liberated the holist hero for art by placing him *between* cultures.

↳ The Renegade and the Mock-Renegade Figures

The "renegade" archetype—a deserter, traitor, wanderer, or, to use Leatherstocking's favorite term of opprobrium, the "vagabond"— is fundamentally a holist conception, although it also represents an escape from holist social categories. The renegade and his heroic double, the mock-renegade, are ambiguous, resonant figures because they are culturally two-faced creations. In the first place, each represents a genuine "sociological" type, with a recognizably objective historical equivalent; for example, the Indian debauched by contact with white men, the hunter-trapper who preceded the farming frontier, or the actual espionage agents of eighteenth-century warfare. The "realism" of Leatherstocking as an historical type was justly praised by as knowledgeable an historian as Park-

man, even while the later writer was taking exception to the lack
of verisimilitude of the novelist's Indians.[1] Yet the inner logic
of the character of the renegade or mock-renegade is always formed
by his perpetual striving for self-definition in a fictive world in
which the self can scarcely be conceived to exist outside of a stable
social matrix. A character who is an acceptable "historical type,"
drawn from a dynamic and fluid historical situation, may be without the credentials of social respectability in Cooper's world: that
is, without a culturally defined role in a stable society. The renegade or mock-renegade can transcend the typical to approach
mythical status in Cooper's best fiction.

↪ The American Scott

If there is one assured event in nineteenth-century literary history,
it is Sir Walter Scott's "invention" of the historical romance in
1814 with the publication of *Waverley*. To overlook the antecedents of the "American Scott" would be doubly misleading, for
not only did Cooper help develop the new genre as a popular
vehicle, but he was close enough in time and world-view to Scott
(unlike Melville, say, or Twain) to give their differences significance. While recognizing that the attention of literary critics and
historians to the "influence" of Scott has probably been the greatest single obstacle to an understanding of the manifold forms of
the historical novel, one may still probe those significant differences in searching for the essence of Cooper's historical art.

C. Hugh Holman has found the essence of Scott's formula for
the historical novel to consist of an historical event or events seen
from the point of view of a fictional character or characters whose
lives are in turn shaped by history.[2] The shaping of the fictional
protagonist may be either more or less deterministic depending
upon whether he is a Waverley or a Jeanie Deans, but there is no
doubt that the central narrative line of a Scott novel depends
entirely upon that protagonist's encounter with forces of history

he cannot materially affect. "Heroes" like Ivanhoe, Quentin Durward, and Frank Osbaldistone have been criticized for their colorlessness, yet Georg Lukács has found great merit in the "middleof-the-road hero" as the novelist's analytic tool for revealing the forces operating in any given historical situation.[3] Lukács also indicated the role of the Great Man in Scott's fiction: setting right the consequences of the protagonist's encounter with history at a critical juncture. Cooper's most signal departures from Scott's formula are occasioned by his relegating both event and middleof-the-road hero to a relatively minor place in his novels, without ever abandoning them entirely.

The Cooperian archetype, the renegade or mock-renegade, tends to supplant the middle-of-the-road hero in Cooper's historical romances and at the same time to remove the necessity for a Great Man or world-historical individual. With a few important exceptions, Cooper does not attempt to depict authentic historical individuals, and in one novel, *The Pilot*, the Great Man himself (John Paul Jones) is a semi-renegade. The specific historical event, again with a few important exceptions, also does not have the value, or perhaps one should say the historistic value, that it possesses for Scott. The historical *situation* counts for everything with Cooper, and the "associations" of historical atmosphere count for comparatively little. Cooper's effort was directed in each of his novels towards defining that situation through one dominant theme, and matching his simplicity of historical theme by a narrative line that, compared to Scott or even to the Scottish master's other American pupil, Simms, is simple and sparse, without the complexity, diffuseness, and richness of social milieu that can be evoked by elaborate subplotting.

Cooper's dominant themes extend over the whole spectrum of the nineteenth-century historical imagination, from subjects that are typically "progressive" to those that are typically "holist." The divided intellectual allegiance of the American artist mocks these categories, and in every one of the writers I examine there are

strong traces of both structures. To cite one example, the fictive
world of *Huckleberry Finn* by the progressive Twain has a denser
social matrix than was ever created by Cooper. In every case, the
apparent inconsistency is the result of the novelist's struggle with
the diminished sense of reality that adherence to one frame of
the historical imagination alone entails. Thus, the most coherent
way of approaching Cooper's historical fiction—which comprises
the bulk of his writing—may be under the rubrics of both of these
frames.

The Idea of the State and the problems of progressive change
pervade the Revolutionary and European novels, just as one can
trace the great holist theme of decline and fall through the Leatherstocking tales and the Littlepage trilogy. The historian of ideas
would find variations on the concepts of progress and the self-
determined integrity of society throughout Cooper's work; yet as
fiction, as narrative art, its treatment of the imaginative *structure*
of society is most significant, and so I have grouped Cooper's
historical fiction with an eye to the closeness of each to the holist
or progressive frame.[4]

⌐ The Revolutionary Novels

The Spy: A Tale of the Neutral Ground, Cooper's 1821 novel of
the American Revolution, exemplifies the contradictions and peculiar power of his historical imagination. The contradictions
arise from the very meaning of the Revolution for Cooper, and
the power from his attempt to reconcile through symbolic and
mythic means the conflict between his social ideals—the structure
of his social vision—and the realities of historical change which
he could not ignore.

The Revolution presented a thorny problem for Cooper the
fierce patriot and for Cooper the lover of good social order: how
to distinguish the process of national birth from the accompany-
ing throes of dangerous philosophies and social upheaval. Cooper

tries twice to meet the question head on in *The Spy*. The first time is in a discussion between the British Colonel Wellmere and the American army surgeon Sitgreaves. Wellmere chides the American for a lack of "consistency" on the part of the American leaders who have declared "the equality of political rights" but have said nothing of the emancipation of their slaves. The doctor's equivocal answer to the charge lays the blame for the introduction of slavery on England's colonial policy, and makes the naive assumption (from the date of Cooper's writing) that slavery will someday end through gradual manumission. What is rhetorically significant is the strictly limited justification advanced for the Revolution:

We deem it a hardship to be ruled by the king of a people who live at a distance of three thousand miles, and who cannot, and who do not, feel a single political interest in common with ourselves. I say nothing of oppression; the child was of age, and was entitled to privileges of majority.[5]

The doctor makes the shift from the progressive question of "liberty" to the more holist question of nationalism; from the doctrine of natural rights to the metaphor of natural growth. Cooper's desire to define the essential purpose of the Revolution as narrowly as possible is shown with considerable low humor in another colloquy, this time between Katy Haynes, the "Yankee" housekeeper, and Frances Wharton, the genteel patriot sympathizer:

"If I could but see anything to fight about," said Katy, ". . . I shouldn't mind it so much. 'Twas said the king wanted all the tea for his own family, at one time; and then again, that he meant the colonies should pay over to him all their earnings. Now this is matter enough to fight about—for I'm sure that no one, however he may be lord or king, has a right to the hard earnings of another. Then it was all contradicted, and some said Washington wanted to be king himself; so that, between the two, one doesn't know which to believe."

"Believe neither—for neither is true. I do not pretend to understand, myself, all the merits of this war, Katy; but to me it seems unnatural, that a country like this should be ruled by another so distant as England." [6]

The book's central conflicts do not really revolve around the reasons for the Revolution (since Cooper regards that problem as settled), but rather concern the problem of honorable behavior in a chaotic historical situation. The Neutral Ground—a no-man's-land alternately overrun by the British and Americans—was Cooper's first great experiment in making his landscape play an active and even symbolic role in his work. It is, of course, the scene of divided loyalties, as with the Wharton children, as well as of prudent non-commitment, the course of Mr. Wharton, the Trimmer of the Neutral Ground. The Neutral Ground is a prize to be possessed by the opposing armies which clash on it. It is a victimized region ravaged by raiding parties of "Skinners" and "Cowboys" who pillage farms and battle one another. It is a center of social anarchy, signalized by the unscrupulous confiscation of property for political crimes. Finally it is the scene of espionage, masked identities, and betrayal.

Cooper has transformed Revolutionary Westchester County into a controlled chaos symbolizing the destructive disorder of revolutionary change. The most typical denizens of the Neutral Ground are the Skinners—false patriots and thieves who are the leaders in confiscating Tory, or suspected Tory, real estate. It is characteristic of the novel that Cooper exposes the venal motives of the confiscators without examining the "progressive" subject of the *right* of confiscation.

Against this background of revolutionary disorder Harvey Birch assumes his significance. Harvey has been described by Charles A. Brady as "the first of Cooper's guardian presences, a mythopoeic emanation, almost, of the American landscape . . . a celibate hero, a tutelary wandering spirit, a protecting demigod, a redemptive figure." [7] With a less rigorously Christian frame of reference than Brady's, one may see Birch as a prototype not only of Natty Bumppo, but of Melville's Confidence Man and Ralph Ellison's Rinehart, the "master of chaos" of *Invisible Man*. The earmarks of the archetype are disguises, freedom of movement, and omniscience.[8]

Harvey is a peddler, and therefore an intermediary and transient by profession. Beyond that, Constance Rourke has shown that the peddler was already established as a folk figure by the early 1820's.[9] This native American type was a symbol of ambiguity, the valued itinerant who was never quite respectable or trusted. His unerring judgment in appealing to feminine taste was not his least suspect quality. Cooper could hardly have chosen his Spy better.

As a "master of chaos" with his link to "Mr. Harper," Harvey redeems the anarchy of revolution by symbolizing the principle of nationalism. The other face of the "demigod," however, is the servant of the Republic, "hunted like a beast" by his countrymen. Harvey is an Ishmael with a Cause. (A full reckoning of the Cooper factor in Melville discovers a great deal of Harvey Birch in Israel Potter.) Most significant for Cooper's later work is the introduction of the image of the mock renegade. In the Neutral Ground of masked loyalties and betrayal, where all virtue is identified with open and steadfast commitment, Harvey must assume the deceptions of the double agent. Vindicatory speech is barred to him, and he must take consolation that there is *"one"* to whom he has made promises, "and to him I have never yet broken my word." [10]

This note of divine omniscience, constantly reinforced by Harvey's fears "that HE had forgotten that I lived," may serve to introduce the figure of the Great Man, Washington.[11] Unfortunately, for Cooper's contemporaries Washington was the great man *par excellence*, and even the implied humility of his assumed disguise as Mr. Harper drew protests. Such criticism now appears unreasonable. Idealized almost out of all humanity, Washington is here the touchstone of Republican virtue that he was to remain for the nineteenth century, and that Henry Adams would look back to wonderingly in *Democracy*. Yet he is not entirely the progressive Great Man, the pure embodiment of an Ideal, for Cooper shows that Washington too is bound by artificial laws— in this case, the usages of war regarding spies. Washington preserves the facade of law amidst anarchy, justifying the narrowly nationalistic and legitimist view of the Revolution.

In order to take advantage of its wealth of associations, Cooper introduces an historical event into *The Spy*, as he later does from time to time in his other novels—for example in *The Last of the Mohicans* and *Satanstoe*. Here, discussion often hinges on the death of Major André, the dashing British officer who intrigued with Benedict Arnold. Washington had been entreated by many on both sides to spare André when he was captured. Despite André's rank, high breeding, and popularity, Washington did not relent. Cooper's allusion to the affair has a fine aptness, as the outcry over the fate of the aristocratic André contrasts ironically with Harvey's miserable existence. The associations of Arnold's treason make all the implications of the Neutral Ground reverberate.

When confronting the underlying conflicts of *The Spy*, it is easy to make the mistake into which a preoccupation with the "international theme" leads Marius Bewley; that is, to see Cooper weighing English against Americans, and to see Harvey's "ambiguity" arising from his role as a line of communication between the opposing sides.[12] This theme has no relevance for the "progressive" *Spy* although it has some for the more thoroughly holistic *Satanstoe*. The contrast between the British and the Americans is for the most part typical, superficial, Cooperian "plot." The tension which makes history come alive in the novel results from the shifting faces of deceit, neutrality, and commitment. The social and intellectual forces released by the Revolution bring the moral problem of political behavior to greater intensity. Through the symbolic figures of Washington and Harvey Birch, Cooper offers the conservative a means of preserving a vital essence from the destructive chaos of violent historical change.

Cooper's success with *The Spy* inspired him to attempt a much more elaborate treatment of the Revolution. *Lionel Lincoln, or the Leaguer of Boston,* was Cooper's most ambitious attempt at what may be called the "historistic novel." Researched in depth, it was to have been the first installment in a series of thirteen novels on the American Revolution in each of the colonies.[13] The novel is endowed with a wealth of historical detail, including the logistics of the siege (or "leaguer"), the personalities of prominent officers on both sides, and, especially, superb descriptions of the battles of Lexington and Bunker Hill. Yet the novel as a whole is badly botched, a strange mismatching of historicism and Gothicism which might have marked a new departure for Cooper but which was ultimately such a confused failure that he abandoned his projected chronicle of the Revolution. The failure is instructive, however, both for the revealing possibilities of Cooper's approach and for exposing the irresoluble difficulties to which it led him.

The novel begins with the re-entry of the hero, Lionel Lincoln, into Boston—his native home—from England, where he has received a baronet's education. Though an officer in the British army, Lionel has family ties to the rebel side, and seemingly by chance finds himself the protector of a militantly patriotic and Calvinist half-wit who, immune to reason and intimidation, is constantly threatened by the redcoats with punishment or death. This imbecile object of the hero's constrained affection (rather unfortunately revealed late in the novel as his own half-brother) helps to create the atmosphere for a psychological romance as he moves against the background of a besieged Boston which lies somewhere between the London of *Journal of the Plague Year* and the Philadelphia of Brockden Brown's *Arthur Mervyn*. Cooper employs an absurdly complicated Gothic plot to bring about the dénouement, but even his bungling cannot obscure the psychic disintegration of the hero who, at the melodramatic crisis of the novel, literally "loses his mind" and goes over to the rebel side.[14] The hero's encounter with the Revolution—as opposed to the author's *presentation* of the Revolution—is a journey into madness, from which Lionel eventually is rescued and returned to England where he lives out his days as a conservative peer and Member of Parliament.

The novel fails because Cooper completely lacked the talent of a Brockden Brown, a Poe, or a Hawthorne for evoking abnormal states of consciousness. (It is possible, however, that Hawthorne took a hint from the novel's structure for "My Kinsman, Major Molineux.") Despite Cooper's weakness in execution, *Lionel Lincoln* points towards a method of internalizing historical conflict in the novel *through* Gothic "machinery," a method which is to become dominant in the historical fiction not only of Hawthorne but of Faulkner. As many critics have pointed out, Cooper's historistic presentation of the Revolution in the book seems to have too few rational and unambiguous points of contact with the Gothic melodrama of Lionel's search for his identity for the novel to possess any viable unity. Whereas, in *The Spy* Cooper constantly redeemed the disturbing phenomenon of revolution by reference to a national Ideal, in *Lionel Lincoln* he attempts to take the dangerous implications of social chaos latent (to his holistic mind) in the Revolution as the *basis* for his view of the event. This makes the novel a risky experiment in control of meaning for an author usually given to over-explicitness. Cooper had also taken a holistically negative view of revolution in *The Pilot* (1823), but in that novel he had removed the scene of the conflict to England, where most of the intimations of social disorder become academic. Not progressive and Idealistic, the threatening overtones of the Revolution are not resolved in *Lionel Lincoln* through the holist frame either, for the subplot shows Lionel's family (the repository of virtue and stability in the holist view) honeycombed with corruption and madness. For Cooper, success required a thematic blending of contradictory attitudes at the center of his historical conception. *Lionel Lincoln,* with its schizophrenic mixture of modes, is one of his most fascinating failures.

↴ The European Novels

Cooper's three "European" novels, *The Bravo* (1831), *The Heidenmauer* (1832), and *The Headsman* (1833), have received increasing attention from recent critics of Cooper such as Marius Bewley and Donald A. Ringe.[15] *The Bravo* had been especially commended by Ringe as on a level with the Leatherstocking tales, and Bewley has found *The Heidenmauer* to contain the essence of Cooper's criticism of the growing money power within the United States itself. There is more binding these novels together than a Continental locale and the avowed republicanism of their author at the time of their composition. They stand as a self-contained trilogy, flawed and inconsistent in many of the details, yet representing Cooper's most sustained attempt to discover and reveal the pattern of Progress in the Western world. The American Revolution had proven to be too close and ambiguous a subject for Cooper clearly to express his ideas on the theme of historical progress, and the European background allowed him the license he needed for didactic fiction. That his pattern eventually collapsed, notably in *The Headsman,* is due to his failure to recognize that the same contradictions in his progressive subject matter that had plagued him in his novels of the Revolution would reassert themselves even in an Old World setting.

It is well to reiterate the distinction between the genuinely progressive social and historical imagination and the merely typical subject matter of progressivism. Thus even when Cooper is concerned with such eminently progressive themes as the Idea of the State, he tends to make his points through the observation of nuances of manners, as in this passage from *The Heidenmauer*:

Whoever has had much intercourse with Asiatics, or with Mussulmans of the southern shore of the Mediterranean, must have frequently observed the silent, significant manner with which they regard each other, when disposed to court or to yield confidence: the eye gradually kindling, and the muscles of the mouth relaxing, until the feeling is fully betrayed in a smile. This is one of the means employed by men who dwell under despotic and dangerous governments, and where the social habits are much tinctured with violence and treachery, of assuring one another of secret faith and ready support. There is a sort of similar freemasonry in all conditions of life, in which frank and just institutions do not spread their mantle equally over the powerful and the weak, superseding, by the majesty of the law, the necessity of these furtive appeals to the pledges and sympathies of confidants.[16]

The Bravo is by far the most didactic novel of the trilogy, and yet, despite the modern aversion to the didactic in art, it has probably survived the best as fiction.[17] Its success, however, does not represent any imaginative innovation for Cooper, for this novel of eighteenth-century Venice is actually a sophisticated variation on the structure of The Spy. Venice, like the Neutral Ground of the earlier work, is a complex and treacherous domain of fear, masks, and subterranean passageways, where the faces of the rulers are always concealed and where deception and disguise are the modes of survival. While the Neutral Ground and Harvey Birch had been redeemed by the national Ideal, there is no escape from the totalitarian chaos of Venice, for in The Bravo Cooper's subject is the betrayal of the ideal of the Venetian republic by the ruling oligarchy. In this false republic, the goal of policy is the unrestrained power and wealth of the commercial ruling classes, and the chief qualification for statecraft is the ability to deny human feeling whenever the interests of the State are involved.

Jacopo, the Bravo, is a true "mock-renegade" descendant of Harvey Birch. He is distrusted by everyone for his reputation as a hired assassin, but actually he is the innocent and unwilling agent of the state, forced to maintain his "renegade" pretense lest his imprisoned father suffer. Like his predecessors, the Spy, the Pilot, and the Leatherstocking of *The Pioneers*, he possesses a "secret" identity which he may not divulge, and which validates his claim to "civilization," a claim denied to the genuine renegade. Jacopo is sinister enough, however, as the servant ("innocent" or not) of the false republic, and the burden of true republican apostleship is borne by the old fisherman, Antonio. It is as if Cooper had split the character of the mock-renegade in two, to get the benefit of both forthrightness and suffering silence as witnesses against the regime. Perhaps the loquaciousness of mock-renegade Natty Bumppo, permitted to him alone of these most typical figures of Cooper's imagination, is a key to his survival and development as a character through a series of five novels. The others, trapped like Jacopo and Harvey Birch in the necessity for concealment endemic in the world of Cooper's "progressive" historical novels, never endure beyond a single book.

The Heidenmauer is the most genuinely original novel of the three in its conception. The austerity of its presentation, however, together with the lack of panache which had leavened the didacticism of *The Bravo*, make it less congenial than the earlier novel to Cooper's talents, which were those of a romancer and political raissoneur rather than a philosophical novelist. The anti-utopian *Bravo* had presented in the decadent republic of Venice a metaphor for those evils of the past which must be eradicated by the march of progress. *The Heidenmauer* is Cooper's attempt to dramatize historical progress itself, to "represent society, under its ordinary faces, in the act of passing from the influence of one set of governing principles to that of another." [18] The historical subject of the novel was the quintessential one for the American progressive imagination, much more vital than the possibly ambiguous American Revolution or the positively dangerous French one. This subject was the Reformation, venerated by Bancroft as the shining example of the progress of Truth and by Motley as the opening of the modern era of Liberty. *The Heidenmauer*, however, illustrates how a thoroughly holist imagination may transform a progressive theme so as to leave it virtually unrecognizable.

The chief action of the novel, which is set in sixteenth-century Germany, is a contest between the powers of church and state which culminates in the destruction of an abbey and the eventual reconciliation of the opposing factions. The antagonists, Prince Emich and the Abbot Benedictus, are pitted against one another as cultural and political types rather than as the embodiments of different philosophies (Cooper was perhaps aiming somewhat unsuccessfully at the kind of contrast Scott had achieved in Louis XI and Burgundy in *Quentin Durward*), for their struggle grows out of a desire for personal power and long antedates the new theological opinions of the age of Luther. Cooper is quite effective in this regard as he shows by inference the political usefulness of the Lutheran heresy to the German barons. Brute force and the customs of the day are far more important than Ideas or the conflicting claims of legitimacy in the power struggle which begins, revealingly, with a drinking contest between Prince and Abbot.

There is a third party to the conflict, in the person of Heinrich Frey, the burgomaster of Duerckheim (a character who may also owe something to an original in *Quentin Durward*), who as representative of the perpetually rising middle class attaches himself and the "popular party" to the side of the Prince. This bourgeois revolutionary is emphatically not a representative of the historical type described by Weber and Tawney, nor is he properly seen, as Marius Bewley claims, as the exemplar of a rampant money power.[19] Gullible, easily flattered, equally the slave of wealth and rank, Frey is no more the hardheaded, grasping bourgeois than he is a democrat; unwilling or unable to seek the causes of the quarrel in which he has been enlisted, he is eventually sold out by Emich when the Prince reaches his inevitable settlement with the

Church. The true significance of this naive champion of the third estate is different, for he and his wife Ulricke (one of the few figures of flawless religious devotion in the book) allow Cooper to indulge his favorite metaphor for historical change and disturbance—the crossing of customary boundaries and the breaking of taboos. This is especially effective in the comic scene in which Emich forces the reluctant burgomaster to sit in the Prince's chair, and in the revelation that both Prince Emich and the penitent ex-iconoclast and noble Odo von Ritterstein had desired to marry the commoner Ulricke but had been barred by their rank. Manners have more sway here than the "law of progress."

If there is a law in history, Cooper seems to be saying, it is a law of flux, in which contending forces are constantly seeking a new equilibrium, and in which sometimes one and sometimes another "spirit" appears to dominate society. *The Heidenmauer* is in part a travelogue, and like the other European novels, it contains a good deal of pedantic commentary on the proper way to observe, compare, and evaluate different cultures and civilizations. In the world of these novels, all is relative both within and among cultures, and even terminology is not constant. There are no philosophically absolute terms of description such as Twain will pugnaciously insist upon in his debunking of the European past in *The Innocents Abroad*.[20] Cooper also denies the validity of historical symbolism such as that to be practiced by Hawthorne and Melville in which act, event, and sign are perceived as one. Although Cooper himself at times utilized historical symbolism, he contends in this novel that symbols are merely "idle significations" that mask the contradictory mixture of interest and principle which guides the actual history-makers.

What Cooper was attempting to evoke was the complicated nature of historical change and the falseness of any attempt to polarize historical conflict into the forces of Truth vs. Superstition, while showing society so intimately bound together by inter-

ests, beliefs, habits, and manners as to force "progress" to pursue
a very devious path indeed. This passage, probably Cooper's fullest statement on historical change, shows that such a holist analysis as his may be developed to some complexity:

It has been seen that Emich, though much disposed to throw off the
dominion of the church, so far clung to his ancient prejudices as se-
cretly to distrust the very power he was about to defy, and to entertain
grave scruples not only of the policy, but of the lawfulness of the step
his ambition had urged him to adopt. In this manner does man become the instrument of the various passions and motives that beset
him, now yielding, or now struggling to resist, as a stronger induce-
ment is presented to his mind; always professing to be governed by
reason and constrained by principles, while, in truth, he rarely con-
sents to consult the one, or to respect the other, until both are offered through the medium of some engrossing interest that requires
an immediate and active attention. Then, indeed, his faculties become suddenly enlightened, and he eagerly presses into his service
every argument that offers, the plausible as well as the sound; and thus
it happens that we frequently see whole communities making a moral
pirouette in a breath, adopting this year a set of principles that are
quite in opposition to all they had ever before professed. Fortunately,
all that is thus gained on sound principles is apt to continue, since
whatever may be the waywardness of those who profess them, principles themselves are immutable, and when once fairly admitted, are
not easily dispossessed by the bastard doctrines of expediency and
error. These changes are gradual as respect those avant-couriers of
thought, who prepare the way for the advance of nations, but who,
in general, so far precede their contemporaries, as to be utterly out of
view at the effectual moment of the reformation, or revolution, or by
whatever name these sudden summersets are styled; but as respects
the mass, they often occur by a *coup de main;* an entire people awakening, as it were, by magic, to the virtue of a new set of maxims, much
as the eye turns from the view of one scenic representation to that of
its successor.[21]

The Headsman, set in eighteenth-century Switzerland, forms a
logical sequel to the novel of the anti-utopian past and the novel
of progressive change, for it is concerned with the effort of a group

of "enlightened" people to cope with the dead hand of the past. The claim of the past consists in the office of headsman, or executioner, once an honorific gift to a favored family but at the time of the novel a mandatory entail in a more squeamish age. Although the novel is badly marred both by its insecure mixture of modes (being roughly one-third "nautical"—in Switzerland!—and one-third travelogue) and more especially by its claptrap mixed-identities resolution, at its best it offers a serious attempt to grapple with the unwieldy heritage of the past.

The heart of the novel is a domestic dilemma in which a conventional problem—the "inappropriate suitor"—is given resonance by the circumstance that he appears to be disqualified as a result of historical wrong and prejudice. In this basically sentimental novel the outcast is not, as is usual with Cooper, a romantic exile; for once the problem of the mock-renegade is seen from within the family circle, thus developing a greater complexity of moods and attitudes than usual. Unfortunately, Cooper dodges the entire problem at the end, making the suitor the true son of the Doge, rather than of the headsman. The most promising character in the book, Il Maledetto, a genuine renegade, is then revealed as the suitor's illegitimate half-brother. The spectacle with which Cooper leaves the reader is of the author attempting to fight one prejudice of birth (hereditary office) with another (illegitimacy). Cooper's own holist sympathies and associations have become too implicated in the argument he is supposedly trying to combat.

The trilogy as a whole does show how Cooper was able to adapt the apparently stereotyped formula of his historical romances with some flexibility to suit his theme. Thus in his novel of ideas, he concentrated the interest of his tale in the image of one man against a system; in his novel of change he emphasized the three more or less equal effective forces of one era of the past in their complex interactions; and in his study of the partially unwholesome historical residue inherited by the modern world, the crux of his drama is the struggle of three families with a moral and emotional predicament. As his miniature panorama of progress approaches the modern situation, there is in every case a broadening and normalization of significant milieu, an effort to restore stability and cultural complexity to the center of the social spectrum.

⌐ Some Versions of Pastoral

Cooper's conservative optimism in the face of historical progress is matched, in his work, by a stoicism which threatens to collapse into shrill declamation in the face of the decline of valued dominant cultures. Cooper's intrinsic fatalism appears most strikingly, however, when he is not dealing directly with the major themes of the progressive and holist imaginations, but instead is probing the possibility of an escape from historical chaos. This possibility seems to be offered through the figure of Leatherstocking; but the lone man, torn from his cultural matrix, is too ambiguous a cultural alternative to be acceptable. In *The Wept of Wish-ton-Wish* (1829) and *Wyandotte* (1843), Cooper tries to extract entire patriarchal communities from the disorder of two different revolutionary ages, creating rustic but hierarchical societies reminiscent of that of the exiled Duke in *As You Like It*. (Apropos of Shakespeare, it is only Polonius' example which keeps me from designating these novels "historical-pastoral.") Combining the issues of revolution and the frontier, and representing both the first decade of Cooper's career and the last, the two books may serve in this discussion as a bridge between his progressive and holist concerns.

The Wept of Wish-ton-Wish, set in the Connecticut valley of the seventeenth century, and *Wyandotte*, set in western New York at the time of the American Revolution, are each centrally concerned with communities which maintain a high standard of civilization in an extremely primitive environment. Cooper's conventional requirement of upper-class characters in his wilderness situations is often, as Henry Nash Smith has shown so well, an acute artistic embarrassment.[22] Here the presence of "artificial" characters does not encumber the novel with a debilitating convention, but rather places it within a viable literary tradition, the ancient pastoral theme of highly sophisticated individuals seeking and finding a simpler and truer mode of existence in rustic surroundings. At the center of the structure of each novel is the community (the Wish-ton-Wish of one title and the "Hutted Knoll" of the other's subtitle), which acquires symbolic value as a sanctuary of civilization in the wilderness. The basic movement of each novel consists of a series of threats to that sanctuary, culminating in its penetration and destruction. Whether knowingly or not, Cooper placed these two novels precisely in the tradition first delineated by Crèvecoeur's "epistolary romance" *Letters from an American Farmer,* with its progression from pastoral to a renewed awareness of the evils of man's history and the invasion of the rustic retreat by History in the form of savage–civilized warfare.

The Wept of Wish-ton-Wish represents Cooper's effort to study the psychology of two "alien" cultures, for Puritanism was almost as distant from him—or so he would have the reader believe—as the Indians themselves. This meant that he faced a problem similar to that of Prescott in *The Conquest of Mexico.* In the early part of the novel the Puritan is signally represented by Mark Heathcote, the patriarch of Wish-ton-Wish and ex-member of Cromwell's army who has abjured the military life, and, finding even Massachusetts too worldly, has settled with his family in the wilderness. Although Heathcote lacks any of the subtlety and psychological depth of Scott's Calvinists, he must be seen as at least a precursor of stern American frontier patriarchs down to Thomas Sutpen. The wilderness offers him a non-utopian opportunity to set up a community governed by his own law. Cooper's attitude towards him and his community, at least as far as their

Puritanism is concerned, is the typically half-admiring, half-super-cilious stance of the civilized pastoral artist before rude virtue.

The action of the novel is divided into two parts. In the first, set in the years immediately following the Restoration, the settlers establish their community. Heathcote's motive for leaving his position in "civilization" is dramatized by the visit of an old comrade, one of the regicides who signed Charles I's death warrant, and by the set of roguish soldiers who pursue him. The settlement is at last destroyed by Indians, who burn it to the ground, apparently immolating the settlers within. The Puritans save themselves by artifice, however, by finding refuge in a well, and their reappearance has been appositely likened by Donald A. Ringe to the reemergence of the phoenix from the flames.[23] Yet the world into which they are reborn provides no escape from history, but rather is a world of unremitting war for survival between red men and white. Like *The Yemasee* by William Gilmore Simms, *The Wept of Wish-ton-Wish* is a novel of the last *serious* threat—King Philip's War—to the existence of the conquering white civilization. It represents the decisive turning point after which the doom of the red man is clear.

Writing about two "alien" cultures as he is, Cooper reveals the historical causes for the position of each group impartially, without the cynicism about the rights of opposing sides shown in *The Last of the Mohicans*. He also furnishes each group with an ideology which justifies the extermination of the other, whether spoken by the Wampanoag chief Metacom or by the Puritan divine, the Reverend Meek Wolfe. After the rebirth of the community into history in the New World, the only survivors are desperate Indians and Borderers, with a small group of original settlers who still possess the Christian love that had sent them into the wilderness and a tragic consciousness forced on them by the destruction of their pastoral dream.

Tacitly skirting the possibility of mock-renegadism as a "middle way," Cooper essays a more intimate study of the competing claims of savagery and civilization through his major subplot of the aborted conversion of a captured Indian boy and the complete acculturation to Indian life of a white girl captured by the Indians. The Indian is marked but unchanged by his captivity and becomes a famed warrior in the struggle against the whites. The girl, however, is completely transformed and becomes the squaw of Conanchet—the captured Indian boy grown to savage manhood. Although Cooper has with some justice been accused of yielding to the taboos of his day for effecting a convenient demise for the miscegenating couple, the novel clearly emphasizes the superior cultural integrity of the red man, not the European. The half-breed child of the couple is to be raised as an Indian. This brings the irony of the pastoral escape from the chaos of European "progress" full circle, for the original purity of purpose which sustained Mark Heathcote in his flight from the high historical complexity of the English Civil War is destined to perish before many generations—his great-grandson is doomed to fight for survival against the white man. History, even in its nascent, New World form, guarantees unrelenting hostility among the descendants of the original community.

Wyandotte represents a renewed pastoral rejection of the trappings of high civilization, a rejection symbolized by the refusal of Captain Willoughby, the head of the household, to accept the baronetcy which he has just inherited. Cooper is no longer writing about two "alien" cultures, for this pastoral outpost in the wilderness has been settled by the same New York gentry whose career he was shortly to chronicle in the Littlepage trilogy. Captain Willoughby, the genial master of the Hutted Knoll, resembles Judge Templeton of *The Pioneers* far more than he does grim Mark Heathcote, and seems to be a paragon of the New York empire-building aristocracy that Cooper admired. The affected sobriety of the Puritan is apparently not the worst of faults, however, for it is clear that the Captain's lack of introspection and reliance on the habits of military discipline rather

than either Christian charity or insight into the positive values
of Indian culture brings about his death at the hands of the of-
fended warrior Saucy Nick–Wyandotte.

The destructive aspect of history in *Wyandotte* has become
even more ominous than it had been in *The Wept of Wish-ton-
Wish*. History comes in the form of the American Revolution,
which appears in the background of the novel as a series of doubtful and confused echoes which bewilder and divide the formerly
harmonious inhabitants of the settlement.[24] The dubiousness of
the struggle itself is symbolized by the invasion of the Knoll by
an irregular force of Indians and masquerading whites, whose true
identity and allegiance is left deliberately cloudy. In collusion with
the invaders is Joel Strides, a Yankee prototype of the upwardly
mobile Newcomes of the Littlepage trilogy. Cooper has his difficulties with the character, for Strides must be contemptible, rather
than a full-fledged villain, and so the book is burdened with
strident denunciations of demagoguery even while that demagoguery is shown to be self-defeating and ultimately ineffective
in the face of the cultural ascendancy of the Willoughbys. As in
Lionel Lincoln, Cooper denies the saving grace of emerging nationalism to the Revolutionary chaos of savage warfare and class
strife. In *Wyandotte* the Revolution is a destructive force which
penetrates the very heart of the pastoral community, setting father
against son and brother against sister at the very moment when
their "servants" (Saucy Nick and Strides) are betraying them. In
The Wept of Wish-ton-Wish the community itself had stayed
whole and endured its trial. The tensions of the Revolution cause
the survivors of the Hutted Knoll to flee again to the order of the
Old World.

⤙ The Leatherstocking Saga

The Leatherstocking novels are quintessential Cooper and are unmistakeably holist in their frame of social and historical reference.

In this series Cooper narrates the decline and fall of the American wilderness and the red man's culture, binding the sequence of novels together through the character of Natty Bumppo, the elegiac agent of progress. If Cooper poses an ideal to justify the fall of the Indian, it is "civilization," not "progress," a seamless whole of established social values, not a transcendent Idea moving through Time. In his holist novels, Cooper's great subject is the ugly rent in the fabric of both white and red civilization made by the cutting edge of history.

The Leatherstocking Tales are too well known as a group to require description here. Yet the difference between the complex tensions and microcosmic society of *The Pioneers* and the ritualized and mythicized wilderness of *The Deerslayer*, composed twenty years later—the change which D. H. Lawrence called a "*decrescendo* of reality and a crescendo of beauty"—prohibits any attempt to find meaningful generalizations for the special quality of Cooper's historical imagination throughout the whole canon.[25] The best course may be to examine the one novel in the saga which most closely approaches conventional definitions of historical romance in an effort to uncover the historical themes which control Leatherstocking's fictional world.

The Last of the Mohicans: A Narrative of 1757 was published in 1826, the second volume of the series in order of composition and in the "myth" of Leatherstocking's life. The novel opens with an historical introduction, sketching the French and Indian Wars as a contest of those who "had pledged their blood to satiate their vengeance, or to uphold the cold and selfish policy of the distant monarchs of Europe." [26] The frontier is depicted as a region terrorized by the Indian allies of both sides, the English are accused of bungling and "imbecility," and the colonials are shown in suffering subordination. The corrupting effect of Old World diplomacy and statecraft in the New World wilderness gives the book its historical unity.

The wilderness of upper New York plays a role as active in its way as that of the Neutral Ground in *The Spy*. On the scenic level it is a somber and sublime land of cataracts, dense forests, and rocky cliffs. On the military level it is a cockpit. The destiny of the land is obscured, for from even a short historical perspective, it is clear that the Powers were contesting for land "neither was destined to retain." [27] Significantly, there are no "Yorkers" in the novel. French, British, Yankee, Virginian, Delaware, and Huron—all, including Natty, are transient. *The Last of the Mohicans* is concerned exclusively with the passing of the old order.

Natty Bumppo is like Harvey Birch, subject to the suspicion of being a renegade—in this case a racial renegade. Blessed with the privilege of speech on the subject, he exercises it incessantly in describing himself as "a Man without a cross." Natty's social value as a scout and guide is never called into question, yet his fundamental moral and personal problem—like Harvey's—is related to the uncertain and ambiguous status attached to a role which is unexceptionable in historical perspective.

The characterization of Montcalm is drawn with explicit attention to the limited holist conception of the Great Man and to the theme of Old World corruption. Although Montcalm "bore a high character for courage and enterprise, he was also thought to be expert in those political practices which do not always respect the nicer obligations of morality, and which so generally disgraced the European diplomacy of that period." [28] The portrait with which Cooper illustrates this description is rendered with considerable humanity. Although Cooper condemns Montcalm for want of "moral courage," the French general's failing is also attributed to the curse of European diplomacy.[29] The exigencies of the balance of power have forced both sides to enter into "barbarous" alliances with the Indians, allies who cannot be restrained to the ordinary usages of European war. The substance of the Old World power struggle has been imported into the New, but without the carefully developed sanctions which alone can make balance-of-power politics appear humane. Montcalm is thus shown nego-

tiating with the British with consummate skill but is stymied
completely in a confrontation with Magua. The Indian leader's
moral and political standards make Montcalm's diplomacy ring
false, and not merely because Magua is diabolical and cunning.
Bewilderingly for Montcalm, the rules have changed.

The central historical event of the novel is the massacre at Fort
William Henry, the inevitable result of the unnatural alliance.
Cooper economically represents the massacre in one scene of infanticide and murder, and achieves the book's most powerful
dramatization of the savagery underlying this war conducted by
"civilized" powers. The lamentation scene of the pursuers searching the field of the dead is one of Cooper's most successful and
telling exploitations of "raw history" in order to put the iron of
reality in his romances.

With the William Henry episode the formally "historical" section of the novel concludes. The pretensions of the two Great
Powers to the New World are undermined, if not devastated. The
deficiency of "moral courage" on the part of Montcalm is balanced in a small way by the blundering Scot Munro, who misun-
derstands the racial nature of the new continent so badly (according to Cooper's lights) that he has an Indian chief flogged
and marries a mulatto. Whatever their individual merits, Cooper
seems to say, neither of these holistic civilizations is fit to rule in
America.

The great historical countertheme in *The Last of the Mohicans*,
alluded to earlier, is what Georg Lukács has called the decline of
Gentile, or tribal, society. Here, the downfall of the Delawares is
carefully attributed to treacherous treaties made with the Dutch
in the earliest colonial era. In the French and Indian wars their
subversion has been completed, and they are now allied with the
French and their traditional enemies the Hurons, or Mingoes.
(The effect of the original treaties was to make "women" out of
the Delawares.) Whether this is a fair or "accurate" historical
account is unimportant. The essential point is that Cooper has

intimately linked the downfall of the Delawares to their intercourse with the Europeans. Thus by the logic of the European balance of power, the Iroquois (the main "Mingo" tribe) are the allies of the British, the "good" imperial power. Cooper's audience was well aware that this alliance continues through the Revolution, when the frontier was again subject to barbarous warfare. Natty complains that "white cunning" has thrown everything into disorder, "destroying all the harmony of warfare." [30]

The ambiguous benefits of white contact are central to the meaning of the decline of Indian civilization. As always in the holist frame, the division between savage and civilized is absolute and unbreachable; though the Indian may be "idealized," his culturally determined nature is of a different order from that of the Europeans.[31] While Uncas is shown as partly ennobled by an engrafting of white and Christian attitudes, Magua attributes his own corruption and downfall to the same "civilizing" force. Magua, in fact, seems to be the prototype for Cooper's innumerable evil authentic renegades. As an historical type he is that half-Satanic, half-Napoleonic figure, the Romantic Evil Genius. Like his fictional descendants (Arrowhead, Mahtoree) he is an alien among his own people. He is grave, cunning, a superb orator and politician. Characteristically, his overreaching spirit must attempt the final fulfillment of the ego through the race-sex nexus.

The patriarchal figure of Tamenund is the historical antithesis of Magua, as Cooper contrasts the soundness of the old order of the red man with the Romantic explosion of corrupt decay. The pitting of Delaware against Delaware at the concluding council scene imbues Tamenund's decrees on his captives with the full weight of history. He is obliged to yield his friends to his enemies by the dictates of tribal law. The tragedy proceeds from the alliance which accompanied the downfall of the tribe. Significantly, the death of Uncas, the last of the Mohicans, is marked by a final assertion of tribal identity in battle with their traditional foes.

The Last of the Mohicans is not merely an elegy, but an exorcism of the ghost of the past. The era appears here as a dark and transitory age of mutual corruption of the Europeans and the native races of the continent. Cooper's views on the true destiny of the continent itself make no appearance.

⤳ The Littlepage Trilogy

In none of his historical fiction does Cooper attempt so directly to define the quality of a civilization as in the Littlepage novels, *Satanstoe* (1845), *The Chainbearer* (1845), and *The Redskins* (1846). By the 1840's Cooper had come to rest his sense of values exclusively in the conservative verities of the holist imagination. After his return to America in 1838, he abandoned the progressive subject matter of the preceding period and sought to demonstrate as vividly as possible in fiction the integrity and superiority of the civilization of his New York State gentry. The holist categories of social immobility predominate in his contemporary satires (*Homeward Bound, Home as Found*) as well as in the Littlepage trilogy. At the same time, the historical dimension saves at least *Satanstoe* and (partially) *The Chainbearer* from the flat caricatures and insufferable "gentlemen" of *Home as Found*.

Inspired by the Anti-Rent agitation of the 1840's, Cooper makes the land itself the true historical protagonist of the series, as it had been for the Leatherstocking books. Civilization is the product of a certain relationship to the land, in Cooper's holist conception, and if that relationship is destroyed, the Republic's nascent civilization must infallibly crumble. Cooper's position is not founded so much in the idea of fee-simple ownership and the sanctity of private property (though he makes tedious rhetorical use of both) as it is in his sense that civilization is more a matter of relationships—of men to the land and to each other—than it is of transcendent rights. Cooper, like Faulkner, sees the land as beyond "ownership" in any metaphysical sense, and through the Indian Susquesus he provides an ironic reminder of the indifference of the land to human claims.

The Chainbearer, to be sure, is a melodrama, but a vintage one. Close in mood to *Wyandotte* (both have the dislocations of the American Revolution in the background), its subject is the proper use of the land, with all the dimensions that theme possessed for Cooper—wastefulness versus nurture, anarchy versus ownership, cash value versus spiritual value. Of all his novels of the Revolution, *The Chainbearer* is most pregnant with the possibilities of the alternative civilizations for the Republic. Cooper taps the strongest vein of his imagination when he creates characters who do not fit into the holist web of civilization and who are doomed to extinction like Leatherstocking and his fellow mock-renegades, or who threaten the values of society in an "inadmissible" way, like Aaron Thousandacres and his Borderers. The tribe of Aaron Thousandacres, like that of Ishmael Bush in *The Prairie*, is dangerous because of its wasteful ways in relation to the land. In this they are joined by Hurry Harry of *The Deerslayer*, infected by renegadism as he is, and by Billy Kirby, the attractive but wantonly destructive backwoodsman of *The Pioneers*, who is probably the prototype of them all.

The challenge to the holist matrix represented by these "Borderers" (to use Cooper's name for Bush's clan) combines upward mobility and border transgression (class renegadism and culture renegadism) with something yet more powerful—the challenge of a new society. Unlike the solitary deviant renegades who people much of Cooper's fiction, Borderers like Ishmael Bush and Aaron Thousandacres seem to be themselves system builders, to be forming the nucleus of a new society. That society may be perverse, rapacious, and atavistic, according to Cooper, but within it egotism is suppressed by community rule, and as a holist he must respect the nascent society of the Borderers even as he respects the settlement of Wish-ton-Wish and the Hutted Knoll.

In short, Aaron Thousandacres represents for Cooper an instance of perverted pastoral, and an instance of great social import. (It is worth noting that the English edition of *The Wept of Wish-ton-Wish* was entitled *The Borderers.*) These Borderers represent a parody of the existing society, extending the dangerous and rapacious aspects of civilization as the Hutted Knoll and Wish-ton-Wish extend the communal spirit and mutual responsibility of civilization.

This sense of alternative possibilities of civilization, formulated in holist terms, gives Thousandacres' arguments[32] their currency and power in this trilogy in which cultural hegemony is celebrated and egalitarian ideology is scouted. Cooper's counterpoint of voices on the fate of the American soil—the law-and-tradition bound Chainbearer, the anarchic and egocentric Aaron Thousandacres, and the mocking, dispossessed Indian Susquesus—has the intensity of the dialogue of Faulkner's McCaslins, though Cooper lacks the economy and grace of the later author.

Susquesus himself is the final incarnation of Cooper's mock-renegade. Under suspicion because he has left his tribe to live among the whites, he becomes nevertheless the spokesman not only for the vanquished red man (who at the time Cooper wrote *The Redskins* faced complete cultural extinction in the Indian Territory) but also for the purity of civic virtue and civic faith of the almost mythical Early Republic. The false way in which Cooper relates the demise of the red man to the decline of the New York gentry as the unchallenged cultural arbiters of the region prevents *The Redskins* from being a good novel, yet it was almost inevitable that Cooper should make the attempt to relate the two declining cultures.

For Cooper's conception of the ideal relationship of man to the land, one cannot do better than to look to *Satanstoe*, the first volume of the trilogy. The order and harmony of New York society gives *Satanstoe* a radically different tone not only from its sequels but also from *The Last of the Mohicans*, although the two are about largely the same era and region—upper New York, 1757–58.

It is not that Cooper has mellowed—which indeed would be a curious way to describe the evolution of his temper from the mid-1820's to the mid-1840's. The harmony is present structurally in the novel as the author shows his characters in correct and unstrained familial relations with one another. Politics and history have not yet shattered the basic social unit. The blight affecting the family groups of the Whartons, of Major Munro, of Chingachgook and Uncas was not the result of a defect of family love, but of the impingement of politics and history. In his earlier historical novels Cooper was showing the destructive force of historical conflict and change (à la Crèvecoeur) in its most immediate form, through the family group; both *The Spy* and *The Last of the Mohicans* return constantly to the ritual image of the bereaved father, broken in spirit or stoically mourning.

In *Satanstoe* the emphasis on the family is expressed not merely in terms of dutiful sons and "excellent parents" but also extends to the many degrees of kinship which form an endless source of speculation, complication, and satisfaction in the novel. This is proper, for *Satanstoe* is the first part of the saga of a dynasty. Cooper must establish the family as the center of moral health, and so the protagonist, Corny Littlepage, is virtually circumscribed by his familial relations and responsibilities. Most of his "adventures" are in fact built around the twin goals of the would-be empire-builder: matrimony (perforce a "good match") and the establishment of his land title.

In its action, the novel moves constantly out to greater reaches, flinging Corny ever farther from the bosom of his family: from Satanstoe to New York, to Albany, and at last to the woods. It is a tale of initiation in stages, each stage fitting the novice better for his role as the head of a family and the master of an estate. Each step is also signalized by some sort of historical color, conflict, or event, for in *Satanstoe* the role of history is to reaffirm the family, not to destroy it. History appears static and benevolent, because the characters are on the brink of change which they do not understand. Among the elaborate historical color and antiquarian memorabilia of the novel, there is only one historical event in the classic sense. In contrast to the use of historical event and personage in many of the earlier novels, the battle at Fort Ticonderoga appears as almost pure adventure. To be sure, the defeat can be seen as adding to Corny's "character," and it reflects poorly on prospects of permanent British control of the American colonies, but it is hard to see the adventure as more important to the basic themes of the book than the sleighride on the ice or the fictional battle at Ravensnest. The historical event is shorn of its genuinely historical significance, however well integrated it is on the most superficial plot level. The event does not illuminate the great subthemes of the book. As one phase of the hero's initiation, however, it does link his destiny to that of the land, and this is perhaps all one may hope for.

One of the important subthemes of *Satanstoe* is allegorized in the contest between the British officer Bulstrode and Corny for the hand of Anneke Mordaunt. The result, of course, is foreordained, and the Briton, with his wealth, title, and "fashionable" taste, is rejected. Though well handled, the theme of growing provincial maturity and independence of the cultural standards of the mother country, like the reflections on the fortunes of imperial military power in the New World, never acquires genuinely formal importance.

The other historical subtheme involves the possession of the same land that was contested with such obvious fruitlessness in *The Last of the Mohicans*. The battles of Ticonderoga and Ravensnest, however, include the future "owners" of the soil— symbolically, the future ruling class of America. The conflict over the land between Corny and Jason Newcome is rendered only sketchily here, as a Yankee-Yorker clash, but one must not forget that this is only the beginning of a three-section historical novel.

Corny's animus towards Jason, apparent long before the New Englander has done anything "evil," illustrates perfectly how the holist world-view elevates differences in manners to moral distinctions. Unfortunately, Cooper lacks the comic sense for combining absurdity and danger which Faulkner displayed so well in creating the breed of Snopes, and Corny's strictures on Jason tend to wear on the reader fairly early. Cooper is always effective, however, in his use of the terrain as a structural element in his work. In *Satanstoe* the woods of upper New York again become sublime setting, disputed object, and prize.

For Cooper, not only was war politics carried on by other means, but law was war carried on by other means. Law is the mode by which he instinctively attempts to sharpen his conflicts and bring his forces into confrontation. Although legalism does not really flower in the trilogy until *The Chainbearer*, in *Satanstoe* Cooper has already drawn the lines for the central conflict of the Littlepage novels, and he has drawn them on legal and cultural grounds. The underlying historical process shown in *Satanstoe* is not the struggle between England and America, nor that between the two imperial powers, nor is it the decline of a noble race, though all three figure importantly. Rather Cooper dramatizes a conflict between two coexisting American philosophies of society, a cultural conflict framed in the language of progressive legalism. The dialectics of history guarantee that it will constantly generate new conflicts.

The distinction of *Satanstoe* among Cooper's historical novels, however, cannot be explained simply in terms of the themes with which the novel grapples. Cooper is always remarkable, in his superior work, for his grasp of the problematic and ambiguous aspects of historical change and is always alert to intimations of conflict in the most apparently placid historical ambience. George Dekker has indicated a common critical stricture against *Satanstoe* as being in effect too well-made, with the characteristic ambivalence of the author held too well in hand, and an absence of the "mythic power and grandeur of conception" of the Leatherstocking Tales. As he says, "One can scarcely complain about the serenity of *Satanstoe*, but it is not Cooperesque." [33] The remarkable thing about *Satanstoe*, I believe, is precisely in this discipline. In truth, it had taken Cooper his entire career to imitate "the novel as written by Scott," and I would like to probe farther into the implications of this deliberate imitativeness, and the literary motives behind it.

Cooper's most striking innovation on the formula of Scott, and the one that in great part is responsible for the esteem in which his work has continued to be held, is his creation of the mock-renegade as the resonant figure at the thematic center of his best work. It is for the sake of this figure, Spy, Bravo, or especially Deerslayer, and for the sake of his growing mythic significance, that readers have been willing to overlook the artificial and creaky Romantic plot-interest with which Cooper unfailingly furnishes his work. As I indicated earlier, for Cooper this meant that the passive, middle-of-the-road hero of Scott was shunted off to a position of dull propriety on the fringes of his fiction. Though clearly the ladies and gentlemen of Cooper are essential to the author's holist sense of literary and social propriety, they rarely seem to have engaged his energies as an artist.

Satanstoe changes all this. With Corny Littlepage, Cooper succeeds in placing the middle-of-the-road hero in the center of his own stage. His reasons for doing so are complex, but will repay close attention, for to a remarkable extent Cooper's attitudes towards history and his novelistic method jell for one single moment in this work. The formal benefits of the middle-of-the-road hero to Cooper are immediately apparent. Corny is a figure of destiny in his stolid way, without being either mythicized or idealized. In this connection, Cooper reaps two great dividends from the memoir device. Firstly, Cooper's own stilted style comes off quite well as the personal manner of an opinionated eighteenth-century gentleman. This allows Cooper to air even his

crankiest views without subordinating character and story entirely
to them. Secondly, the memoir form allows Cooper's historical
imagination to expose sympathetically the motivations, prejudices,
and blind spots of a young man of the aspiring New York gentry.

Though Corny as a narrator enhances Cooper's control of the
tone of *Satanstoe*, his formal significance is not merely technical,
but flows from his function as a character in the world of the
novel. Donald Davie, in writing about one of Scott's other followers, Pushkin, describes the protagonist of *The Captain's
Daughter* this way:

> Grinyov is realistically drawn, is no Faustian or Promethean prototype,
> serving to symbolize in his own conflicts the extreme conflicts of man-
> kind. He is, on the contrary, a Russian country gentleman of the
> eighteenth century, conducting his internal argument at no more than
> normal intensity, with no more than normal honesty and courage.
> As such, he may be allowed to embody an ideological conflict, but not
> to resolve the conflict, nor to push it to the limit.[34]

The internalized conflict of the middle-class gentleman, origi-
nating in the "wavering" protagonist of Waverley and continuing
through the most characteristic work of Scott and his followers,
had for Cooper always been lodged not in his gentlemanly characters but in the mock-renegades who people his fiction. The
mock-renegade's conflict is entirely a feature of his social role,
rather than his disposition. Only in Leatherstocking does there
gradually emerge a tendency for the mock-renegade's soliloquies
to evoke an image of internalized conflict, precisely because of
the vehemence of his loyalty to the holist values of white American civilization. Cooper's problem in *Satanstoe* is to create a holist
protagonist who embodies not value conflict but value assertion.

The middle-of-the-road hero must perform a new function for
Cooper; his embattled sense of historical change had crystallized
in the 1840's, the Anti-Rent wars being only the immediate occasion for Cooper's long-standing conservative apprehensions.

Alexander Welsh, in his excellent study of the hero of the Waverley Novels, points out that Scott's protagonists are typically
subject to situations in which their status as gentlemen is not
recognized or not believed, situations which are an abundant
source of titillation and anxiety in Scott's role-conscious holist
world.[35] This anxiety is akin to that of Cooper's mock-renegade
who always fears that his genuine cultural allegiance will be obscured by his ambiguous cultural role. In Corny Littlepage, we
have a deeper anxiety than that of the Scottian hero as to whether
he will be recognized and accepted in the role of a gentleman:
Cooper's New World anxiety as to whether the role of gentleman
any longer exists.

The hero of Scott is notoriously passive, and Welsh argues
persuasively that this is not only because he is essentially an observer, but because his very claim to his property and the gentlemanly status that it entails is dependent on his acquiescing in the
non-aggressive and non-acquisitive stance that his role demands.
The Scott hero is passive and yielding to society so that he will
deserve society's rewards. Cooper's hero, created from the perspective of the 1840's, attempts to *create* a sense of society in which
he may securely repose. Unlike the Scott hero he is edgy, opinionated, combative. Far from being passive, he is constantly a
savior; overcoming butcher's boys, lions, the rampaging Hudson,
and bloodthirsty savages in order to earn his bride and his estate.
Obviously in America rights to a wife and property do not exist
unless they are aggressively asserted, and it is vain to place all
hopes in the rewards of "gentlemanly" status. Cooper has ex-
changed the divided loyalties of the Scott hero for the divided
self-image of his own hero.

In the mute character of Susquesus, as noted earlier, *Satanstoe*
has its mock-renegade. An exile from his people, almost consistently distrusted by our middle-of-the-road hero, the Indian proves
to be a faithful, shrewd, and invaluable guide. Unlike Natty, but
like Harvey, Susquesus is denied the privilege of explaining his

status. He remains stoically silent until almost the end of the trilogy. The historical role of the indispensable but misunderstood guide always had great significance for Cooper, who was throughout his life torn between the desire to be an individualistic critic and the desire to be conventionally respectable and orthodox. Corny Littlepage is a more direct expression than the mock-renegade of the tensions between Cooper's two images of himself: as holist scion, the passively rewarded squire of Cooperstown, and as combative conservative, actively defending his position against an upstart challenge to social order.

It is Cooper's profound recognition of the meaning of historical change for himself—a kind of historical self-recognition—which is the source of the formal and tonal integrity of *Satanstoe*. In the Littlepage trilogy, history is not to sweep away the life of the highlands, as in Scott's border fiction, nor the life of the red man, as in the Leatherstocking tales, leaving the wavering middle-of-the-road gentleman to carry on, a symbol of historical continuity in this triumphant new order. History is to sweep away the gentleman himself. Thus Cooper's imagination, for once, is not working against its own best instincts, and *Satanstoe* is conceived with entire consistency as a picture of manners serving an idea.

Cooper points to this intention clearly in his preface, where he claims a "certain value" for his "chronicle of manners" and says that when "customs are connected with principles, in their origin, development, or end, such records have a double importance." The extent to which manners are put to the service of an ideological argument may be best illustrated perhaps by a lengthy quotation from Corny's thoughts on the demeanor of the irrepressible Jason Newcome:

Jason was always a moral enigma, to me; there being an absolute absence, in his mind, of everything like a perception of the fitness of things, so far as the claims and rights of persons were connected with rank, education, birth, and experience. Rank, in the official sense, once possessed, he understood and respected; but of the claims to entitle one to its enjoyment, he seemed to have no sort of notion. For property he had a profound deference, so far as that deference extended to its importance and influence; but it would have caused him not the slightest qualm, either in the way of conscience or feeling, to find himself suddenly installed in the mansion of the patroons, for instance, and placed in possession of their estates, provided only he fancied he could maintain his position. The circumstance that he was dwelling under the roof that was erected by another man's ancestors, for instance, and that others were living who had a better moral right to it, would give him no sort of trouble, so long as any quirk of the law would sustain him in possession. In a word, all that was allied to sentiment, in matters of this nature, was totally lost on Jason Newcome, who lived and acted, from the hour he first came among us, as if the game of life were merely a game of puss in the corner, in which he who inadvertently left his own post unprotected, would be certain to find another filling his place as speedily as possible. I have mentioned this propensity of Jason's at some little length, as I feel certain, should this history be carried down by my posterity, as I hope and design, it will be seen that this disposition to regard the whole human family as so many tenants in common, of the estate left by Adam, will lead, in the end, to something extraordinary.[36]

This is as clear an expression of the apprehensions of the landed gentry before the rising entrepreneurial class as one could hope to find. Especially striking is the way in which a lack of holist appreciation of manners, sentiment, and the fitness of things is seen as a profound symptom of economic and ideological heresy. In *Satanstoe* customs are indeed connected with principles.

Cooper was enabled to sustain such a holist view by his elegiac motive. Marvin Meyers has suggested that the key element in the rhetoric of Jacksonian Democracy was the concept of an agrarian Golden Age in the time of the Founding Fathers. Perhaps one source of the power of the Democrat Cooper's historical imagination lies in his need to create an ideal society in the past. Corny

Littlepage could not exist in the 1840's. Like his great-grandson or like Cooper himself, Corny would be too embattled with lawsuits and land claims to exhibit the genial and self-assured air which clothes all historical conflicts in *Satanstoe*.

A revealing comparison may be made of *Satanstoe* with *Pan Tadeusz*, the masterpiece of Cooper's friend, the Polish poet Adam Mickiewicz. *Pan Tadeusz* is in part a beautiful nationalist idyll set in the context of the campaign of 1812, when for a brief period Napoleon's armies, including Polish legions, liberated much of partitioned Poland from Russian rule. The work is filled with vivid pictures of the manners, customs, and way of life of the Polish gentry, all shown not in order to contrast them with the manners of another culture, but in tribute to the organic wholeness of the community. In the last scene, a ball and feast in honor of General Dambrowski of the Polish Legions, the appropriate symbol of the moment is an ancient cookbook which supplies the recipes for the occasion. Dambrowski recognizes the meaning of the presentation of this true Polish banquet, the secret of which had been lost until his reappearance. The customs and way of life are inauthentic except within the context of a national Ideal of which they are the expression.

The special elegiac note of the last scene of celebration is attained when it is borne in on the reader that Poland actually *existed* only for one afternoon in the life of the author. The holist picture of manners—so like the feasting, sports, and celebrations of *Satanstoe*—is made valid and authentic only by the concluding idyll of the brief Indian summer of the Polish State in 1812, and it is the sense of irreparable loss and exile which gives the novel its poignance.

In *Satanstoe*, Cooper reverses the artistic motive, and attempts to authenticate his idea of the state through appeal to the vision of cultural wholeness which he presents. The beauty of both works is a product of the implied recognition of the impossibility of any hope for a restoration of the unity of ideal and community. Cooper's awareness that one cannot thrive without the other is perhaps his deepest insight, and, as with Mickiewicz, it is the insight of an exile.

It is the sense of exile from the Golden Age of the pre-Revolutionary gentry that makes what is superficially Cooper's most imitative and disciplined novel actually one of his most profound and disturbing. Alexander Welsh has indicated, for example, how much the passive Scott hero is conceived of as legitimized by his unchallengable and "unearned" right to private property. The notion of Property, of course, is given its full sociological and historical value in the Littlepage trilogy, anticipating, as it does, Faulkner's *The Bear*. Cooper shows his awareness, through the Newcomes, Thousandacres, and especially Susquesus, of the ambiguous legitimacy of property in land, an ambiguity that shakes still further the doubtful tenure of the idea of the gentleman in the New World.

The trilogy in large part is a subtle assessment of the special ways in which New World history has modified and subverted the *a priori* precepts, definitions, distinctions, and categories of the holist frame. This is Cooper's special quality: having accepted the holist categories from the first, he found them in conflict with the stresses and tensions of the historical process as he imagined it. Holism is a view of stasis, and hence insufficient to Cooper's genuinely historical vision.

The progress of his work is a progress of insight into the sources of his own dilemma. His intuitive imagination probes the holistic verities of authority, law, custom, property, and social role, and his work shows the evidence of a sharp consciousness of the extent to which those verities are modified or rendered arbitrary by history. Yet all this strikes against Cooper's powerful need as a writer and as a "gentleman" to affirm the importance of those verities as an ideal, sustaining them by an appeal not to history but to a standard of self-cultivation richly represented by himself. In *Satanstoe* he has not banished this dilemma, but he has subtilized it by frankly recognizing that it is a dilemma.

Thus Cooper's belated return to Scott's form of the historical novel is not a mere aping of the master, but a possession of the secrets of his art. *The Spy* is as much a "political" novel, free of the special consciousness of an age, as one that shows the force of *history* on the conscience as Scott's works do. One never has a sense, for example, of *why* Harvey Birch is a "patriot," and the discussions of the reasons for the Revolution itself are largely academic. The political stances of Cooper's characters rarely grow out of historically conditioned backgrounds. In *The Last of the Mohicans,* race or nationality determines almost all moral decisions. This novel is not concerned with problems of conscience, for the burden of the book is to deny free will and to show nations and individuals trapped by history.

In *Satanstoe*, Corny also appears driven by historical forces he does not understand. On the verge of the Revolution, he can see the "popular party" only as *canaille*, and he is more irritated than concerned by the threat posed by Jason Newcome. He is as bemused by what passed for gentility as Cooper himself ever was. There is no tragedy where there is such obliviousness, but the irony of Cooper's awareness relates far more to his own situation than to Corny's. This renders *Satanstoe* the very considerable achievement it is as an historical novel. If it does not reach the heights of a time-bound battle of the conscience, it presents a memorable and poignantly nostalgic picture of a time-bound consciousness. It is this which entitles *Satanstoe* to stand with the Leatherstocking Tales as the greatest realizations of Cooper's historical imagination.

Chapter Four

HAWTHORNE: THE LIMITS OF
THE HOLIST IMAGINATION

7HE distance from *Satanstoe* to *The Scarlet Letter* is only five years in the chronology of American literary history, but an epoch in the artistic recognition of the qualities and strengths of the holist historical novel. The conscious historical artist is present in Hawthorne as in no other nineteenth-century novelist. *The Scarlet Letter* is such a perfect, "closed" work of art that the imaginative historical issues it raises are cheated of their intrinsic importance by critical analysis which starts from the novel itself. Consequently, I have attempted to work upwards from brief examinations of Hawthorne's historical aesthetic, his philosophy of history, and his interpretation of New England history to the art of the tales and his only historical novel.

⌐ The Aesthetics of the Past

"Alice Doane's Appeal" is Hawthorne's most elaborate early exploration of the meaning of the historical imagination. In this story Hawthorne, through the device of the story within a story, attempts to dramatize the problems involved in developing an aesthetic of historical fiction. The complexity of his response indicates that he is the first writer not only in American, but in

Western literature to realize how thoroughly problematic such an aesthetic could be. The fragment of a story that gives the whole piece its title was originally one of the "Seven Tales of My Native Land" which Hawthorne wrote and then destroyed in despair in the 1820's. By the middle of the next decade, however, Hawthorne was writing and publishing his finest historical tales, and when the fragment appears in the new context of this sketch it is as a remarkable facsimile of an historical artifact, an artifact presented to illustrate the power of the historical imagination.

The resonant meaning of the fragment is augmented by the outer "shell" of the sketch: "The Author of 'The Gentle Boy'" takes two young ladies to Gallows Hill (the scene of Salem's witchcraft executions) in order to regale them with his art, and more especially to awaken their sensibilities to "the historic influence of the spot." [1] He laments that "we are a people of the present, and have no heartfelt interest in the olden time." [2] The necessity for imaginative transformation of the present guides the three, who "threw, in imagination, a veil of deep forest over the land, and pictured a few scattered villages, and this old town itself a village, as when the prince of hell bore sway there." [3]

The fragmentary story follows, with the narrator commenting upon his own techniques and the effects at which he aims. The narrator manifests a self-conscious and occasionally condescending attitude towards his "tale" that cannot be simply attributed to the apparent juvenility of the piece, for the tale is still psychologically arresting.[4] Moreover, the narrator declares that it was written when he was possessed by stronger creative impulses than those that now govern him. The story, however, depends—as does none of Hawthorne's other serious historical fiction (excepting such whimsical pieces as "Feathertop")—on an unblushing and unquestioning acceptance of the existence of the supernatural —ghosts and witches—not as the license of fancy, but as part of the unambiguous meaning of the story itself.

The narrator draws attention to this twice, the first time as he describes the specter of the wizard "gliding" along a path, and then checks the reaction of his feminine audience to see if they have maintained their willing suspension of disbelief "even on the hill where so many had been brought to death by wilder tales than this." [5] The trance induced by the tale breaks at last after the mild Walpurgisnacht of the finale, however, and the women laugh off the effect, leaving the narrator "indeed, a little piqued that a narrative which had good authority in our ancient superstitions, and would have brought even a church deacon to Gallows Hill, in old witch times, should now be considered too grotesque and extravagant for timid maids to tremble at." [6] Taking a new resolve, the narrator "detained them a while longer on the hill, and made a trial whether truth were more powerful than fiction." [7]

Here one becomes aware that the narrator's aesthetic problem includes both the justification of the "tale as tale" and the achievement of an imaginative and emotional effect from "raw history" —in this case the exemplary meaning of the witchcraft hysteria of 1692. The narrator fails in his first, subtle attempt imaginatively to recreate the past for the present. His method was nothing less than persuading his audience to assume the imaginative positions of the "afflicted," of momentarily adopting the psychology of those who believed in and so persecuted the "witches." The narrator, having succeeded only partially in *reproducing* the hysteria, then attempts to *portray* it by describing the execution of "witches":

With such eloquence as my share of feeling and fancy could supply, I called back hoar antiquity, and bade my companions imagine an ancient multitude of people, congregated on the hillside, spreading far below, clustering on the steep old roofs, and climbing the adjacent heights, wherever a glimpse of this spot might be obtained. I strove to realize and faintly communicate the deep, unutterable loathing and horror, the indignation, the affrighted wonder, that wrinkled on every brow, and filled the universal heart.[8]

The narrator describes first the "martyrs" and then the "guilty and miserable band" of persecutors, with their demonic leader

Cotton Mather, "the one bloodthirsty man, in whom were concentrated those vices of spirit and errors of opinion that sufficed
to madden the surrounding multitude." [9] Where fictional evocation of the inner psychology of the time had failed, the impas-
sioned narration of the outer, or conventionally "true" history,
succeeds:

But here my companions seized an arm on each side; their nerves
were trembling; and, sweeter victory still, I had reached the seldom
trodden places of their hearts, and found the well-spring of their
tears. And now the past had done all it could. [10]

The historical imagination must bring the past into confrontation with the present, and unless the encounter touches the "seldom trodden places" of the heart, it is incomplete. The narrator,
in proposing that there be a monument on Gallows Hill as well
as Bunker Hill, is not merely enlarging the ethical value of the
past, but is ironically commenting on the difficulty of bringing
about that encounter in fiction.

In 1849 Hawthorne returned to the aesthetics of the historical
imagination as a literary subject in his sketches "Main Street"
and "The Custom-House," both of which were originally to be
included in the volume which contained *The Scarlet Letter*.
"Main Street" is a reconsideration of the uneasy resolution of
"Alice Doane" at the same time that it looks forward to Hawthorne's first mature novel. In place of the deliberately archaic
"witch tale," Hawthorne presents an ultra-modern show box, with
a showman-impresario in place of the "author." Like the fragmentary tale of "Alice Doane," this creation of art is designed to transmute nineteenth-century Salem into the village of the Puritans,
and both presentations reach their climax in the witchcraft affair.
Although "Main Street" contains trenchant historical observations which make it a fit companion piece to *The Scarlet Letter*,
Hawthorne's tone is light throughout, comic where it is not
sardonic. The difference from "Alice Doane" lies in the "artifice,"

which presents History as a pageant-like procession, and thus is doomed to falsity from the start. The machine inevitably breaks down, leaving "Salem" buried under the blizzard of 1731, and the critical audience quite untouched and rudely demanding its money back.

"Main Street" was Hawthorne's way of announcing his rejection of the attempt to bring about the encounter with the past through "presentation," as he had done in "The Legends of the Province House" or the Cotton Mather section of "Alice Doane's Appeal." Dissatisfied with "pasteboard," and having never accepted the notion of an extraneous historical "setting" for the dramatic action of his tales (excepting "Rappaccini's Daughter"), Hawthorne seems to have been defining by exclusion the historical quality of his finest tales, in which the reader confronts the past through the very consciousness of the characters. The man and the nation lacking a meaningful understanding of their past are like the old Inspector in "The Custom-House," who recalled only certain gourmandizing exploits "while all the subsequent experience of our race, and all the events that brightened or darkened his individual career, had gone over him with as little permanent effect as the passing breeze." [11] The historical artist cannot recapture the inner reality of the past by the representation of history as mere spectacle.

⌐ "A Dark Enthusiasm"

With historical fiction as complex as Hawthorne's, it is imperative that some analysis of the major themes and imaginative structures of Hawthorne's historical and cultural thought precede discussion of his artistic achievement.

Hawthorne's ideas about history are intricately bound up in his work with his more universal images of man as a social and political animal. Yet there are a few leading notions which inform all his writing and govern his treatment of historical types and arche-

types. The thrust of Hawthorne's historical judgment is so clear
that although it became "complicated" in the course of his writing
career, its basic character never changed. This may be seen by
comparing the early sketch "Mrs. Hutchinson" (1830) with "The
Life of Franklin Pierce" (1852), written after the American tales
and novels, and "Chiefly About War Matters" (1864), which is
virtually the author's last testament on the meaning of history.

"Mrs. Hutchinson" is a sketch of the dispute which led to the
expulsion of Anne Hutchinson from the Bay Colony in 1634. The
central vignette is what one may call the prototypical Hawthornean
historical situation: the struggle of an individual who emphatically
insists upon a radically different interpretation of reality from that
of a social structure which, whatever its ideology, retains the great
holist virtues of cohesion and continuity. In this all but dramatized
tableau, Anne Hutchinson confronts her accusers. Among the witnessing authorities of the Bay Colony is the sympathetic governor
Henry Vane. The description of Vane reveals what is to become
the most familiar of Hawthorne's historical figures: "In his mysterious eyes we may read a dark enthusiasm, akin to that of the
woman whose cause he has espoused, combined with a shrewd
worldly foresight, which tells him that her doctrines will be productive of change and tumult, the elements of his power and delight." [12]

In this Ur-confrontation Hawthorne has dramatized the peculiar
stresses of his basically holistic conception of society. In Hawthorne, for the first time in the development of the historical
novel, the "progressive" world of Ideas impinges upon characters
through overmastering passions rather than through an outlook
conditioned almost entirely by the character's "type" and fictional
role. Where Cooper saw upstart "revolutionary" types motivated
by material interests and characterized by vulgarity, Hawthorne
emphasizes the power of Ideas to inspire a character to acts of social dislocation.

"Enthusiasm" appears in many forms in Hawthorne, but its

specific application here—in an essay which begins by moralizing
on the dangers of "public women"—seems to reveal Anne Hutchinson as the ancestress of a line of "heroines" which includes Catherine, the Quakeress of "The Gentle Boy," Hester, Zenobia, and
Miriam. Though "enthusiasm" can be a masculine characteristic
too, as in Hollingsworth, Hawthorne is much sterner with women
who allow "inner promptings" to challenge the prevailing values
than with men, perhaps because for Hawthorne the distortion of
the holist web of civilization was so much more seriously threatened by the feminine enthusiast. It is easy to appreciate Hawthorne's advance in maturity over the work of Cooper, whose every
volume seems to deny that such women could even exist. At the
same time one must not discount the savage animus betrayed by
Hawthorne's rather hypocritical piety after narrating the massacre
of Anne Hutchinson and her party:

It was a circumstance not to be unnoticed by our stern ancestors,
in considering the fate of her who had so troubled their religion, that
an infant daughter, the sole survivor amid the terrible destruction of
her mother's household, was bred in a barbarous faith, and never
learned the way to the Christian's heaven. Yet we will hope that
there the mother and child have met.[13]

The accusers of Anne Hutchinson merit more than passing attention because of Hawthorne's comparatively unequivocal endorse-
ment of their position. The most significant historical individuals
for Hawthorne's later work, John Winthrop and John Endicott,
are paired in a neat antithesis, Winthrop among the "blessed
fathers of the land, who rank in our veneration next to the evange-
lists of Holy Writ," and Endicott among those "unpurified from
the fiercest errors of the age, and ready to propagate the religion
of peace by violence." [14] Hawthorne ironically marks out a com-
promising relationship between Truth and Policy. He finds the
dispute "a most remarkable case, in which religious freedom was
wholly inconsistent with public safety, and where the principles

of an illiberal age indicated the very course which must have been
pursued by worldly policy and enlightened wisdom." [15] Yet he
hints at the identity of "enlightened wisdom" with cowardice in
the next breath, as he describes how "Mr. Cotton began to have
that light in regard to his errors, which will sometimes break in
upon the wisest and most pious men, when their opinions are un-
happily discordant with those of the powers that be." [16]

Saving irony or not, the values of civilization are always bound
up in one knot for Hawthorne, and there can be no historical
"progress" through ideas which threaten the unity of the holist
structure. As in Hawthorne's "Life of Franklin Pierce," the error
of the new "enthusiasts" of abolition is attributed to their failure
to recognize the impotence of "merely human wisdom and human
efforts [to] subvert" slavery without breaking up the Union.[17]
Lawrence Hall has shown the growth of Hawthorne's belief in
"progress" in the 1850's and his increasingly unambiguous preference for "the statesman of practical sagacity" over the "theorist." [18] The Hawthorne of the fifties and sixties may be read, like
Bancroft, for a conservative Democrat's statement of the progressive faith. Hawthorne declared that not men, but "Providence,"
would cause slavery to "vanish like a dream." In Bancroft's history
—unlike his politics—men appear as direct, effective agents of the
Divine Will. In contrast, Hawthorne's historical and fictional
characters appear as indirect, temporally frustrated agents of the
will towards progress. Man's only hope for direct and effective
living is in personal relationships.

The Civil War put Hawthorne's ideas on history—as it also
put Melville's—to a bitter trial. Hawthorne was shaken by the
war, but unlike the younger writer, he did not alter his attitudes.
The pervasive irony of "Chiefly About War Matters" is no different in essence from his treatment of the Louisbourg expedition
in "Sir William Pepperell" (1831), written more than thirty years
before. More significant than the irony—which occasionally yields
under the strain and becomes mere facetiousness—is Hawthorne's

reformulation of his original world-view in a way which would sound platitudinous were it not implicit in the entire body of his work. Hawthorne states his belief that the true beneficiaries of the war will be the "peasants," the poor Southern whites, rather than either blacks or Northerners, and that the "justification" of the war is in the "regeneration of a people," not in the achievement of the goals of "enthusiasts." Providence may advance Progress, but progressive ideas themselves are sure to be intrinsically false and of an effectiveness that is literally incalculable:

No human effort, on a grand scale, has ever yet resulted according to the purpose of its projectors. . . . We miss the good we sought, and do the good we little cared for.[19]

⌐ The Contours of New England History

Even a superficial reading of the tales of seventeenth- and eighteenth-century New England reveals that Hawthorne's grasp of the region's past extends far beyond his much-vaunted base in the "facts" and "sources" of the colonial era, and that these "facts" find their significance in a highly developed understructure of historical understanding. One may abstract an historical schema of pre-Revolutionary New England from the tales, a schema strikingly consistent at all points. Just as the three American novels form a continuous social and cultural history, so do the tales—a history which begins before the arrival of the mass of Puritans in "The Maypole of Merrymount" and ends with the first Massachusetts governor under the new Republic taking possession of the Province House in "Old Esther Dudley."

More than anything, seeking the pattern in Hawthorne's New England past brings a heightened awareness that for him it was not monolithic, and that in tracing changes over the generations Hawthorne was illustrating many cultural fissures, tragedies, and new departures almost as pregnant with meaning as that sym-

bolized by the first great migration. If Hawthorne is as Provi-
dentially deterministic as he appears to be in regard to "macro-
historical" cultural changes, the stories should be related as they
fit into his grand pattern, or sight will be lost in a very real sense
of what happens in the individual narrative. Hawthorne's historical schema is a genetic myth of the New England past, in
which he pinpoints a few critical turning points in its cultural
temper.

The first period is the founding era of the Massachusetts colony.
In stories like "The Maypole of Merrymount" (c. 1629) and
"Endicott and the Red Cross" (c. 1634), Endicott's sword prunes
the cultural heritage of "pagan" Maypoles and "popish" crosses.
The first of these stories concerns the rivalry of two cultures for
the New World, the second the complete rejection of significant
Old World traditions and loyalties, combined with an ominous
forecast of the new orthodoxy. The first crucial turning point
comes, as I shall try to show, in *The Scarlet Letter* (c. 1642–49),
as the first generation departs and the second becomes dominant;
when, as Hawthorne says in "Main Street," "these lamps began
to burn more dimly, or with a less genuine lustre; and then it
might be seen how hard, cold, and confined was their system,—
how like an iron cage was that which they called Liberty." [20] The
nadir of the New England consciousness lasts roughly from the
death of Winthrop in 1649 to the next turning point, that of
1688–92. The meaning of Hawthorne's lone story set in this era
of consolidation will be discussed elsewhere.

The second turning point of New England cultural history is
marked by the schism represented by the two great events that
followed so close upon one another, the rebellion against Andros
and the witchcraft trials. Already the question has become not
the fate of the heritage of Old England but that of the Puritans
themselves. "The Gray Champion," in which Hawthorne's spectral
regicide is revived as the allegorical representation of Puritan
Strength, is an explicit omen of the American Revolution. It is,

incidentally, a fine example of holist treatment of a progressive subject. The complement of Strength in Endicott and in Hawthorne's first American ancestors is of course Intolerance, and although this image of self-righteous power certainly appears in stories like "Young Goodman Brown" and "Alice Doane's Appeal," it is in a degenerate form, outwardly hysterically brutal and exclusive and internally full of self-mistrust. The heirs of the dark night of the New England soul, the Puritans who succeed the second generation, retain their strength for meeting enemies, but are crippled for other human intercourse.

The third and last turning point is set in the second quarter of the eighteenth century, a period to which Hawthorne devoted several of his sketches as well as three of his most famous stories. "The Minister's Black Veil," set in the 1730's, shortly before the Great Awakening, is at least in part a commentary on the final *cul-de-sac* of Puritan introspection and exclusiveness. Beyond adopting a symbolic black veil it is indeed hard to go. Of the other two, "Roger Malvin's Burial" and "My Kinsman, Major Molineux," the latter affirms the outward direction of that impulse towards forceful assertion and revolutionary strength that has been transmitted to the latter-day "Yankees" directly from Endicott. The two traditions of New England—brutal assertiveness and self-destructive mistrust—are once again separate though intertwined. This third turning point in fact creates a new nation, signalized by the emergence—in "Drowne's Wooden Image" (c. 1763–75)—of the American artist. Thus the "Legends of the Province House" are, historically, little more than pageants, costume representations of a *fait accompli*; for the new national consciousness, which was Hawthorne's true historical subject, has already been created.

There is, of course, another chronology of Hawthorne's historical short stories, equally important for their evaluation: the order in which they first appeared. The most striking facts about the historical tales are that, bulking so large in our estimate of Hawthorne, they bulk so small in the corpus of his work (being little more than a fourth of his published stories), and that all but a few of these tales appeared between 1832 and 1838. Though the exact dates of composition are uncertain, the order of publication shows, if anything, an attrition of power and an increasing tendency towards schematized or "moralized" stories as the decade passed.[21] The stories of 1832, "Roger Malvin's Burial," "My Kinsman, Major Molineux," and "The Gentle Boy," reveal the range of radical experimentation in Hawthorne's early work. The skillful combination of realism and sentiment of "The Gentle Boy" seems closer to the imagination of a Dickens or a Dostoevsky than to that of the author of "Rappaccini's Daughter." On the other hand is the extreme artistic sophistication and complexity of "My Kinsman, Major Molineux" with its companion study of guilt and compulsion, "Roger Malvin's Burial."

Whether one may refer the decline in Hawthorne's historical fiction to the demands of a conventional audience or to his organic development as a writer, the decline was absolute. The static ironies of "The Maypole of Merrymount" or "Endicott and the Red Cross" are vastly weaker than Hawthorne's earlier attempts to render history as lived experience, and I believe that Hawthorne's rejection of the historical mode in 1838 after the publication of the highly polished but superficial "Legends of the Province House" was a tacit recognition of a loss of power. Except for "Drowne's Wooden Image" (1844), which properly belongs to Hawthorne's tales of artists rather than his tales of history, he did not return to historical subjects for serious fiction until *The Scarlet Letter*—when he was working from a quite new artistic impulse. In examining Hawthorne's historical art in his short fiction, therefore, I would prefer to concentrate on his earliest major tales, "My Kinsman, Major Molineux," "Roger Malvin's Burial," and "The Gentle Boy."

"The Gentle Boy" is of especial interest for the study of Hawthorne the novelist, because of all his short fiction, it most nearly approaches the "open" form of the novel. This very fact probably accounts for the comparative lack of attention it has received, since criticism of Hawthorne's novels has usually used the short fiction as a source for themes, imagery, and the development of Hawthorne's allegorical-symbolic aesthetic in the novels without considering the very different demands of the two fictional genres. "The Gentle Boy" indicated the form that *The Scarlet Letter* would take; a narrative featuring a dynamic relationship between its characters and a highly unified, particularized, and hostile "society," as well as a narrative method which allows these characters—a rare occurrence before the novels—to develop and change in time in response to a complex pattern of drives, social and personal. Here, as nowhere else in Hawthorne's early fiction, is man in society equated with the social roles of the holist frame.

The tale is set in 1659, that most dismal period of Hawthorne's New England history, which emerges, roughly, after the death of Winthrop. Hawthorne elaborated on the effects of the period of consolidation at greatest length in "Dr. Bullivant," describing the Bay Colony of the 1670's and 80's:

The early settlers were able to keep within the narrowest limits of their rigid principles, because they had adopted them in mature life, and from their own deep conviction, and were strengthened in them by that species of enthusiasm, which is as sober and as enduring as reason itself. But if their immediate successors followed the same line of conduct, they were confined to it, in a great degree, by habits forced upon them, and by the severe rule under which they were educated, and, in short, more by restraint than by the free exercise of the imagination and understanding.[22]

None of the major characters of "The Gentle Boy," it is worth noting, belongs to the second generation, the "immediate successors." Both the Quakers and the household of Tobias are recent emigrants, who bring to Massachusetts a rich experience of the political and religious strife of the Old World. The society

which they enter is remarkable chiefly for its unity and implacability. Except for the Quaker-hating minister and the monstrous
boy whom Ilbrahim attempts to befriend, Puritan society presents
a purely anonymous aspect in the tale: a phalanx of hostility drawn
up before the church as Tobias and Dorothy try to enter with Ilbrahim; a crowd of children who turn into a bloodthirsty mob;
a mocking, threatening voice heard in the wood.

The facelessness of the society makes the historical individuals
mentioned in the tale all the more significant as representatives
of the culture. The governor is unnamed but easily identifiable as
Endicott: "a man of narrow mind and imperfect education, and
his uncompromising bigotry was made hot and mischievous by
violent and hasty passions; he exerted his influence indecorously
and unjustifiably to compass the death of the enthusiasts; and his
whole conduct, in respect to them, was marked by brutal cruelty." [23] This is one of the horns of an historical dilemma, for,
Winthrop being gone, Endicott is the price of stability, the price
of New England's escape from the dialectics of old English
change: a "voluptuous" [24] Charles II for an "ambitious" Cromwell.

In such a society—conceived by its ruling orders as a rigid
structure governing everything from politics and creed to manners (the Quaker refusal to uncover their heads is a superbly
holistic gesture)—it is impossible to separate nonconformity, de-
viancy, and revolutionary will to overthrow the entire system. At
least it is impossible for Hawthorne's Puritans. It is a holist frame
that precludes "progressive" ideas, such as those that Tobias fled
from in fleeing the aftermath of the Puritan Revolution. This social structure, unlike Wish-ton-Wish and the Hutted Knoll, is a
definitely non-pastoral "escape" from history. The chief characters, none of whom can maintain a defined role, are delineated
in uneasy attitudes of conflict with the society.

Hawthorne tells us that the conflict is between Quakers and
Puritans, but this should not misdirect the reader into believing

that the historical problem of the story is to discover which "side" is to blame. Seymour Gross has shown that when Hawthorne revised the tale he did so with an eye towards balancing the scales between the two parties. But is the real conflict between autonomous sects or is it a struggle of individuals with the premises of a certain type of culture? [25] Hawthorne's dominant urge in the revision of "The Gentle Boy" and in his later historical short stories is towards schematizing cultural conflicts, and then making them resonant by the ironical juxtaposition of images.[26] The schematization is a means of undermining the holistic imagination of Endicott and his peers; the high consciousness of culture as system which Hawthorne brings to his anatomies of cultural clashes exposes the congeries of fixed and unquestionable assumptions which always underlie the holist frame. Cooper is capable of showing conflict and paradox within the bounds of the frame, and the archetypal focus for such conflict is the mock-renegade. For Hawthorne, who recognized the possibility of characters "stepping outside" the frame and creating a new identity through the power of progressive ideas, the archetypal figure of historical conflict is the "enthusiast."

What then is the meaning of the conflict of Quakers with Puritan society which so dislocates the characters of "The Gentle Boy"? For the Puritans it was a struggle to repress what they felt to be a threat to the holist web of their society. Hawthorne's attitude is more complex, since he believed (as did his audience) in such "progressive" notions as religious liberty. His position is much like that of Gibbon, writing satirically about the early Christian martyrs and justifying his irony by saying that he was not trying to "palliate the severity" of the Roman magistrates but to "discover their motives." [27] Gibbon's *Vindication* thus attempts to demonstrate why the "progressive" concept of the "unalienable rights of conscience and private judgment" could not have touched either the believers or the philosophers among the Romans. Hawthorne, who wrote of Quakers "indulged" with martyrdom, is similar in attitude to Gibbon. However, both writers are covert moralists as well as masters of historical narrative. Gibbon's irony is so devastating because it implies that the enlightened Christian gentlemen of his day would have acted as "Roman persecutors," not "Christian martyrs," in a similar situation.

Hawthorne's standard for judging the Quakers is not enlightened reasonableness but "human" sentiment. Where Gibbon, for example, ridicules the early Christian denial of "lust," Hawthorne exposes the dark power of the enthusiasm of the Quakers to wither natural affection. Most interesting is Hawthorne's attitude towards the Puritan establishment, immensely complicated by feelings of guilt inherited from his Quaker-baiting ancestor. Hawthorne cannot declare with the equanimity of a Gibbon that he and his audience would have acted like his Puritan forefathers. The shocking betrayal of Ilbrahim to a mob by a Puritan lad he had befriended owes its force to Hawthorne's—and our own—sense of complicity in the blow the "foul-hearted little villain" strikes.

Hawthorne's Quakers (and by extension all "enthusiasts" from Anne Hutchinson to John Brown) reveal the real meaning for him of "the sanctity of a human heart": it does not extend to the demands of conscience but only to a basic sense of privacy. The Quakers incite to persecution, they tempt to wrath, just as the "extreme" reformers of Hawthorne's era threaten not only the State but the emotional economy of the "moderate" individual. This is the essence of Coverdale's rebuke to Hollingsworth, who would turn his personal hold on Miles' heart to the advancement of his reformist schemes. In this way Hawthorne turned the Victorian cliché of the heart versus the head *against* "earnestness."

In the case of Catherine, her fault lies in the way she tempts to wrath. Her verbal violence violates the privacy of the Puritans who are content within their social and religious roles. Yet one should not, I believe, see her as completely condemned and blindly accept the rationalized moral of the tale to which the author points, for though Ilbrahim lives in the home of Rational Piety, he expires in the arms of Unbridled Fanaticism.

Ilbrahim himself is so obviously created on a different plane of fictional reality from the other characters that—as with Hester's Pearl—it is not proper to subject him to the same kind of critical analysis. The appeal of a saintly child to the sentiments of Hawthorne's audience is obvious, and there are many ways in which the Quaker boy anticipates the child-victims of Dickens and Dostoevsky. One character in which it is worth regarding Ilbrahim is as an artist, a teller of "outlandish" tales, for the portrait of the persecuted child-romancer reveals Hawthorne's consciousness of the precariousness of the condition of all nonconformists in a rigidly holist defense society.

Probably the most interesting aspect of Ilbrahim is his relationship with Tobias. Ilbrahim's call originally draws Tobias from the homeward "path" into the dark "field" and so begins and abets the process of Tobias' alienation from his role within Puritan society. When Tobias first encounters Ilbrahim, he identifies himself as a "friend" and is addressed in turn by the boy, Quaker-style, as "Friend." The change in meaning in the common word from a conventional role to a definition of existence is indicative of Ilbrahim's crucial agency in undermining Tobias' uncertain sense of his role in the Puritan commonwealth. Yet, though inspired by his "awakened sympathies" for a "sweet infant of the skies that had strayed away from his home," Tobias' conversion to the creed of the Quakers is not only not commended by Hawthorne but is treated as the culminating failure of an ill-starred life. Tobias' response to Ilbrahim eloquently illustrates the danger in reasoning too literally from Hawthorne's declared moral premises, and the necessity of seeking at least some of the answers to the motivations of his characters in the structure of the author's social imagination.

Tobias Pearson is the earliest of Hawthorne's role-seeking individuals. The cause of Tobias' initial weakness or failure to fit any of the roles he has attempted is obscure, but the dramatized effect, his anguish at his lack of satisfaction in any of the social roles available in the Old World or the New, is pathetically evident. First he leaves England and his position in the New Model Army for politically conscientious reasons.[28] By accepting Ilbrahim to replace his dead children who "like roses had perished" in the hostile climate of New England society, he implicitly rejects his role in that system. He is acknowledging duties which transcend the conformity expected of "a man of some consideration, being a representative to the General Court, and an approved lieutenant in the trainbands." [29] The progress of his alienation is clear enough. What is remarkable is Hawthorne's insight into Pearson's role apostasy. In the scene in the church, for example, Tobias "was agitated and uneasy, but a certain feeling like the consciousness of guilt oppressed him, so that he could not go forth and offer himself as the protector of the child." [30] In what sense is he guilty? In the sense of the Puritans, it would seem, for whom the reunion of Quaker mother and child "did not fail to move the sympathies of many who mistook their involuntary virtue for a sin." [31] Tobias obviously cannot be a "protector" unless he can be so as a *Puritan* —and his sympathies have already made him suspect in that role, especially to himself. Hawthorne is underlining, through the transformation of Tobias Pearson, the anguish of the limbo between social roles in a holist social structure:

But while he was thus becoming assimilated to the enthusiasts, his contempt, in nowise decreasing towards them, grew very fierce against himself; he imagined, also, that every face of his acquaintance wore a sneer, and that every word addressed to him was a gibe.[32]

His new role, of course, fits him no better than any of his old ones. The essence of Hawthorne's moral imperative is revealed in Tobias, and it is no such simplistic admonition as "Do not violate the sanctity of a human heart." Tobias' problem is not "how to act" but how to act given an historical situation over which he has no control and which offers no satisfactory built-in "solutions," or "roles." In this sense his role-seeking is a kind of ethical truth-seeking. Tobias cannot save his own children nor Ilbrahim, but he can refuse to accept those roles which would forbid him to grieve. Tobias represents the third member in Hawthorne's inventory of salient types possible in an entirely holist society: cruel role enforcer, dark enthusiast, anguished role-seeker. In slightly modified form, as I shall try to show, these types reappear in the major characters of *The Scarlet Letter*. The essence of the social imagination which governed Hawthorne's historical fiction was complete at the beginning.

To turn from "The Gentle Boy" to the other tales of 1832— "Roger Malvin's Burial" and "My Kinsman, Major Molineux"— is to turn from the definition of the Puritan culture in its age of faceless consolidation to the problems of historical change implicit in the third crisis of New England history according to Hawthorne's schema. "Roger Malvin's Burial" is intimately related to the undercurrent of psychological meaning in "My Kinsman, Major Molineux" and provides as well a complementary insight into the ambiguous "freeing" of the New England mind.[33] Both tales are set in the 1720's and 1730's, like "The Minister's Black Veil," which Hawthorne was to write later. The "historical subject" of each, or rather the "source" in historical lore for each, concerns violent defense of the then century-old New England culture against the ancient and new masters of the land. The central situation in each story involves a failure of filial duty by a young man to a father-figure in an extremely agitated historical moment. And finally the names of the two protagonists are intriguingly similar: Reuben (Hebrew—"Behold! a son") and Robin (diminutive for Robert; Teutonic—"Glorious in battle"). That Reuben's last name is Bourne, the archaic term for a limit, a boundary, and that Robin is carrying the name of Molineux on towards the future in the New World are indications of the Janus-like relationship between the two stories: "Roger Malvin's Burial" facing backwards and "My Kinsman, Major Molineux" facing towards a future free of the parental restraint of England.

"Roger Malvin's Burial" also illuminates "My Kinsman, Major

Molineux" in another way, for it introduces in a particularly potent way the concept of an historical "categorical imperative" as a force governing human behavior. Reuben fails to see his prospective father-in-law buried, and thus breaks ancient taboos which are specifically reinforced by the existing historical situation, in which the danger of mutilation of bodies at the hands of foes is to be feared. Reuben unsuccessfully tries to *rationalize* his failure in the face of Dorcas' and the community's expectation (he is congratulated by all for having risked his life to perform the last rites over Roger Malvin) but, caught in an historical situation in which community taboos radically conflict with private desires, he cannot relieve himself of his sense of guilt. My reading is obviously not incompatible with Frederick Crews' Oedipal one, but I would tend to place the emphasis on the psychological sanctions of the community—where Hawthorne placed them—rather than on an imagined desire on the part of Reuben to "do away" with his father-in-law.[34]

Historical "categorical imperatives" which are extremely difficult to discover, much less to fulfill, constitute one of the most significant levels in the richest of all Hawthorne's stories, "My Kinsman, Major Molineux." Part of the greatness of this tale is its resistance to any exclusive explication. Much can be learned about the depth of Hawthorne's art from Freudian interpretations like that of Simon O. Lesser, mythic interpretations such as Daniel Hoffman's, and the readings from cultural history of Q. D. Leavis and Roy Harvey Pearce.[35] All these interpretations, like the present one, are partial, and in concentrating upon a few themes in the tale I do not pretend to explicate its "whole meaning" or even to claim inevitability for the meaning I find in those themes I examine.

If "The Gentle Boy" strives for a definition of the New England community, how much more so does "My Kinsman, Major Molineux"; Hawthorne was not to match its wealth of concrete social and physical observation of a city until he came to write his novels. Yet Hawthorne's anatomy of the "Puritan metropolis" is not presented for its own sake, but rather to dramatize the complexity and irresistible force of historical change, just as young Robin Molineux dramatizes the complexity of responses and attitudes towards the imaginative spectacle of that change.

Taking these matters one at a time, what is the character of historical change in "My Kinsman, Major Molineux"? The royal official is expelled through the efforts or complaisance of virtually the whole town. To rehearse all Robin's encounters with the citizenry is probably unnecessary, for most of these figures (the woman with the scarlet petticoat, for example) bear an obvious social or historical role as well as an allegorical significance in Robin's "initiation." The man with the parti-colored face, who appears as "war personified," is the clearest instance of the representative of *violent* historical change in Hawthorne; but none of those who have analyzed the tale have made any effort to discover what social elements in the town are concerned to bring the change about.

The most mysterious individual Robin meets is the elderly gentleman of the sepulchral hems. He is the first one Robin accosts in seeking his kinsman—familiarly, seizing the skirt of the man's coat—only to be warned off by the gentleman, who says he doesn't "know" the Major, that he himself has "authority," and that Robin stands in danger of the stocks for his lack of respect for his "betters." As Robin wanders after this rout, he again hears the gentleman's "sepulchral hems" and flees "to pursue his researches in some other part of the town." [36] Much later, when Robin has taken his post before the church to await his kinsman, he vaguely perceives that he is watched by a face—"one which he seemed to remember, yet could not absolutely name as his kinsman's" [37]—from the Gothic window of an imposing mansion directly across the street from the church door. The silent watcher emerges during the final scene when his laugh "sailed over the heads of the multitude," as he "supported himself on his polished

cane in a fit of convulsive merriment, which manifested itself on
his solemn old features like a funny inscription on a tombstone." [38]
Who is this old gentleman who appears more often in the story
than any of the other townspeople?

The juxtaposition of his rank, his age, the location of his home,
his apparent role as *éminence grise* in the doings of the evening,
and not least the aura of death which surrounds him, suggest that
he undoubtedly represents the Church of New England. In stories
of three separate epochs of New England history—"Endicott and
the Red Cross," "The Gray Champion," and "Lord Howe's Masquerade"—Hawthorne reveals that the driving force against Royal
rule is not "democracy" but Puritanism. For in all Hawthorne's
vague assertions of the power of the People, he is clearly not talking of what in the parlance of a later generation would be referred to as "the masses" but of a complete culture embodied in
a discrete society.[39] Hawthorne always expressed his ideas of progressive change in a holist vocabulary.

Understanding this mysterious personage helps one to comprehend what is actually happening in the seaport this night; and
an awareness of Hawthorne's historical schema can help one to
see the implied meaning of this change for Hawthorne. The People are not beginning a new "revolution" in their own eyes (or in
Hawthorne's), but resisting a recent usurpation. The trouble began with the turning point of the late seventeenth century, when
"the kings of Great Britain had assumed the right of appointing
the colonial governors." [40] The gentleman—or clergyman—of the
sepulchral hems is the symbol of the Old Order, unable to discover
in his raucous glee at the expulsion of the interloper that the
writing on the wall is also for himself. The future belongs to
another breed of Molineuxes who have left the piety and order
of their fathers (for Robin's father is also a clergyman) forever.

Hawthorne explores attitudes towards historical change through
the eyes of Robin, and Robin's responses are recorded as atten-
tively as those of the "female auditors" in "Alice Doane's Appeal."

The process of historical change is presented to him in a guise analogous to, but far more vigorous than, the magic theater of "Main Street."

After Robin's spirited reactions to the rebuffs and blandishments of the early part of the evening (in many ways so similar to the mishaps of Melville's Redburn trying to use his father's outdated gazetteer as a guide to Liverpool), he settles almost into a trance, and his whole sense of reality is transformed. No longer blinded by his obtuse "common sense," which had enabled him to dismiss ("shrewdly, rationally, and satisfactorily") such extraordinary phenomena as the parti-colored stranger, he gives way to "the moon, creating, like the imaginative power, a beautiful strangeness in familiar objects, [that] gave something of romance to a scene that might not have possessed it in the light of day." Musing on his adventures and home, "his mind kept vibrating between fancy and reality." [41] At last, partly warned by the distant noises and the equivocal commentary of the "kindly" gentleman, he sees the procession appear. Since the image of processions, of "streams" of people, is Hawthorne's characteristic metaphor for the whole of mankind, the "magnetic chain of humanity," the reader is alerted to the more than political meaning of the "riot." In fact "the whole march" has "a visionary air, as if a dream had broken forth from some feverish brain, and were sweeping visibly through the midnight streets." [42]

Robin is one of Hawthorne's armed historical witnesses, capable of apprehending history as more than a meaningless spectacle. There are a number of such figures in the tales: Tobias Pearson, Roger Williams in "Endicott and the Red Cross," the old Puritan in "Lord Howe's Masquerade," Captain Lincoln in "Edward Randolph's Portrait," and the Doctor in "Lady Eleanore's Mantle." All, like Horatio in *Hamlet*, are witnesses and commentators and are meant to represent in essence the reaction of the audience to the tragedy. Yet it is not tragedy which Robin is called to witness.

The climax of the story, the confrontation of Robin and his
kinsman, is properly subject to readings on a number of levels,
one of the most important of which is the one Hawthorne *presents*
—what Robin has seen and sees on this one night. Robin's first
reaction is unmistakably meant to represent the emotions of
tragic catharsis: "Robin's knees shook, and his hair bristled, with
a mixture of pity and terror." This first reaction is subverted by
another, for "more than all, a perception of tremendous ridicule
in the whole scene, affected him with a sort of mental inebrity."
Joining the crowd—which, as Hawthorne makes clear, begins by
laughing *at his reaction*, not at the Major—Robin caps the merriment by a "shout of laughter that echoed through the street." [43]
The Major might quite properly feel insulted at Robin's yielding
to one categorical imperative of history (loyalty to place) rather
than to another (loyalty to blood). Yet Robin laughs at least as
much at the spectacle of historical change, in which he perceives
"tremendous ridicule," as at the pain of his kinsman. Like Hawthorne—and like the Melville of *Israel Potter*—Robin is strongly
impressed by the comic aspects of national emergence, but not so
strongly as to forget that history cannot be observed entirely as a
spectacle.

↶ *The Scarlet Letter*

The themes suggested by [William Gilmore Simms] viewed as he
views them, would produce nothing but historical novels, cast in the
same worn out mold that has been in use these thirty years, and which
it is time to break up and fling away.[44]

Hawthorne, 1846

I would hope that this entire chapter might be taken as a series
of notes for the appreciation of Hawthorne's historical art, revealing the themes and methods brought to full flower in *The Scarlet*

Letter. It is intended to complement other interpretations. Unlike Cooper, who was so dominated by the holist frame that his most profound intuitions stem from his struggles to free himself from it, Hawthorne was able, in such stories as "The Gentle Boy," to write *about* the holist imagination as an astute critic and observer. One of Hawthorne's most telling criticisms of New England Puritanism is conveyed by his portrayal of it as a civilization which believed that its obsession with forms and appearances brought it closer to "pure" religion. In *The Scarlet Letter* Hawthorne was able to use the holist frame in order to dramatize an historical situation. At the same time he consciously explores the meaning of that frame by recognizing the social imagination it expresses as the distinguishing mark of a particular society. Thus he makes holism his subject as well as his implicit method.

What is meant by saying that Hawthorne's Puritans *themselves* had a holist imagination? The scene with which the novel opens, of the woman with the scarlet letter standing on a scaffold and confronting the assembled community (so similar to the setting of "Mrs. Hutchinson") is as dramatic a representation of a society incapable of separating "private" and "public" concerns as one can imagine. The scaffold, which was "held . . . to be as effectual an agent in the promotion of good citizenship, as ever was the guillotine among the terrorists of France," [45] is a somber expression of the holist matrix of society; Hawthorne's anecdote of the dispute over a pig which altered the frame of government is the ludicrous complement. The web of interrelationships of a society in which all surface manifestations of behavior carry social significance has not only dramatic and comic possibilities, but opportunities for perversity, too; Hester serves the hierarchy with her needlecraft on all ceremonial occasions, literally stitching herself into the society which "frowned on her sin." The tale is of "a people amongst whom religion and law were almost identical, and in whose character both were . . . thoroughly interfused." [46] To the nineteenth- or twentieth-century mind the concept of a civilization attempting to realize transcendental ideals by reinforcing the formal matrix of society is highly ironical. That the paradox would not have been apparent to the seventeenth century is no matter; Hawthorne was writing genuinely historical fiction, embodying the perspective of his own time, not fictionalized chronicle.

Another aspect of this ironic situation, well illustrated in the opening tableau on the scaffold, is the Puritans' inability to appreciate the distance between man's social appearance and the reality of his intellectual and psychological life. The distinction between the inner and the outer spheres of human existence is such a pivotal intuition of Hawthorne's writing that it is difficult to overestimate its impact on the holist frame, in which the interlocking surfaces *are* "society." A character's position within or outside this matrix dictates the content and pattern of his thought.

Hawthorne reveals the scaffold as a place where personal and public history intersect. The public cannot see that "the scaffold of the pillory was a point of view that revealed to Hester Prynne the entire track along which she had been treading, since her happy infancy." [47] Matching the blindness of the crowd is the utter incompetency of the great men of the colony, the history-makers, to "meddle with a question of" the human spirit.[48] Hawthorne's suggestion is a revolutionary one, threatening to explode the holist frame of Cooper and Scott: there are living actors as well as demanding roles, and a fictional view of history which neglects this dimension, which advances the art by an insatiable absorption of new historical subject matter, "it is time to break up and fling away."

Hawthorne makes the distinction between holist and inner reality very effectively through the symbol of the scarlet letter itself. Hester is required to wear it as a stigma bearing an absurdly obvious social signification. What is at first taken by the community as a sort of algebraic sign for a quality of the personality, however, is transformed almost immediately by the author from the allegorical to the symbolic level. To an imagination dominated by literal readings of natural and social phenomena, nothing could be more subversive than symbolism. The symbolism of the letter makes another rent in the seamless whole of Puritan life by demanding *immediacy* of perception and judgment by artist and reader, a "progressive" absolutism challenging the "comparative" judgments encouraged by the holist historians. Moreover, as I shall try to show, where the sign appears most blatantly allegorical, in the specter of a letter "A" in the sky during Dimmesdale's vigil, Hawthorne was actually engaging in the richest kind of historical symbolism.

The central pattern of relationships among the characters implicitly demonstrates the meaning for a holist society of self-conscious awareness of secret "lives." That pattern is not, as is commonly thought, a triangle, for it has four, rather than three, poles of tension. The relationship of Hester and Dimmesdale is at the heart of the novel, yet neither character is defined entirely by that relationship, for Hawthorne shows each of them responding throughout the major part of the action to two other forces of varying power. Hester is in direct and intimate contact with the rulers of the community, whom I shall call the role-enforcers, represented by Governor Bellingham and John Wilson. At the same time she yields a sanction—unexamined by her during most of the seven years' action—to Chillingworth, as the price of secrecy. Dimmesdale is locked in mortal combat with Chillingworth, the searcher of the inner man, just as Bellingham and Wilson are the censors of the outer. Dimmesdale too yields an almost unconscious sanction, but his is to Bellingham and Wilson, whom he allows to prosecute Hester alone in exchange for being able to keep his secret. Hester and Arthur each turn almost violently at one point in each of their careers to challenge their dominant adversary at a moment when their personalities seem in danger of open violation. Hester does so in the scene in which she fights for her child: Arthur lashes out in the scene in which Chillingworth presses him too closely for his secret. Finally each yields to the more insidious sanctions of the "weaker" influence (Chillingworth for Hester, Bellingham for Dimmesdale) until the climax.

My point is not merely to illustrate the notorious symmetry of *The Scarlet Letter*, but the premises upon which that symmetrical structure is reared: roles and role-playing. The tensions created by probing the essential character concept of the holist frame— the social role—transform the various historical types of Hawthorne's short fiction into characters with intrinsic psychological depth, capable of sustaining a great novel. Bellingham and Wilson —always together—appear at four strategic places in the book: first as punitive, role-enforcing figures, questioning and exhorting Hester on the scaffold; then at the Governor's suggestively luxurious mansion; again at the scaffold on the night of Dimmesdale's vigil; and at last attempting to support Dimmesdale in his role and place in the procession at the conclusion before he breaks free to "confess." Though they are history-makers and role-enforcers, they have no insight into the inner life. When Dimmesdale cries from the scaffold during his vigil, Bellingham stares from the window of his mansion but can "see but little farther than he might into a millstone." [49] John Wilson passes within a few feet of him, "looking carefully at the muddy pathway before his feet, and never once turning his head towards the guilty platform." [50]

Hawthorne never brings the charge of hypocrisy against them (as he does against Dimmesdale), for they come very close to fitting their roles perfectly. Their very form of thought is holist (whatever its theological premises), and they have difficulty accepting the outwardly penitent Hester because their "prejudices" were "fortified in themselves by an iron framework of reasoning. . . . Thus it was with the men of rank, on whom their eminent position imposed the guardianship of the public morals." [51] Rank, morals, and logic are all parts of one inflexible system. For Hawthorne, the separation of "heart and head" was not the chief fault of the history-makers of New England; it was, rather, their inability to imagine a human reality behind the masks of society, an imaginative, not an emotional, failure:

But it is an error to suppose that our grave forefathers—though accustomed to speak and think of human existence as a state merely of trial and warfare, and though unfeignedly prepared to sacrifice goods and life at the behest of duty—made it a matter of conscience to reject such means of comfort, or even luxury, as lay fairly within their grasp. This creed was never taught, for instance, by the venerable pastor, John Wilson, whose beard, white as a snowdrift, was seen over Governor Bellingham's shoulder; while its wearer suggested that pears and peaches might yet be naturalized in the New England climate, and that purple grapes might possibly be compelled to flourish, against the sunny garden-wall. The old clergyman, nurtured at the rich bosom of the English Church, had a long established and legitimate taste for all good and comfortable things; and however stern he might show himself in the pulpit, or in his public reproof of such transgressions as that of Hester Prynne, still, the genial benevolence of his private life had won him warmer affection than was accorded to any of his professional contemporaries.[52]

In other words, to be a role-enforcer with equanimity one must have a "comfortable" attitude towards role-playing, and not be troubled by, or even be able to distinguish, the distance between ideal forms and reality.

The parallel to the conflict of the "deviant" Hester with the Puritan role-enforcers is the inner, hidden struggle of Dimmesdale with Chillingworth. Two scholars—the man of skill and the man of faith, the doctor of the flesh and the healer of the spirit—serve to introduce one of Hawthorne's most consistent historical themes into the novel: the struggle of competitive cultures for the New World, here the struggle of the Reformation with the Renaissance. Chillingworth, though he may represent the darker side of the English Renaissance—a student of the flesh, whose "higher and more subtile faculties . . . were materialized"[53]—nonetheless also bears the fate of "art" in America.

Even the most generous interpretation of the "demonic" cannot redeem Chillingworth as a "realistic" figure. Existing almost exclusively on one plane in the structure of the novel, like Bellingham and Wilson, it is impossible for his characterization to be more than schematic in some respects. He is indeed a figure out of melodrama, but high melodrama: an Archimago, a Richard III, an Iago. The melodramatics are Jacobean, and Hawthorne provides for him the most elaborate Jacobean background of any of his characters.[54] Like the great Elizabethan and Jacobean villain figures, he is a born dissembler and simulator, and is already a veteran of many roles—among the Indians, in court intrigue—which are as much his identity as his "true" life as a quiet but ambitious scholar. As an indication of his adeptness at role-changing we never learn his true first name and he is never addressed by his last.

A man for whom the social role has no *intrinsic* importance, he stands at the farthest remove from Bellingham and Wilson. Like Burckhardt's Renaissance man, his very personality is a work of art, and part of Hawthorne's message seems to be that the self-made personality can be made very ill. More importantly, the mere role-changer is not really free. Like the Puritans, among whom he at first numbered himself, he is a kind of dark progressive, acting through the social roles of the holist world but believing in the immanence of Will. In proclaiming his predestinarian "old faith" Chillingworth is declaring a significant attitude towards history:

By thy first step awry, thou didst plant the germ of evil; but, since that moment, it has all been a dark necessity. Ye that have wronged me are not sinful, save in a kind of typical illusion; neither am I fiend-like, who have snatched a fiend's office from his hands. It is our fate. Let the black flower blossom as it may! [55]

An alternative attitude is expressed in the character of Dimmesdale. Dimmesdale is not so much of a "Calvinist" as Chillingworth for the bulk of the narrative, and despite his mortifications of the flesh (or abetted by them), he is less concerned with his ultimate end than with worldly "vanities." Hawthorne piercingly analyzes the effects of Dimmesdale's concealment of his "sin," but never takes for granted the "shame" the clergyman so zealously avoids. Hester did not take it for granted, for she was so well able to live with "shame" that in the end she could not live without it, returning to New England and her scarlet badge in later life. The idea of "shame" of course is a corollary of the conception of personality as defined by social roles. Perhaps the extent to which *The Scarlet Letter* is about the effects of "sin," and not "shame," has been overemphasized in past interpretations. Dimmesdale's uniquely central role in the social structure of the community— he is, to all appearances, especially at the Election Sermon, a history-maker and role-enforcer himself—neither absolves nor condemns him in the reader's eyes for his failure to reveal his "sin." An understanding of Dimmesdale's attitude towards this role, however, is basic to an appreciation of his character. His social role as a minister appears to be a far surer prop for his weakness than Hester's affection and support, and the conclusion of the novel, with Dimmesdale, in the just and witty phrase of D. H. Lawrence, "dodging into death" rather than fleeing with her, proves it.[56]

Dimmesdale's tragedy is that he cannot be secure in either his faith or his role. His faith is impotent before social imperatives. Chillingworth, like a charlatan, assumes new roles with ease. For him, man is made by art, not by faith; he accepts social imperatives and roles at face value, to pun seriously. In the social ascendancy of Dimmesdale over Chillingworth Hawthorne epitomizes a New World which eschewed art to choose a faith it could not live with. Hawthorne is never more ambiguous than when he is subtly questioning whether the much-vaunted "faith" of the Puritans was simply an "iron framework" of ideology which prevented the examination of New England society and the roles men played in it:

Mr. Dimmesdale was a true priest, a true religionist, with the reverential sentiment largely developed, and an order of mind that impelled itself powerfully along the track of a creed, and wore its passage continually deeper with the lapse of time. In no state of society would he have been what is called a man of liberal views; it would always be essential to his peace to feel the pressure of a faith about him, supporting, while it confined him within its iron framework. Not the less, however, though with a tremulous enjoyment, did he feel the occasional relief of looking at the universe through the medium of another kind of intellect than those with which he habitually held converse. It was as if a window were thrown open, admitting a freer atmosphere into the close and stifled study, where his life was wasting itself away, amid lamplight, or obstructed day-beams, and the musty fragrance, be it sensual or moral, that exhales from books. But the air was too fresh and chill to be long breathed, with comfort. So the minister, and the physician with him, withdrew again within the limits of what their church defined as orthodox.[57]

Dimmesdale's ultimate rationalization for secret sin is precisely the necessity of an unblemished social mask as the prerequisite for doing social good. Pleading the case of secret sinners with Chillingworth, he asks, "can we not suppose it?—guilty as they may be, retaining, nevertheless, a zeal for God's glory and man's welfare, they shrink from displaying themselves black and filthy in the view of man; because, thenceforward, no good can be achieved by them; no evil in the past be redeemed by better service." [58]
Like all rationalizations, this is not a lie but rather a distortion of the subject's true situation. Dimmesdale is so wedded to his *conception* of his role (as shown by his deferment of escape until *after* the Election Sermon) that he consciously recognizes it as having an independent agency of its own.

More aware than Tobias, Dimmesdale becomes the first completely self-conscious role-playing holist protagonist, aspiring constantly to his role but never filling it. Self-conscious role-playing, for Hawthorne, was psychologically fatal to anyone but a practical charlatan:

It is inconceivable, the agony with which this public veneration tortured him! It was his genuine impulse to adore the truth, and to reckon all things shadow-like, and utterly devoid of weight or value, that had

not its divine essence as the life within their life. Then, what was he?
—a substance? or the dimmest of all shadows? [59]

The peculiarly modern *angst* over the true locus of the personality is not the only possible outcome of a sharp awareness of role-
playing in a holist society. Hester's awareness of the externality of
social roles is the most profound, as it is the most central to the
meaning of the book. More than anything else, it is indicated by
the badge:

The effect of the symbol—or rather, of the position in respect to
society that was indicated by it—on the mind of Hester Prynne herself, was powerful and peculiar. . . . Some attribute had departed
from her, the permanence of which had been essential to keep her a
woman. Such is frequently the fate, and such the stern development,
of the feminine character and person, when the woman has encoun-
tered, and lived through, an experience of peculiar severity. [60]

In other words, the effect of the social stigma—her character as
defined by the role-enforcers of the community—has been to alien-
ate Hester and cause her to question the validity of any such definition. Like Dimmesdale's guilt, her alienation does not affect her
performance in her role, and she seems to thrive on this dualism.
As Hawthorne observes, "persons who speculate the most boldly
often conform with the most perfect quietude to the external reg-
ulations of society." In a revolutionary age, whose spirit she had
"imbibed," she "cast away the broken chains" of her dependence
on society's definition of reality. "The world's law was no law for
her mind." [61] This is a fair description of the Hawthornean "dark
enthusiast." Only the alleged influence of Pearl keeps Hester
from developing into a specimen of this—for Hawthorne—extremely unsympathetic type. Otherwise

she might have come down to us in history, hand in hand with Anne
Hutchinson, as the foundress of a religious sect. She might, in one of

her phases, have been a prophetess. She might, and not improbably would, have suffered death from the stern tribunals of the period, for attempting to undermine the foundations of the Puritan establishment.[62]

Hester's speculation, then, carries all the social dynamite and aesthetic repugnancy of an Anne Hutchinson, a Catherine, a Zenobia—even a John Brown. And as with Brown, the wreck of the hopes fed on this speculation is "in requital of [a] preposterous miscalculation of possibilities." [63] Hester's inner rebellion belies her outward obedience, and Hawthorne's verdict convicts both her and the implicit reliance on the "truth" of social roles so necessary to the holist imagination: "The scarlet letter had not done its office." [64]

The *dramatis personae* are thus in large measure defined by their own attitudes towards history: Bellingham and Wilson, the holist history-makers and role-enforcers; Chillingworth, the "dark progressive" fatalist; Dimmesdale, the holist role-player *manqué*; and Hester, the frustrated genuine progressive. She is frustrated because she must watch Dimmesdale flee his "role" to embrace "Fate," for the course of the tragedy of the novel lies precisely in this cycle she had attempted to break. Pearl not only exists on a different fictional level from the other characters, but stands outside the holist social world of *The Scarlet Letter*. She is not a mere renegade but a "born outcast," and her character is a standing reproach to the holist imagination. Having a nature which "lacked reference . . . to the world into which she was born," her escape to Europe is a rejection both of the Puritans and of the conception of character as purely a function of "culture." [65]

The Scarlet Letter shows the novelist in command of the holist historical novel, and in his two chief protagonists he registers significant attacks on the holist frame that all but break it apart. In Dimmesdale, Hawthorne illustrates the almost intolerable limits which the holist conception of roles places on the human personality. In Hester, he allows the "enthusiast," for the only time in his work, to assume very nearly heroic proportions, and so finds a place in the historical novel for progressive Idealism. In the end, Hawthorne was unable to transcend the limitations of the holist frame of the historical imagination, but he created a work of art in which the tensions within that frame are wrought to the very highest intensity.

In addition to giving a new dimension to the characters of historical romance, *The Scarlet Letter* relates their tragedy to the inner history of New England's cultural disaster. Hawthorne has placed the action of the novel at the first decisive turning point of New England history, when the not unmellowed "ponderous sobriety" of the first settlers gave way to "their immediate posterity, the generation next to the early emigrants, [who] wore the blackest shade of Puritanism, and so darkened the national visage with it, that all the subsequent years have not sufficed to clear it up." [66] There is a tragic inevitability to the coincidence of the night of the minister's vigil and disturbing vision of "A" in the sky and the deathwatch of Winthrop, whom Hawthorne had elegized in "Mrs. Hutchinson" as "a man by whom the innocent and guilty might alike desire to be judged; the first confiding in his integrity and wisdom, the latter hoping in his mildness." [67] From this point in the novel, the tragedy rushes swiftly to its conclusion. There is a painful irony in the Election Day rejoicing that greets Dimmesdale's sermon on "the relation between the Deity and the communities of mankind, with a special reference to the New England which they were here planting in the wilderness." [68] And the full weight of the irony cannot be grasped without knowing that the rejoicing, "as if a good and golden year were at length to pass over the poor old world," [69] heralded in fact the rise to rule and dominance of John Endicott.

As the people are unaware of the nemesis overtaking their own culture, so they can scarcely comprehend the tragedy of Hester Prynne and Arthur Dimmesdale.

The witnesses of Hester Prynne's disgrace had not yet passed beyond their simplicity. They were stern enough to look upon her death, had that been the sentence, without a murmur at its severity, but had none of the heartlessness of another social state, which would find only a theme for jest in an exhibition like the present.[70]

They do not function like a Greek chorus, for although they proffer diffuse judgments and interpretations of many events in the novel, their judgments are exceptionally limited and timebound. They do not sense, see, or apprehend the tragedy enveloping the central characters. This tragedy does not involve overtly the destiny of a people. Rather it is a covert manifestation of a dynamic historical situation which will affect them more than they will ever know; and as such, can only be apprehended from the vantage point of historical perspective. Thus, there is no Roger Williams, Robin, or Tobias in the tale. The historical witness is not in the seventeenth century, but in the Custom House, poring over moldy documents and a tattered letter "A."

Chapter Five

MELVILLE: REBELLION, TRAGEDY, AND HISTORICAL JUDGMENT

ELVILLE, no less than Cooper and Hawthorne, has an historical focus which sets the pattern of his work. Cooper's peculiar theme is the decline and fall of civilizations, red and white; Hawthorne's is the splitting apart of cultures, both national and generational. For Melville violent revolution was the significant historical event and he was preoccupied with questions of change rather than the limitations of roles.

His awareness of the significance of cultural systems, deepened by his voyages to South Sea Islands, seems to have prompted him to seek the basic root of all civilizations. He consistently concerned himself with the inner destruction of identity that all societal forms may inflict at times on the individual and with the impulse to escape from such damage or to revolt against it. The social organization of roles and the need to resist closed, authoritarian definitions of reality for the self-preservation of the individual were Melville's central themes and they marked the emergence in American historical fiction of the progressive frame. Melville reflected that sense of injustice and willingness to revolt violently that has been a part of American history from colonial days to the present.

Two of his historical novels, *His Fifty Years of Exile* (*Israel*

Potter) (1854–55) and *Billy Budd* (unfinished in 1891), are attempts to give imaginative form to the two great revolutions of the
preceding century that had done so much to determine the shape
of his own time. A third, *Benito Cereno* (1855), is an omen of
the civil war and social revolution about to overtake America.
More than this, these novels chart the rise of the progressive
frame of the historical imagination in the nineteenth century.
Melville's changing imaginative conception of revolt came more
and more to mature as a rebellious critique of what a character in
Redburn calls "snivelization." This development is complex and
may be traced through the decade of fecund creativity from *Typee*
(1845–46) to *The Confidence Man* (1855–56).

Melville's first book exemplifies the curiously indistinct line
that exists between "history" and "fiction" in his work, for he
claimed that his adventures among the cannibals of Typee were
literally true. It has since become clear that many of his assertions
about the customs of this Polynesian culture owed their accuracy
to Melville's later bookish researches rather than to his capacity
as an eyewitness and field researcher.

Typee invites comparison, as Howard Doughty has shown, with
other anthropological narratives, like *The Oregon Trail*, in which
the motivation and stance of the investigator towards the host culture become as vital a source of interest as the "facts" that are
presented about an alien people.[1] In his narrative, Melville is
clearly exploiting the tensions of the holist frame which sustained
Cooper before him. The narrator, Tommo, is alternately seduced
by the Edenic life of the Typees and drawn back to the European-
American civilization that he condemns for its imperialist rapa-
ciousness and repression but values for its "seriousness." Constantly tempted by the role of renegade, he is at last brought to
the point of decision. He resists the Typees' attempt to tattoo
him, for were they successful, he avers, he would not have "the
face" with which to return to civilization.[2] Then he recklessly
pushes on to discover what D. H. Lawrence might call the "dirty

little secret" the Typees have been at pains to conceal from him: that they are in fact cannibals. Having raised again the absolute holist bar of cultural difference between himself and his hosts, Tommo can at last force himself to escape, nearly killing one of his old "friends" in the process.

Although initially holist in its terms, *Typee* constantly makes the distinction between civilization and savagery ambiguous and value judgments between them doubly doubtful. Thus Tommo may hold the opinion that war is but ancient cannibalism writ large, yet still flee the eaters of human flesh for the culture of wholesale massacre. Though Melville apparently begins as a holist, the consistent element in his view of society is not a stable frame of cultural values; indeed, he insists throughout his writings on the interchangeability of savagery and civilization, that cultures exist on a scale of development, and that often, in the imagined words of Queequeg, the "cannibals must help these Christians." [3] The regularly sounded note is that of the psychically threatening quality of all culture forms and the impulse either to escape from their destructive pressure on identity or to rebel against them.[4] This escape from history, imaged in Tommo in the arms of Fayaway or Ishmael in the arms of Queequeg, is a recurrent theme in Melville, but it is the minor one.

Melville first confronted what was to emerge as his major theme, the problems of social revolt and revolution, in *Mardi*. As Merrell R. Davis has demonstrated, Melville wrote *Mardi* in three sections, adding the last, the "travelogue-satire," after June 1848, by which time the forces of reaction had gained the upper hand in Europe.[5] In this part Melville expresses his view of the future prospects of America through a thinly disguised allegory. He reveals, among other things, a grudging respect for England's ability to maintain her Empire while confounding her Chartists and a sympathy with revolutionaries on the continent tempered with skepticism about the substantial achievements of the abortive revolutions of 1848. The note which dominates Melville's discourse on America itself is the rawness and lack of historical sense of the American people, a fault of youth which permits Americans to believe themselves an original historic phenomenon. The high point of Melville's commentary, in a "Voice from the Gods," presented as an anonymous scroll fixed to a palm tree, warns an assembly of national expansionists against the fallacy of trying to spread "freedom" by the sword. The "Voice" speaks of man's pride in his freedom as a kind of hubris, and stresses the real limits on man's power in a way that presages *Moby Dick:*

It is not the prime end, and chief blessing, to be politically free. And freedom is only good as a means; is no end in itself. Nor, did man fight it out against his masters to the haft, not then would he uncollar his neck from the yoke. A born thrall to the last, yelping out his liberty, he still remains a slave unto Oro [God]; and is it well for the universe that Oro's sceptre is absolute.[6]

The "Voice" further says that freedom in Vivenza (the United States) has been a result of the frontier and the spirit of the founding fathers, not merely a product of democratic codes. In this way, the scroll warns against attempting to transplant democracy all over the world, and also against mistaking license for liberty:

For the state that today is made up of slaves, cannot tomorrow transmute her bond into free; though lawlessness may transform them into brutes. Freedom is the name for a thing that is *not* freedom; this, a lesson never learned in an hour or an age. . . . freedom is more social than political. And its real felicity is not to be shared. *That* is of a man's own individual getting and holding.[7]

As the voyagers continue their quest through Vivenza, all their observations tend towards the same point: that freedom is not an absolute or progressive Ideal, and that it is not to be attained by merely doing away with the trappings or institutions of tyranny. To be free, a nation must possess freedom of spirit, which is to be achieved only by a process of evolution, by a combination of challenging environment and social heredity. Rebellion against the existing social order is always vain, and barren in results for real —that is personal—freedom.

Turning to Melville's novel of 1849, *Redburn*, one finds a much less Olympian attitude towards questions of social injustice. Melville's mode has been conspicuously transformed in the later book, for its narrator is a young man who undergoes the experiences of a social outcast and encounters the seamy side of civilization full face. Through what has been regarded as a technical lapse on Melville's part, the narrator often speaks in the voice of a mature man reflecting on the society that the boy observes. Both man and boy seem to contradict *Mardi* by demonstrating that the miseries of the poor and the resentment of the working classes against the privileged are not problems to be deferred to the actions of "all-healing Time." The depravity of the sailors, the horrors of Liverpool, the revelations caused by a shipboard epidemic, are presented as vividly as possible, and heated with the author's anger. Melville's *Redburn* is hot with the immediacy of injustice. *Redburn*, and, to an even greater extent, its successor *White Jacket*, show a radical difference in tone from *Mardi*, as F. O. Matthiessen has noted:

The waking of Melville's tragic sense is more apparent in *Redburn* and *White Jacket* than in the wooden allegory of Yillah and Hautia. These books reveal that the actual sufferings of mankind had been so impressed upon his consciousness that none of the optimistic palliatives or compensations of his age could ever explain them away.[8]

◜ Transition: Holist to Progressive

Certain events in Melville's life provide insight into the heightened tone and almost classical expression of progressive outrage in these works. In the spring of 1849, Melville had been drawn into a literary circle of dissident Democrats known as Young America.[9] They included Evert and George Duyckinck, Cornelius Mathews, and W. A. Jones. Asserting the existence of American artistic talent, they sought to throw off English domination of American literary and cultural life and adopted the seaman-turned-writer Melville as a valuable protégé.

Yet there were marked differences between their backgrounds and circumstances and Melville's. The Duyckincks and their colleagues were all established literary men, while Melville was a struggling young author. They were college graduates with elegant tastes and the economic means to be professional literary gentlemen, while Melville's formal education had been abandoned on his father's death and he had twice survived hard times by sailing before the mast as a common seaman.[10]

Despite their views on Young America, when the long-standing feud between William Charles Macready and Edwin Forrest, the leading tragedians of England and America, culminated in the Astor Place riot, these dissident Democrats sided with the Englishman. The intemperate quarrel reached its climax on May 7, 1849, when a group of Tammany followers drove Macready from the stage of the Astor Place Opera House. A few days later well-to-do Whigs, led by Washington Irving, issued a public letter denouncing this action and swearing to "sustain" the British actor in new appearances. This letter was signed by three Democratic writers— Evert Duyckinck, Mathews, and Herman Melville.

Thus supported and well advertised, on May 10 Macready reappeared, and a well-organized Tammany crowd so violently assailed the Astor Place theatre that the National Guard was summoned. It fired into the mob, killing 31 persons and injuring 150. Tammany orators then blamed the signers of the public letter—the "kid glove aristocracy"—for the "murders." Those signing the letter were loudly condemned; Forrest asserted that the "blood will rest on [their] heads." [11] A widely circulated pamphlet called the signers of the public letter *participes crimines* in the deaths of those killed by the troops and accused them of "a desire to appear before the world as champions of law and order, and as the *élite* of New York society, who could and would sustain any actor, especially the pet of the English and American aristocrats, against the lower orders of society—as they are pleased to call the laboring and producing classes of this country." [12] Many newspapers expressed fear of laboring class mobs.

Melville's poem "The House-top" indicates that he probably observed the riots from his rooftop. The shock of the many deaths, the widespread censure of himself and other signers of the public letter as calloused "aristocrats," insensitive to the feelings of poor, hard-working Americans, appear to have shaken Melville profoundly.[13] While the Astor Place riot raised questions and issues inherent in revolution that were to preoccupy him for the rest of his life, his immediate reaction to being called an aristocrat was swift. In the two books he finished during the summer after the Astor Place riots, *Redburn* and *White Jacket*, he reasserted his rebellious proletarian sympathies with vigor.

Redburn, apparently begun before Melville's unwitting plunge into history, is remarkable not only for the step it marks in Melville's artistic growth, but for the warm professions of democratic humanism that supplant the aloof skepticism of *Mardi*. Written from the point of view of a boy who is an "outsider" by dint of youth and his anomalous combination of education and poverty, the novel is much more concerned with the urban poor than anything Melville had yet written. He describes the social conditions which breed moral revolt with a bitterness which far surpasses the gentle muckraking of *Omoo*. Liverpool is a revelation of misery and depravity for Redburn—a city of beggars and starvation, of murderers, prostitutes, and thieves. Most important is the identification of Redburn with the poor, even though his sympathy is salted with criticism of the lower classes. In this role of outsider within civilization, Melville begins, in a veiled way, his declaration of independence from the privileged few, a gesture which would extend immensely on the literary level at least, and would eventually include Young America.[14] Although the pervading tone of *Redburn* conveys a deep resentment of the prevailing social order, the tension between Melville's anger at these conditions and his skepticism of reform is never resolved within the work.

White Jacket carries farther the social analysis of *Redburn*.[15] As its subtitle, "The World in a Man-of-War," suggests, the world of a naval vessel is but a microcosm; in Wordsworth's words, "the very world . . . the place where, in the end, we find our happiness, or not at all!" [16] This world is characterized by the conflicts of totalitarian authority and smoldering resentment against it, of officers always eager for war and "the people," as Melville always refers to the crew, who hate it, of two classes perpetually dwelling in "incurable antagonism." [17] *White Jacket*, as a novel of protest, not only strikes out for the abolition of flogging, but penetrates beyond an attack on a single evil to get to the roots of a multiform contradiction between democratic professions and practices of tyranny and privilege. The novel further suggests that in the resolution of that contradiction lies the future hope of the world; in a rhetorical flourish the narrator appeals to his fellow countrymen to abandon all doubts that in America "the political Messiah had come." [18] *White Jacket* caps Melville's five-year transition in his definition of revolt from the holist terms of the renegade's escape to the progressive terms of class conflict.

ᕫ *Moby Dick*: Interrogation of Reality

White Jacket is the apogee of Melville's progressive hope, showing his conscience stung into identification with the victims of repression, and his work almost entirely absorbed in the terms of militant opposition between natural rights and tyranny that the progressive frame alone allows. In his next novels, far more ambitious and artful, he was to press the possibility of revolt to the limits. *Moby Dick* (1851) is composed basically in the terms of progressivism. However, with greater reflection than had been possible in *White Jacket*, Melville was able to shift the locus of revolt from the social plane to the metaphysical. *Pierre* (1852) complements Melville's masterpiece by exploring the same theme, but within the holist order of a society crisscrossed by a net of class, sexual, and racial taboos, its protagonist attempting to rip through a strand of circumstance that ultimately strangles him.

In each of these major works Melville demonstrates the unbridgeable distinction between what the "pamphlet of Plotinus Plinlimmon" in *Pierre* calls "chronological," or ideal, truth, and the "horological," actual world in which we live.[19] For the progressive frame, this means that the Idealist progressive dialectic of Spirit reifying itself appears at best naive, for it is confuted by the lack of demonstrable correspondence between the world of the mind and the world of things and social relations. The "chronologicals" of ideal spirit are fatally alienated from the "horologicals" of human action. The implications of this alienation for the holist frame are no less threatening, for the narrative representation of society becomes a matter of entirely arbitrary invention if the intricately related appearances of the actual social world reflect no essence which can be tested and approved by the mind.

Moby Dick is Melville's greatest novel. It is the unique example, among his many formulations of the dilemma of progressive revolt, of a work in which the social and metaphysical levels of his drama of ideas do not threaten to drown each other out. The crew of the *Pequod* are not ranged against the master and officers of the ship as they are in the progressive class division of *Redburn*, *White Jacket*, *Benito Cereno*, and *Billy Budd*. The crew threaten neither to escape from oppressive authority nor to mutiny against it.

Through two contrasting images of revolt Melville reminds the reader that the willing acquiescence of this crew is a striking exception to the usual rules of the sea. The first is the *Town-ho's* story, a tale of violent repression and successful overthrow of authority. This tale stands out in greater relief by its strategic placement at the very center of *Moby Dick*.[20] Significantly, the tale is related during a gam between the men of the *Town-ho* and those of the *Pequod*, who "kept the secret among themselves so that it never transpired abaft the Pequod's mainmast." [21] The contrasting image is the constant opposition and resistance of Starbuck to what he perceives as Ahab's perversion of the commercial ends of their voyage. Though brought to the brink of the ultimate act of mutiny, the murder of his captain in his sleep, Starbuck's failure to act reflects his ambiguous role as an apostle at once of righteous resistance and of seasoned authority.[22] As Melville says in *The Confidence Man* of the divided consciousness which leads to such "a fall of valor," Starbuck may stand for "the moderate man, the invaluable understrapper of the wicked man."

The *Pequod*, unlike *White Jacket's Neversink*, is not a microcosm of incipiently violent class conflict. The relations of Ahab and his crew rather exemplify a perverse form of democratic centralism than an outright despotism. The crew is not only "commanded" by Ahab, but is wooed and won to his purpose as he converts his formal authority into a nightmare vision of a Jacksonian democratic dictatorship. This unity of will—in which Ishmael shares, though he declares his allegiance is born of the "dread in [his] soul" [23]—is symbolized in the pact of "violence and revenge" against Moby Dick in which they join. Ahab uses a battery of inducements, including the customary forms of command and the lure of cash, as well as the pact of rebellion, to weld the crew into his effective instrument. Since all his means are bent to unnatural ends, however, the forms he manipulates become only empty vessels for his will. The "sultanism" of Ahab's mind cannot become "incarnate in an irresistible dictatorship," on the other hand, without the aid of some version of the holistic forms of shipboard command. "For be a man's intellectual superiority what it will, it can never assume the practical, available supremacy over other men, without the aid of some sort of external arts and entrenchments, always, in themselves, more or less paltry and base." [24]

Ahab's purpose defines his being; it creates him as the personality who can defy the "personified impersonal" in a way his customarily limited role does not permit. This purpose is thus categorically progressive, but it is defined by will and not by historical necessity, thus making it progressive after the dark manner of Roger Chillingworth's fixed purpose. Motivating an action that passes through conflict to a climactic victory or defeat, embodied in forms but not defined by them, at once the creator and servant of the forces he sets in motion, and joined to his followers by the force of intention rather than the habit of formal ascendancy, Ahab becomes in part a sinister parody of the progressive Great Man. For the dark progressive protagonist history moves by the same dialectical means as for Bancroft's Washington; the end, however, is not the comic goal of the realization of public order and freedom, but rather the personally cultivated dark flower of predestined tragedy.

The pursuit of Moby Dick is variously interpreted by the crew (*vide* their "readings" of the doubloon),[25] but for all of them the encounter with the whale suggests a final violent encounter with reality, and so with human history. The "Anacharsis Clootz" composition of the crew, with its spectrum of the peoples of the world, suggests that in the outcome of their quest Melville is indicating a teleological perspective on history which ends in annihilation, even if one takes the voyage of the *Pequod* as a limiting case among eschatological possibilities rather than as a prophetic emblem of spaceship earth.

Having changed the object of the rebellion of "violence and revenge" from earthly authority to a symbol of natural and divine force, Melville makes a further distinction, between the authoritarian and the rebellious intellectual perception. Ahab, as Starbuck meditates, "would be a democrat to all above," who "lords it over all below." [26] Moreover, his reading of nature is vital to his goal. Ahab discerns an "inscrutable" essence behind the whale's appearance, which one must "strike through the mask" to vanquish. "That inscrutable thing," says Ahab, "is chiefly what I hate," [27] and so in piercing the holist world of appearances, he hastens to create a new meta-reality and to enforce its acceptance on his inferiors.

Ishmael joins the quest, but he resists Ahab's limiting definition of reality. Here as elsewhere, Ishmael is content to rest in the mystery of a myriad of meanings possibly inherent in the phenomenal world. In the mind of Ishmael, the zealous interrogator of reality, the "chronological" and "horological" spheres, the ideal and the actual, only meet in tentative fashion. Fleeing the holist world of literal appearance, he yet resists Ahab's specification of an unseen reality. Fleeing the bitter loneliness of an "isolato," he is only fleetingly forged into a mass-man by Ahab, and seeks the rarely attainable ideal companionship he briefly shares with Queequeg. In *Moby Dick* Melville successfully distinguishes between the revolt of "violence and revenge" and spiritual resistance to closed definitions of reality.

⤻ *Israel Potter*: Cultural Clash in a Comic Light

Israel Potter is Melville's first attempt to give the historical dimension to the problem of man's place in society. In a sense this book represents a kind of intellectual and moral holiday for Melville. Utilizing comedy and irony, he mocked and caricatured the holist certainties of nationalism, and when he next turned to the form of the historical novel, in *Benito Cereno* and later in *Billy Budd*, he continued the development of the progressive frame that marked his work from *Redburn* through *Moby Dick*.

Of all Melville's works, *Israel Potter* has received the least critical attention. The most repeated explanation, which blames this neglect on its comparatively inferior quality, is neither adequate nor correct. *Israel Potter* is not a failure of "art," for it is probably Melville's most "well-made" novel. The difference between *Israel Potter* and Melville's other historical fiction is one of complexity. *Israel Potter* is comparatively so fresh, fluid, and self-explanatory that it seems to make interpretation superfluous; the fragmentary, ambiguous nature of the later novels provokes explication. The simplicity of *Israel Potter*, usually attributed to its "derivative" character, is one of its most fascinating aspects as an historical novel, the result of a uniquely fruitful coalescence of historical and fictional method.

His Fifty Years of Exile (*Israel Potter*) is a picaresque tale. It purports to be a revision of a Revolutionary soldier's own "little narrative of his adventures, forlornly published on sleazy gray paper," probably not written by him but "taken from his lips by another." [28] Historiographically, Melville, like a Henry Adams who has substituted poetic license for scientific method, is placing the original document, in emended form, before our eyes, identifying himself as "The Editor" in the book's mock dedication to the Bunker Hill Monument. Structurally, the book consists of two narratives. One is the "adventure" tale, the second describes his fifty years of exile, to which the opening and the brief closing chapters belong; in the opening chapter he is in a sense "exiled" from his family and his true love by his father's determined opposition to his marriage.

What significantly distinguishes *Israel Potter* from the traditional picaresque novel is Melville's use of comedy and critical ironic commentary, directed particularly towards the patriotic mythology developed by the Young America movement of which Melville had once been a member. Potter is a perfect foil for such an ironic treatment. He is the epitome of the mythic American: a farmer, hunter, trapper, clearer-of-the-wilderness, surveyor, and peddler. Unable to marry because of his tyrannical father's opposition, which is unexplained, he wanders, becomes a sailor, then a whaling harpooner, returns to farming, and answers the patriotic call of his countrymen at Bunker Hill. Wounded and captured, he is carried to England where he escapes, but betrays himself by addressing Sir John Millet as "Mr." Nevertheless, Sir John helps him gain employment in the "securest asylum"—the

King's gardens.[29] The King promptly recognizes him as a Yankee and, in a burlesque on the Idea of Equality, they have a comic dialogue which hinges on manners and forms of address—the subject is no longer the subject to whom the king is not the king. This leaves Israel feeling that "it could not be the warm heart of the King, but the cold heads of his lords in council that persuaded him so tyrannically to persecute America. Yet hitherto the precise contrary of this had been Israel's opinion, agreeably to the popular prejudice throughout New England." [30]

Forced to flee, lest he be impressed into service, Israel finds some of America's secret friends in England and becomes their courier to Dr. Franklin in Paris. This enables Melville to present the encounters of this heroic common man with Benjamin Franklin, Captain John Paul Jones, and Ethan Allen—heroes drawn from the young nation's pantheon. Melville uses the deceit required by Potter's role as a courier to expose the reality behind these mythical figures. For example, although always in awe of Dr. Franklin, Potter nevertheless becomes aware that the wise old man's simple, "highly ingratiating air" is actually a strategy.[31] Indeed, he concludes, "Every time he comes in, he robs me, with an air all the time, too, as if he were making me presents." [32]

In presenting these figures, Melville draws upon Franklin's *Autobiography* as well as *Poor Richard,* upon Ethan Allen's *Narrative,* with its racy prose and Revolutionary rhetoric, as well as upon the scandalous memoirs of John Paul Jones recorded by Jones' first mate, Nathaniel Fanning.[33] These primary documents are not only important as literary "sources." Historical method here corresponds perfectly with Melville's special method of composition, which often included wholesale appropriation of materials from his reading. He never lost sight of the service that fact can pay to fiction, and his work bristles with affidavits, authentic and invented, from his first novel to his last. In *Israel Potter,* the sources are documents presented and arranged for our inspection. One is referred to them, and can almost examine the originals embedded in the text, a technique that prefigures that of William Carlos Williams in *In the American Grain* (1925). The incidents involving Potter with Franklin, Jones, and Allen are interwoven to reveal a meaning not hidden in any one alone. The novelist-as-historian's task is to regroup the documents and rethink that meaning, following Emerson's dictum that history is subjective biography. Since Melville was habitually a heavy borrower of materials and usually worked within a loose "personal narrative" tradition, these procedures when applied to an historical subject tend to create a more self-conscious work than is at first apparent. Thus *Israel Potter* is in one sense a self-reflexive novel, the temporary identity of historical and fictional narrative voices constituting an oblique commentary on the craft of the author.

These highly publicized American heroes are revealed in marked contrast to the forgotten hero, the common Revolutionary soldier, and what happens to him. In the culminating battle of the British frigate *Serapis* and Jones' *Bon Homme Richard*, Potter is knocked by chance aboard the English ship and returned once again to England. For the next forty years, trapped by circumstances, he leads an impoverished existence in London, befogged and grimy: "Nor marble, nor flesh, nor the sad spirit of man, in this cindery City of Dis abide white." [34] At last, he comes home to America, arriving on the Fourth of July amidst a celebration of the battle of Bunker Hill. Like Rip Van Winkle—another bit of Melville's mockery—he finds everything changed or vanished, the old family homestead long gone. Melville, as "The Editor," refers to the graves on Bunker Hill as a "true Potter's Field." [35] And there Israel is buried, "his scars . . . his only medals," assured of "a posthumous pension, in default of any during life, annually paid him by the spring in ever-new mosses and sward." [36]

The third-person narrative is not Melville's only vehicle, for the early and late chapters are mediated by a narrator with a more fully developed persona, a mask submerged for most of the novel. These chapters, as imagistically packed as the rest of the book is fluid, possess the sense of historical distance and reflectiveness that is missing in the "first-hand" account. These two stances of "The Editor" *vis-à-vis* his subject differentiate the "adventure" and "exile" narratives. The "exile" narrative, with all its stylistic richness, is an exploitation of the idea first embodied in Cooper's Harvey Birch: the lonely, self-imposed silence of the truest patriots, and the author's tacit accusation of his nation for a cold-hearted betrayal of warm-hearted patriotism.

The "adventure narrative," however, provides the clearest picture of the kind of social imagination working in *Israel Potter*, for in it the terms of Israel's revolt are defined. In Melville's view the American Revolution is nationalist, not philosophically progressive, and his somewhat impudent depiction of the irresistible emergence of national "types" far outweighs the importance of any incidental Ideas implied in that rebellion. For example, the Idea of Equality is presented through the humorous dialogue between Israel and George III on the etiquette of forms of address. The social imagination which dominates *Israel Potter* is holist, and the Revolution is treated as a form of accommodation of two cultures in a complex *contretemps*. As in the historical fiction of Cooper and Hawthorne, the Revolution finds what Kenneth Burke would call a comic frame of acceptance.[37]

Yet individuals' strategies of revolt continue within the larger Revolution, and those of Israel, Franklin, Jones, and Allen are constantly threatening to break through the comic confrontation with human error which this limited conception of revolution implies and become a savage assault on Evil. Israel's revolt seems to cross this boundary in the scene in which he massacres the crew of a British revenue cutter on which he is temporarily serving in a fight as brutal as anything Melville wrote. Israel's action, though it bears the aspect of a treacherous mutiny, is not condemned by the narrator, and John Paul Jones even compliments it profusely.

Why is Israel's violent overthrow of his superiors (initiated by a deathblow to the captain reminiscent of the abortive assault upon the captain of the *Neversink* in *White Jacket*) sanctioned by Melville? This is like the conundrum, "When is a revolution not a revolution?" To which the answer is: "When it is [only] a war of national liberation." Just before Israel attacks the unsuspecting officer, he puts the Britisher on guard, declaring himself an "enemy" and a "Yankee." The national grievance sanctifies the act, just as it does the violence at Bunker Hill, and, much more dubiously, the battle of the *Bon Homme Richard* and the *Serapis*. The "frame of acceptance" is not law- and tradition-centered as in Cooper, yet it retains much of Cooper's "nationalism," greatly purged of the older author's "romanticism." This distinction is made most forcefully in what has been critically deemed the great success of the "adventure narrative," the battle at sea in which Melville combines a brilliant description of naval action with a capsule definition of nationalism.

The battle between the *Bon Homme Richard* and the *Serapis* is the literary set piece of the novel, yet it never really extends beyond the limitations of the set piece to become a metaphor for the theme of revolt—as Bunker Hill does. The description of the naval engagement does something more trenchant, however, by questioning the nationalist frame of acceptance itself. The sea battle is a death struggle between two *nations*, and it signifies "war," not "revolution." Melville brackets his description of the fight between two of the most significant passages of the novel. In the first the narrator suggests that this conflict between "the Englishman and the American" reveals that "intrepid, unprincipled, reckless, predatory, with boundless ambition, civilized in externals but a savage at heart, America is, or may yet be, the Paul Jones of nations." [38] At the conclusion of the conflict, so wasteful of human life, Melville returns to his theme in another way, asking, "Is civilization a thing distinct, or is it an advanced stage of barbarism?" [39]

Melville is using the historical event as a metaphor for *emerging* civilization; here the culture clash is a means of revealing the roots

of culture itself rather than the elaborated surface manifestations
of two civilizations. It is this drive toward a theoretically radical
portrayal of society which distinguishes Melville from Hawthorne
and Cooper. Melville, like Parkman, had observed "savage" and
"barbaric" life as a self-consciously civilized visitor, and he has the
awe and horror of genuine renegade behavior which is a touchstone of the holist imagination. Instead of imposing a rigid barrier between savagery and civilization, however, a barrier without
which "civilization" is to be taken as meaningless, Melville attempts to find one root for all society in an effort to account for
the senseless violence of man in all stages of "development." [40]
The rhetorical question quoted above indicates fully the transitional role of *Israel Potter* among American historical novels; it
is a "holist" novel whose inquiry into the meaning of an historical
event is framed in language indistinguishable from that of the
thoroughly progressive ethnologist Lewis Henry Morgan.

It has been customary for critics of *Israel Potter* to attempt to
seek Melville's statement about American civilization through his
remarkable portraits of "representative men" in America's Revolutionary past: Benjamin Franklin, John Paul Jones, and Ethan
Allen. This designation is more than a critical cliché, for there is a
more direct relationship to Emerson's *Representative Men* in
Israel Potter than is commonly recognized. *Representative Men*,
published in 1850, seems indeed a likely and appropriate philosophical point of reference for Melville as he first essays the definition of the role of the individual in history. The similarity of
Melville's drawing of Franklin and Paul Jones—the two historical
personages Melville treats at length—to two of Emerson's representative men suggests, moreover, that for Melville Emerson's
book was a source of direct inspiration, if not parody.

Melville finds a number of historical analogies to Franklin, including Jacob, Hobbes, Machiavelli, and particularly Plato; he
refers to Franklin's "Plato-like graciousness," and calls him a
"household Plato." [41] Yet there is little similarity between Emer-

son's Plato and Melville's Franklin, though there is a strong resemblance between the latter and the Concord philosopher's portrait of Plato's "double-star" Socrates. The resemblance is increased when one remembers Franklin's injunction to himself in the *Autobiography* to "imitate Jesus and Socrates," and his employment of Socratic questioning in civic disputation. Socrates, according to Emerson,

was plain as a Quaker in habit and speech, affected low phrases, and illustrations from cocks and quails, soup-pans and sycamore spoons, grooms and farriers, and unnamable offices—especially if he talked with any superfine person. He had a Franklin-like wisdom.[42]

Emerson was most impressed by the combination of high seriousness and earthiness in this "tyrannous realist," this "Aesop of the mob." His portrait of the historical Socrates provides the synthesis of contradictory qualities at which Melville was hinting in his Franklin. Melville wishes to show Franklin's "real" life as it was hinted at in the *Autobiography*; in *Israel Potter* the precepts of the sage, especially those of his Poor Richard, do not reflect the actions and attitudes of his own life, but rather an "ideal" simplicity. Melville's portrait is not merely a satiric thrust at hypocrisy, but an exposure, mellowed by appreciation, of Franklin's self-generated myth. To criticize the myth is not, as Melville is at pains to state, to impugn the great man himself.[43] The profile of Franklin casts a shadow on Israel, for he too has a real and hidden life as well as a public one. Like Franklin in his *Autobiography*, Israel Potter in his personal narrative is retrieving reality from the secrecy and deceit imposed upon him by his historical role.

Melville's Paul Jones also finds a partial prototype among Emerson's representative men. Emerson's Napoleon is the coarse, unscrupulous, brave incarnation of the power of democracy and the middle class. Paul Jones fits this Napoleonic conception in many respects, and in none more so than the narrator's Carlylean appreciation of him as a Reality:

Much subtle casuistry has been expended upon the point, whether Paul Jones was a knave or a hero, or a union of both. But war and warriors, like politics and politicians, like religion and religionists, admit of no metaphysics.[44]

And on "self-reliance" in history:

He sought to conciliate fortune, not by despondency, but by resolution. And, as if won by his confident bearing, that fickle power suddenly went over to him from the ranks of the enemy—suddenly as plumed Marshal Ney to the stubborn standard of Napoleon from Elba, marching regenerated on Paris. In a word, luck. . . .[45]

Like his Socrates, Emerson's bourgeois Child of Destiny helps us to resolve the paradoxical nature of the Melvillean counterpart.[46] Jones, the "barbarian in broadcloth," the savage with aristocratic linen, represents the political and social upheavals to come after the Revolution in America's nascent nationhood. As he paces in Paris he is

a sort of prophetical ghost, glimmering in anticipation upon the advent of those tragic scenes of the French Revolution which levelled the exquisite refinement of Paris with the bloodthirsty ferocity of Borneo; showing that broaches and finger-rings, not less than nose-rings and tattooing, are tokens of the primeval savageness which ever slumbers in human kind, civilized or uncivilized.[47]

A savage aping aristocratic manners, Melville's Paul Jones reveals to the full his creator's apprehensions of "the agent or attorney of the middle class of modern society"—as Emerson dubbed Napoleon—and of the enterprising and rapacious class which he represented.[48]

There are also less extensive historical "cameos" from the Revolutionary period in *Israel Potter*—an idea which may well have been borrowed from Thackeray's *Henry Esmond* (1852), in which the narrator-protagonist encounters most of the memorable personages of Augustan England. Certainly Israel's confrontations with George III and Horne Tooke have only this "antiquarian" interest, and are in fact rather closely based on Potter's original narrative. Ethan Allen, the possessor of all the characteristically "American" and "Western" virtues, is indeed, as Richard Chase has indicated, a kind of mythic folk-hero.[49] A bellicose giant in chains, he exemplifies for Israel an alternative strategy for survival in a hostile historical situation for the individual who can neither beguile Chance like Franklin nor command it like Jones.

Melville's employment of "representative men" is not altogether consistent or clear. The issue which he seems to skirt constantly, without engaging it, is what makes a man "representative" or "great"—what separates Ethan Allen from the forlorn soldier with whom he has so much in common. Chance, the foe of the common man, cuts short Israel's attempt to contact and succour Allen when the latter is a prisoner, and so Israel too loses his last chance to be saved from exile. Following the Allen episode immediately with the "exile narrative," Melville seems to be allowing the barrier which separates the "representative man" from the man who is merely represented also to divide the comedy of national emergence from the gentle pathos of the City of Dis.

↱ Focus on Authority

Melville's tales of the mid-1850's mark a very significant re-orientation towards the idea of revolt. *Billy Budd, Israel Potter* and *Benito Cereno* form a trilogy of extraordinary historical novels of revolutionary violence, all set in the tumultuous last quarter of the eighteenth century. Forming another thematic trilogy, *Benito Cereno, Billy Budd,* and *Bartleby* focus attention not on the rebel but on the crisis of judgment and will in the figure of authority.

Benito Cereno concerns a Spanish slave ship, the *San Dominick,* on which the slaves have successfully revolted. Recognizing their own inability to navigate, they have spared the captain, Don Benito Cereno, and directed him to return them to Africa. The

ship has come to a rarely visited island to take on water for that
voyage when the whaler commanded by Captain Amasa Delano
also arrives at the island's bay. The slaves cover the figurehead—
now the skeleton of their former owner—with canvas and carry
out an elaborate masquerade of normal slave-ship routine in which
Babo, mastermind and chief of the revolt, pretends to be the devoted, intelligent, tireless, and cheerful servant of Captain Cereno
—indeed, his servant counselor. None of this is known to Captain
Delano, who comes on board to offer friendly help. He is mystified
by the Spanish captain's appearance, his weak and sickly responses,
his close, apparently confiding relationship with the black Babo,
and the activities of the crew and the slaves. Yet he cannot establish what is wrong and tries to accept it as a different but natural
situation aboard a Spanish slave ship. When he glimpses signs
of the real power relations aboard the ship, Delano reads the evidence as a conspiracy against himself, which he then rejects as
absurd. The situation is suddenly revealed to him when he prepares to leave and invites Don Benito Cereno to visit his ship. To
his surprise Cereno turns him down but then leaps overboard into
the whaleboat pursued by Babo, who tries to stab him.

Although derived from an authentic incident, as is *Israel Potter*,
and despite their distant date (some sixty years earlier than the
writing—the classic Waverley formula), the events on board the
San Dominick in a curious way seem to take place outside of history. Melville presents the revolt of the slaves as an event occurring
on a floating microcosm, deliberately detached from any particularized historical context and, more significantly, bereft of genuine
historical consequences. Melville sustains throughout a sense of
mystery about the *San Dominick*; the "living spectacle" on its
decks "has, in contrast with the blank ocean which zones it, something of the effect of enchantment. The ship seems unreal; these
strange costumes, gestures, and faces, but a shadowy tableau just
emerged from the deep, which directly must receive back what it
gave." [50]

The situation does not seem to be part of a sequential continuum. Yet for all its sense of isolation and enchantment it is an historical paradigm that concerns the relations among men in time. Such small-scale revolts occurred again and again throughout the Americas, the one best known to Melville's compatriots being the 1835 seizing of the Portuguese ship *Amistad* by slaves who were tried and acquitted in New Haven amid national publicity. Melville's story also boldly explores the issue of race, which had been intensely politicized by the mid-1850's, so that the author can imply a prospective as well as a reflective significance in his historical tale. If an allegory, it is not a metaphysical one. Rather, *Benito Cereno* is an attempt to abstract from historical circumstances the very elements of historical consciousness and judgment.

Israel Potter and *Benito Cereno* are oddly assorted literary twins, though composed consecutively in 1854 and 1855. The former is a comparatively light-hearted comedy of revolt sanctioned by the holist gods of nationality, while the latter is one of Melville's darkest and most tortuous tales. Yet only from the vantage point achieved by examination of the revolutionary comedy, *Israel Potter,* that sport among Melville's literary progeny, does the nature of his achievement in *Benito Cereno* become clear.

Both tales exploit the authenticity of the original narratives on which they are based, with *Benito Cereno* drawing attention to its source with a lengthy affidavit that is not as faithful to its original as it purports. The original source of *Benito Cereno* is Captain Amasa Delano's *A Narrative of Voyages and Travels,* a bulky volume of memoirs and reflections in which the tale of the real Benito Cereno is the most interesting of a lengthy series of episodes in Delano's life.

Melville departs from Delano's text in many details in order to heighten the dramatic effects and symbolic overtones of the tale. Melville's characterization of Delano, however, is most significant, for it is through his consciousness that the details are filtered. In his own book Captain Delano presents himself as a strikingly consistent exponent of progressive common sense. His memoirs recount a life lived on the razor's edge of judgment and will, in which he as master of a vessel exercises his authority in a world of action and reaction where stately ritual and circumstance alone cannot maintain his position. He betrays no squeamishness in discussing either the maintenance of power or the preservation of life, and he balances his views on the proper administration of floggings and rewards with his hard-earned opinions on the proper pickling of bully-beef. This side of Delano—the practical, genial, democratic shipmaster—is faithfully represented by Melville.

What is revelatory is Melville's handling of Delano's views on race and slavery. In *Benito Cereno*, the Yankee skipper, uneasily puzzling over his mixed and contradictory perceptions of relationships aboard the *San Dominick*, entertains a host of holistic fantasies—of Latin decadence so far gone as to conspire with racial inferiors against whites, of noble savages, of black beings, like Babo, apparently exquisitely designed by nature to serve the comforts of whites.

The "innocence" of Amasa Delano is delicately established by Melville through a scene in which Delano recalls boyhood incidents of himself as Jack o' the Beach.[51] Moreover, Delano's illusionary constructions are only partly the result of the deceptive wiles of the blacks, for he is constantly adding to the picture and benignly explaining away the contradictory phenomena that his progressive common sense tells him mean danger. In the relation of slave and master anything is allowed to seem possible, in defiance of Delano's experience of a lifetime.

This contrasts sharply with the original *Narrative* in which Delano's racial attitudes are entirely consistent with his stout New England progressive beliefs that it is man, not culture, that is the irreducible constant, that all men are equal, and that exploitation breeds hate. For example, he meditates on the Spanish contempt for the Indians: " 'Thus,' thinks I to myself, 'goes the

world:—one man robs another of his country, his wealth and his
liberty; and then says he is a brute, and not a Christian.' " [52] This
view is most completely developed in his reflection on a narrow
escape from natives in New Guinea:

The natives of New Guinea and of the adjacent islands are negroes,
or wooly headed, and are well known to hate white people so much
as to reward an individual by making him a chief, when he will bring
them a white man's head. . . . The causes of this hatred are, in great
measure, traceable to our own misconduct towards them. When Europeans first visited New Guinea the natives manifested no spirit of
enmity. But the Europeans seized and carried them away as slaves,
in a most treacherous manner. . . . It is not therefore a matter of
surprise that the natives should encourage and transmit this hatred
toward Europeans. The white people have too often, to their everlasting disgrace, used their arts and force, as members of civilized society,
to betray, to kidnap, or to seize openly and violently, the natives for
the most selfish and inhuman purposes. . . . Happy will it be, when
the time shall arrive, that we ourselves furnish no longer the chief
obstacles to the civilization and moral improvement of the natives, according to the laws and religion of Christian countries. [53]

Thus Melville's attribution of holist illusions about race relations in a slave society to Delano marks the precise point at which
he departs from specific faithfulness to historical source. The implications of this decision, which complicates the consciousness of
Delano by making him an ambivalent combination of holist illu-
sionist and progressive realist, are reflected in all Melville's significant variations from his source. For example, in *Benito Cereno*
the Don is all dependent gratitude after his salvation, an attitude
that fits well with his pictured languid Latin decadence and the
traumatic race mania of which he dies. Melville makes Delano
both suspicious and contemptuous of Don Benito on cultural
grounds, while Cereno echoes the holist illusion in ghastly fashion
by his obsession with "the negro." In Delano's original, Benito
Cereno is an ingrate who unsuccessfully slanders Delano to escape
paying compensation for his rescue. Far from attributing this

moral weakness to cultural qualities, Delano insists that it is an all too common failing of humanity in general and proudly presents evidence that respectable Chilean opinion upheld his claims against the scapegrace hidalgo and, more pertinently, enforced them.

One further comparison reveals the significance that Melville placed on this exquisitely wrought holistic haze of confusion. His Captain Delano forges it virtually as a shield from his own progressive vision of the power realities of slavery, from the moment he sets foot on the quietly unreal, seemingly enchanted island of the *San Dominick* until Babo, knife in hand, leaps after his former master into Delano's whaleboat and is thus revealed as the leader of the slaves. The original Delano must be disabused of a deception only, not of such wilful blindness.

Nothing can be more striking than the difference in tone between the two passages of illumination. In Delano's *Narrative*, significantly, it is Don Benito alone who jumps. Delano continues:

These proceedings excited the wonder of us all. The officer whom I had with me anxiously inquired into their meaning. I smiled and told him, that I neither knew, nor cared; but it seemed the captain was trying to impress his people with a belief that we intended to run away with him. At this point one of my Portuguese sailors in the boat, spoke to me, and gave me to understand what Don Benito said. I desired the captain to come aft and sit down by my side, and in a calm deliberate manner relate the whole affair. . . .[54]

Don Benito corroborates this calm and rational view of the revelation in his original affidavit:

That he instantly told the captain, by means of the Portuguese interpreter, that they were revolted negroes; that the said captain soon understood the affair, and recovered from his surprise, which the leap of the deponent occasioned, and told him, "Be not afraid, be not afraid, set down and be easy." [55]

Here is the scene in *Benito Cereno*:

That moment, across the long-benighted mind of Captain Delano, a flash of revelation swept, illuminating, in unanticipated clearness, his host's whole mysterious demeanor, with every enigmatic event of the day, as well as the entire past voyage of the *San Dominick*. He smote Babo's hand down, but his own heart smote him harder. With infinite pity he withdrew his hold from Don Benito. Not Captain Delano, but Don Benito, the black, in leaping into the boat, had intended to stab.

Both the black's hands were held, as glancing up towards the *San Dominick*, Captain Delano, now with scales dropped from his eyes, saw the negroes, not in misrule, not in tumult, not as if frantically concerned for Don Benito, but with mask torn away, flourishing hatchets, and knives, in ferocious piratical revolt.[56]

In Delano's original *Narrative* one finds confusion clarified and Delano's actions realistically amended. In Melville's account there is guilt associated with that confused picture of reality, an image of masters and black slaves in unholy alliance. Delano feels guilty because he has known all along that slavery is a hateful and hated form of exploitation and that his misreading of the situation on the *San Dominick* is the product of a wilfully false consciousness, a comfortable illusion about slavery that he may entertain aboard the Spanish vessel but would not tolerate for a moment were his own authority at stake.

The deposition concluding *Benito Cereno* has seemed vexingly anticlimactic to commentators unaware of the historical nature of Melville's art. By altering Delano's narrative, Melville brings out the irony that historical hindsight can produce in the very language of the past. Thus the "worst" of the blacks could equally well be called the most intelligent and resolute, depending on one's sympathy for them. Everything has its apparent opposite reflection in *Benito Cereno*; and Melville, with characteristic artfulness, invites us to choose. "The negro" haunts Benito Cereno because the blacks have briefly turned the tables and enslaved him. Delano asks him, "What has cast such a shadow upon you?" "The negro," is all he replies.[57] One may find in this laconic utterance an expression of cultural trauma, the outcry of a holist appalled at the unspeakable savagery of the blacks. Or one may see what Delano and Don Benito have both been forced to see: that the web of affection and sentiment that they accept as the basis of slavery is an illusion masking a merciless dialectic of submission and dominance.

The central problem of *Benito Cereno*, as a picture of man in history, is not whether Melville is "for" or "against" the blacks. The ironies lie far too deep in the tale for any confident assertions on that subject. A conditioned *consciousness* of race and slavery rather than the nature of either constitutes the issue. It is difficult to say whether Melville accepts the full humanity of the blacks. Yet surely if the tale has any moral it is that a failure to accept that full humanity—including a "civilized" desire for mastery and control—invites self-destruction.

Benito Cereno belongs also with *Bartleby* and *Billy Budd*, as indicated earlier, because it centers on the judgment of an authority figure confronting an intractable reality. In each story there is a "rebel" who must be punished, yet that rebel is so far beyond the authority's categories of understanding as to render judgment insecure. The quietistic rejection of Bartleby, the Iago-like implacability of Babo, and the unique combination of subhuman and angelic qualities in Billy Budd—all seem to place them beyond the categories of judgment at the very moment when the authority must act.

Karl Mannheim has defined the varieties of what the Marxian tradition calls "false consciousness" in a way that is pertinent to this situation. He considers ideology to be a set of beliefs that define reality in such a way that it may be acted upon. A "false consciousness" may be characterized as an ideology that is inappro-

priate to the true historical situation.[58] For example, Captain Vere
in *Billy Budd* is a classic case of the ideological strategy that Mannheim calls the false resolution of conflicts by recourse to absolutes.
In *Bartleby*, the narrator is constantly setting his "assumptions"
—those of a "prudent," evasive Wall Street lawyer—against Bartleby's "preferences." Unwilling to take the imaginative leap that
would explain Bartleby's refusal, and the manifest discontent of
his other employees—all "alienated" laborers in Marx's original
sense of the word—he evades the necessity for questioning his own
ideology. In this sense, the narrator of Bartleby is like Captain
Delano in *Benito Cereno*, for the ideology of each is presented as
a form of knowledge that is no longer adequate for comprehending
their situations.

At this time in Melville's career it is most significant that the
inadequate ideology is that of the holist imagination. It is as if
Israel Potter and *Benito Cereno* were two sides in a dialogue, the
first an attempt to find at last a comfortable sanction for rebellion
in the holist terms of cultural liberation and the second an implicit
but decidedly stinging rebuke to the fatuousness of the holist illusion of a revolution that does not upset cultural values.

The Civil War at last presented Melville with an historical correlative for the tragic implications and ambiguities of revolt that
he had been exploring throughout the 1850's. His poems, *Battle-
Pieces*, reveal, in fact, that the tragic stance had completely displaced the spread-eagle messianic democracy of *White Jacket*.
This is most clearly seen in "The House-top," inspired by the
bloody New York Draft Riots of 1863, which occurred while
Melville was visiting the Army of the Potomac. Despite the fact
that he did not return to the city until four months later, the
poem gives a strong sensual impression of the "Atheist roar of
riot"; perhaps he drew upon his earlier experience with the Astor
Place riot against Macready. Melville's vision in the poem is un-
sparing both of the rioters—"ship-rats/And rats of the wharves,"

—and of the measures taken to repress them, referring to the troops called up from Gettysburg who finally quelled the riots:

> Hail to the low dull rumble, dull and dead,
> And ponderous drag that jars the wall.
> Wise Draco comes, deep in the midnight roll
> Of black artillery; he comes, though late;
> In code corroborating Calvin's creed
> And cynic tyrannies of honest kings;
> He comes, nor parlies; and the Town, redeemed,
> Gives thanks devout; nor, being thankful, heeds
> The grimy slur on the Republic's faith implied,
> Which holds that Man is naturally good,
> And—more—is Nature's Roman, never to be scourged.[59]

The last line, of course, is a painfully mocking answer to the question Melville had asked with such assurance in *White Jacket*. Building towards his denunciation of flogging in the American navy, he had asked rhetorically:

Is it lawful for you to scourge a man that is a Roman? asks the intrepid Apostle, well knowing, as a Roman citizen, that it was not. And now, eighteen hundred years after, is it lawful to you, my countrymen, to scourge a man that is an American?—to scourge him round the world in your frigates? [60]

"The House-top" represents the other side of Melville's deep conflict over equality and injustice—the side which maintains that the oppressed and violent classes may need strong and arbitrary regulation. This debate, which found its most serious pro and con arguments as a result of two riots in New York City, was to reach its final balance at the end of Melville's life in his historical parable *Billy Budd*. At the time of the Civil War, however, Melville could only come to moral terms with the problem of revolt and repression through a tragic stance:

Let us pray that the great historic tragedy of our time may not have been enacted without instructing our whole beloved country through

terror and pity; and may fulfillment verify in the end those expectations which kindle the bards of Progress and Humanity.[61]

⌐ *Billy Budd*: The Problem of Historical Judgment

Perhaps the shift in Melville's consciousness can be taken as
symptomatic of a broader shift in literary approaches to historical
reality. He is, after all, the only major writer of American fiction
whose career spans the Civil War. Melville is often seen, with
Whitman, as a kind of witness to the immense cultural change in
American life that accompanied the war, and it is hardly surprising that his writings, so affected by the forces of history, would
also reveal Melville's pivotal position in the evolution of the
American historical imagination in fiction. His turn away from
the comic frame of acceptance of *Israel Potter* led to a development even more important as an omen for American fiction, a
resignation from the holist historical imagination inherited from
Cooper and Hawthorne in favor of a progressive one. While
purely one of emphasis, the change unfailingly reveals a new consciousness.

It is entirely in accord with Melville's metaphysical cast of mind
that his great historical subject should be revolution, whose treatment was usually tinted with Idealism during the full flush of pre–
Civil War American Romanticism. Thus the progressive frame exemplified in Bancroft and Motley was unvaryingly Idealist, almost
Hegelian in its explanation of historical change. This Idealism
was well resisted by Cooper and Hawthorne, though for neither
of them was uncompromising revolt, either personal or political,
a major literary theme, as it was for Melville. And when they did
treat this eminently progressive subject it was always within the
holist frame.

Billy Budd, a novel of revolt framed in the practically ambiguous terms of metaphysical contraries, is a continuation of old
Melvillean themes, but represents a new form of the American

historical novel. However, it is Melville's last work, incomplete
and not fully unified. Consequently this new form must be understood—or perhaps the word should be "discovered"—analytically.
Therefore I have attempted to deal with the varied aspects of this
complex and fragmented novel separately before discussing its implications for Melville's final attitude towards revolt.

Just as the historical subject of *Israel Potter* was the American
Revolution, the historical subject of *Billy Budd* is the French
Revolution, or to be more precise, the reactions and attitudes of
the Anglo-American world to that event.[62] These attitudes are
brought to a focus in the narrator's relation of the mutinies at
Spithead and the Nore, events whose ramifying meaning extends
through the novel in an even more impressive way than the battle
of Fort William Henry in *The Last of the Mohicans* or the battle
of the *Bon Homme Richard* and the *Serapis* in *Israel Potter*. The
Nore mutiny is not dramatized as are these other "events," but instead it is deliberately introduced into the novel as a bit of "raw
history" which is constantly present in the author's commentary
and in the awareness of the characters. A proper understanding of
the mutiny at the Nore is necessary for a true reading of Vere's
actions, so heavily weighted as they are with considerations of
"conditions in the Navy"; but Melville's use of the "macrohistori-
cal" event will also illuminate the small historical world of "the
inner life of one particular ship and the career of an individual
sailor" that he was attempting to relate in *Billy Budd*.[63] Novels
which involve raw history present unusual difficulties. The iron
of historical reality in such books exhibits, as expressed by Stendhal's celebrated remark about politics in the novel, the effect
of a pistol shot in a drawing room, and the responsibilities of the
reader and critic on encountering such explosive material need
some scrutiny.

Kenneth Burke has suggested the admirable formulation "frame
of acceptance" for the set of terms in which an historical situation
is conceived, and that largely determine possible reactions to that

situation.[64] The great danger for the critic when confronted in fiction by an historical event as resonant as the French Revolution or American Civil War is that he will impose his own—not the author's—frame of acceptance on the event. Surely the only way to avoid such serious misreading is rigorously to limit not only the extra-literary impact of the author's political or historical views on the event at hand, but also the critic's tendency to be guilty of his own "pathetic fallacy."

The task in the present case demands a method as strictly textual as possible and an analysis of Melville's frame of acceptance for the French Revolution only in the terms which he himself used. The same standard must be applied when analyzing the acceptance frames of such characters as Captain Vere. Paradoxically, this is the opposite procedure from that to which historical events in fiction usually lead us, namely the cultivation of resonant historical associations by the reader, rather than their restriction. This is a genuine problem of interpretation, for consistency forbids the critic simply to adopt one or the other at his convenience. Generally, and more as a suggestive guide than as a maxim, one may say that resonance is properly a characteristic of the holist imagination, a useful critical concept when discussing, say, Scott or Hawthorne. In Twain, who worked often within the progressive frame, one may see resonance reverberating out of control. Limitation of resonance is in order when reading *Billy Budd* because of the kind of fictional and philosophical tension Melville has drawn from the French Revolution, resting more on the power of Ideas than on details or atmosphere from that event.

Melville's language echoes *Battle-Pieces*, as he describes the Red Flag and its raising at the Nore:

. . . the bluejackets, to be numbered by thousands, ran up with huzzas the British colors with the union and cross wiped out; by that cancellation transmuting the flag of founded law and freedom defined, into the enemy's red meteor of unbridled and unbounded revolt. Rea-

sonable discontent growing out of practical grievances in the fleet had
been ignited into irrational combustion as by live cinders blown
across the Channel from France in flames.[65]

Equally worth noting in this passage are Melville's fastening
upon a *symbol* of revolt as a means of understanding an enormously complex social and historical phenomenon, forcibly re-
calling "Endicott and the Red Cross," and the recurrence of the
image of revolt as a "meteor" from the first of the *Battle-Pieces,*
"The Portent." Melville underlines the symbolic similarity of the
Nore to the Civil War as he discusses the way in which the Great
Mutiny has been glossed over, much as were the New York Draft
Riots; for example:

Like some other events in every age befalling states everywhere, including America, the Great Mutiny was of such a character that national
pride along with views of policy would fain shade it off into the historical background.[66]

Melville's dominant metaphors for this bit of hidden history
give us the surest clue for understanding the significance of the
Mutiny in the "Inside Narrative." In the first quoted passage the
alteration in attitude comes with the change in the quality of the
revolt from the "reasonable discontent" of Spithead to the "irrational combustion" of the Nore. Melville joins the images of fire
and insanity to an equally conventional use of the ancient concept
of "disease" in the body politic, finding the Mutiny "analogous to
the distempering irruption of a contagious fever in a frame con-
stitutionally sound, and which anon throws it off." [67] The danger
presented by the Nore is always imminent madness, and it is this
danger that extends, with proliferating significance, through the
world of the *Bellipotent.* One must be careful not to confuse this
single dominant metaphor with other terms (e.g. "Rights of
Man," "atheism") in Melville's frame of acceptance for the

French Revolution, because only the metaphor of madness, intricately entangled with the historical event, has a major structural role in the tale.

Yet the other items in his frame of acceptance are not unimportant, for when political events are injected into a work of art they reverberate against its moral and metaphysical meaning. For example, the ship from which Billy is impressed early in the novel, the *Rights of Man*, explicitly brings the language of Edmund Burke's and Thomas Paine's debate on revolution to bear on the novel's inquiry into man's essential nature. Burke and Paine are more pertinent sources for the philosophical conflict of the novel than their French contemporaries, for, as noted earlier, the historical subject of *Billy Budd* is not the French Revolution so much as Anglo-American attitudes towards an essentially unnameable revolt. The ambiguity involved in the presentation of the subject was given an earlier embodiment in Captain Delano of *Benito Cereno* and the narrator of *Bartleby the Scrivener*. In both of these tales a revolt that is almost literally incomprehensible (though covertly recognized and overtly feared) becomes a sufficient reason for the blind and brutal assertion of authority.

Burke and Paine are, of course, eminently political philosophers, and application of their ideas to the *Bellipotent*—an application one is invited to make by Melville's allegorical names for his vessels—also involves a temporary assumption that we are dealing with a microcosm, with a "world in a man-of-war." The anti-war message of Paine's *Rights of Man*—an indictment of the usages of war more or less sustained by Melville in the text of *Billy Budd*—is obviously important in its consequences for the *Bellipotent*. What kind of relationship does the state of society on the ship bear to the larger "civilization" of England? In *White Jacket* the *Neversink* was a vestigial wrong in a society based on the progressive Ideas of the Declaration of Independence, but a wrong with a hidden portent for the future urban America. The *Bellipotent*, however, is identified as part and parcel of the "sole free and conservative [power] of the Old World." By removing this conflict in time and space, Melville sharpened his antithesis.

The striking difference between the views of Burke and Paine on human nature is almost too well known to need comment. For Burke the public and the private man were one, and the evils of society could be directly attributed to the corrupt nature of the individual. For Burke:

History consists, for the greater part, of the miseries brought upon the world by pride, ambition, avarice, revenge, lust, sedition, hypocrisy, ungoverned zeal, and all the train of disorderly appetites, which shake the public with the same

"troublous storms that toss
    the private state and render life unsweet." [68]

Paine makes the vital distinction between "civilized" man and natural man—but for him the latter is capable of compacting in a new society based on completely just principles. (Thus one may have an ideal of "sociality" like Melville's without necessarily endorsing existing "civilization.") Calling for a complete reformation of the government of England in *Rights of Man* (which was considered the foremost piece of inflammatory material inciting the Great Mutiny), Paine asserts that "man, were he not corrupted by Governments, is naturally the friend of man, and that human nature is not of itself vicious." [69]

Melville's pointed allusion to Burke and Paine is significant for two reasons. The first is the similarity of Paine's views on society and war to Melville's, as expressed throughout the latter's writing and particularly in *Billy Budd* and *White Jacket*. This puts the burden of proof on those who try to impose the social philosophy of *Reflections on the Revolution in France* upon *Billy Budd*. Secondly, as shall be further elaborated, the Burke-Paine dialogue presents the reader with an "historical" alternative to the usually accepted Miltonic frame of reference of much of the novel. Billy and Claggart represent two absolutely incompatible views of po-

litical man, and insofar as the problem of interpretation is seen
as political and historical rather than theological, they represent
the philosophical extremes which Captain Vere must sift in seeking a basis for judgment and action.

Melville's introductory exposition of the tale not only includes
an historical event, but also a noted individual of the period, Admiral Horatio Nelson. It has been generally recognized in *Billy
Budd* criticism that the portrait of Nelson is of the greatest importance for a correct evaluation of Vere, but the lack of viable
critical approach to Great Men in fiction has led to some rather
surprisingly illogical interpretations.[70] First of all, one must recognize the distance in Melville's thought on the subject from the
"representative men" of *Israel Potter*. In a digression the narrator
of *Billy Budd* makes an unabashedly "literary" use of Nelson.
Instead of humanizing and partially debunking Nelson as he had
done with Franklin, John Paul Jones, and George III, Melville
savors the essentially "superhuman" quality of the Great Man, as
in his reference to Napoleon's appearance to Americans in the
guise of a "French portentous upstart from the revolutionary
chaos who seemed in [the] act of fulfilling judgment prefigured
in the Apocalypse." [71]

This new appreciation of the "great" historical figure grew on
Melville, it is clear, during the years of what appeared to him and
other observers as the appalling mediocrity of public men in the
Gilded Age. Melville gave the problem his fullest exploration in
the very late poem "At the Hostelry," with its image of Garibaldi
as the modern Great Man, and in its sequel, "The Picturesque in
Men of Mark." According to the poet, "picturesqueness" is difficult for a Garibaldi; for the Great Man to come in the future
"Millennium of the busy bee" it is perhaps impossible.[72] As in his
poems on the *Monitor* and the *Merrimac* and "The Temeraire,"
picturesque greatness is posed as an alternative value to the utility
of the Benthamites.

It is important to realize that Melville's apostrophe to Nelson is at least partly directed to the Admiral's value as an object of historical and artistic apprehension. This is worth emphasizing, for if the digression on Nelson is to be taken as a form of reproach to Vere, it need not be seen as a *moral* reproach. It is a mistake to overemphasize the moral distinctions in nineteenth-century novels, as though their authors were solely concerned with separating the sheep from the goats among their *dramatis personae*. There is no need to see a "higher utility" in Nelson's apparently foolhardy recklessness at Trafalgar, for his actions have a "poetic" justification; the historical existence of Great Men actually legitimizes art.[73]

There is a moral question, however, implied in Melville's allusion, culled from Southey's *Life of Nelson*, to Nelson's ability to quell the threat of mutiny by his mere presence aboard a ship in the days after the Nore.[74] For Southey and for Melville, Nelson represents the incarnation of ambition and the lust for glory—a figure very similar to Prescott's Cortez and to Parkman's La Salle and especially his Wolfe, the holist man of action, secure in his role. In contrast, of course, Vere represents *repressed* ambition and Duty—the less generous and less military virtue. Vere, the philosophical maximalist, dies fighting the *Atheist*, while in his copy of Southey's book, Melville's underlining emphasizes that Nelson hated not an Idea but the French.[75] Again, Melville is not necessarily condemning Vere by this example. Nelson is perhaps "flawed" by passion as Vere is by intellect, and the primary martial virtue, like the primary "picturesque" virtue, need not be the first of *all* virtues.

In large part the difference between Vere and Nelson is the difference between the philosophical maximalist and the warrior in the holist mold. The Nelson of Southey's biography is defined completely by his social and historical prejudices, while Vere is defined by his ideas and his studies as much as by his class. Interestingly, "Starry Vere" is born to anti-revolutionary prejudices, while Nelson had to fight his way into the aristocracy. Nelson, to whom the Dansker is linked in much the same way as Harvey Birch was to Washington, offers more of a limiting case than a steady criterion for judgment of Vere.

Understanding Melville's use of the historical event and the historical individual brings one closer to a basis for interpretation of the historical novel itself. *Billy Budd* has traditionally been interpreted through static metaphysical concepts, rather than the dynamic ones of fiction and history—both of which forms are primarily concerned with the *narration* of events, of the way things happen. Thus *Billy Budd*, when not treated as an outright theological allegory, is often discussed as if it were a conflict between "freedom" and "order" or between ideal law and man's law, or as expressing the tension between ideal history and "fallen" history. One need not dismiss these critical formulations entirely to question their value as a means to understanding *Billy Budd* as an historical novel.

In their place, I would propose a set of terms drawn more or less exclusively from the "fallen world" of history and human action. "Revolt," for example (or "revolution" in its political and historical dimension), is dynamic. "Freedom" as a concept is static. My analysis must be prepared to beg some of the metaphysical questions which have perplexed critics in the past in favor of examining how and why things happen in the story. Literature may, as Aristotle maintained, be closer to philosophy in the kind of truth it contains than it is to history, but this does not preclude it from being in its modes and achievements closer to history than to philosophy. In this context, for "freedom" I would substitute "resistance" or "revolt"; for "order" I would substitute "authority"; and "justice" I would supplant with "judgment."

Melville makes this kind of conceptual critical framework even more appropriate by the historian's stance that the narrator takes. The narrative point of view in *Billy Budd*, though less creative historiographically than Melville's interweaving and elaboration of personal narratives in *Israel Potter*, and marred by inconsistencies, is extremely sophisticated. The narrator combines the qualities of an omniscient storyteller and a meticulous reconstructor of the past. Perhaps because the manuscript was never finished by Melville, this discrepancy was never resolved, though Melville had set a precedent for such a mixture of narrative authorities in *Benito Cereno*. Of most interest is the narrator's behavior as a conscious historian. Certainly, his description of Nelson's victory and the reflections this artifact induces in "anybody who can hold the Present at its worth without being inappreciative of the Past" is reminiscent of the fictional Hawthorne in the Custom House, contemplating his souvenir of an earlier age.[76] Elsewhere, Melville alludes to various historical authorities (some of which are himself), giving a mock-scholarly cast to the narrative as a whole.

The cultivated sense of the Past in the narrator's stance goes far towards explaining the obliqueness of the novel and the predominance of exposition and commentary over dramatized action. The Hayford-Sealts "genetic text" indicates that Melville was trying to overcome this obliqueness in his revisions, but I would suggest that one may miss Melville's intent if the specifically historical nature of his narrative technique is not recognized. Significantly, he draws our attention most to that technique at the conclusion of the tale, where he juxtaposes, with only "editorial" comment, the two documents that the reader is to take as primary sources for his account. The first is the magnificently garbled "News from the Mediterranean," which by its distortion gives immediacy to the hysteria and fear of mutiny of the time. The other, the true or "inside" source, is the poem "Billy in the Darbies," allegedly written by an anonymous shipmate of Billy's, and which, faithful to the truths of art rather than to lying "history," gives none of the "facts" of the affair at all.

The essential problem of the art of *Billy Budd* as an historical novel lies, finally, not in any of these tangential matters but in the special character of tragedy conceived in terms of the progressive frame. An adequate investigation of *Billy Budd* as an historical novel should reveal not only the uses Melville made of historical fact and the techniques of historical method, but also some of the ways in which the novelist's art transforms one's awareness and imaginative understanding of these facts and that method. The French Revolution, for example, holds a special place in the nineteenth-century Western imagination as the very incarnation of revolt, and the efforts to comprehend it artistically were many and varied. To mention only some of the major literary treatments of the Revolution in the period between the event and the next comparable shocks to Western values, World War I and the Russian Revolution (and omitting here the special case of Napoleon and *War and Peace*), one has Büchner's *Danton's Death*, Dickens' *A Tale of Two Cities*, and Anatole France's *The Gods Are A-Thirst*. This eclectic group offers several striking points for comparison. For example, Büchner's protagonist is a titan in the chains of historical necessity, while Sidney Carton, like Billy Budd, is associated with the Redeemer, and Evariste Gamelin explicitly evokes Orestes. The progression from Prometheus to Christ to Orestes offers an interesting insight into the intellectual and emotional history of the century, but more significant is the fact that in each case the protagonist is a symbolic sacrificial figure, and that each work ends with the image of the guillotine or the gibbet.[77]

For the major writers of the nineteenth century—including Twain—the French Revolution was best understood as a progressive historical revenge tragedy, steeped in blood and horrors, but impossible to arrest until the People's lust for retribution is sated.[78] As in Carlyle's *The French Revolution*, the emphasis is not on the rational achievements of the insurgents or the conservative opposition, but on the inexorability of the course of revolution, on a necessity which renders even the strongest individuals little more than puppets. There are no Carlylean Great Men in *The French Revolution*. The hanging scene in *Billy Budd* represents at least in part the conventional method for artistically rationalizing revolt and taming it through ritual. However, Melville was not simply readopting the strategy of tragedy with which he had attempted to confront the Civil War.

As I have noted, Burke and Paine seem to offer an alternative system of meaning—the system of political polemic—to the Miltonic analogues of Billy and Claggart in much the same way that Melville's digression on Nelson helps to define Captain Vere. Claggart's "natural depravity" is informed by Burke as well as by Calvin and Plato, and Billy is Paine's natural man just as he is man before the Fall. But this is only part of Melville's technique for giving his characters—who, with the exception of Vere, are but slightly revealed through dramatized action—weight equal to the significances the narrator finds in the tale. Claggart is likened at various points in the story to a Guise, Guy Fawkes, and, twice, to Titus Oates, thus introducing a wealth of reference to Renaissance intrigue, Gunpowder Plots, and false Popish Plots.

These particular references, especially to Fawkes and Oates, were favorite images with Melville, and constitute "image clusters," allusive in much the same way as Hawthorne's historical "scandals" in *The Scarlet Letter* and elsewhere.[79] The allusion to Titus Oates is especially illuminating because Oates was one of the most successful false witnesses who ever lived, a man of demonic power who cowed both King and Commons during the Popish Plot hysteria with his outrageous accusations. Oates' career as an exemplar of the power of unabashed evil provides a telling analogy to Claggart's actions.

Nelson and Vere, Oates and Claggart—it is all the more remarkable that the imagery surrounding Billy himself is *sub*-historical. He is always described as an Adamic figure, a barbarian, or a beast. The animals Billy is likened to—a stallion, a Saint Bernard—are, it should be noted, domestic. The similes are reminiscent of Captain Delano's appreciation of the slaves aboard Benito Cereno's ship as feral but benign, before the rebellion becomes apparent, and of the malignant creatures, tigers and rats, which invest the riot-torn city in "The House-top." The overtones of revolt implied by Melville's choice of imagery for Billy make the "handsome sailor" an even more ambiguous figure than is usually thought. While Claggart's "image cluster" associates the master-at-arms with the overreaching and vicious villains of history, Billy's imagery, combined with his stammer and his death-blow to Claggart, reveal Melville's continuous concern with that flawed and inarticulate revolt of the oppressed, which in his conception could turn a docile beast of burden momentarily into a deranged brute. The revolt that is not sanctioned by the demands of either a holistic role or a progressive Idea can only be non-historical, non-human.

The total effect of this rich association is to make *Billy Budd* a political and historical, as well as a theological, mystery play. It is vital to understand the way in which Melville thus polarized the oppositions and ritualized the action of the story before attempting to assess the central critical problem of the novel: the actions and attitude of Captain Vere. Vere's world-view, which affects and almost completely determines his actions in the crisis of the novel, is marked by a tendency to abstract philosophical extremes from the historical situation and by a preference for tragic "acceptance" as a means for meeting otherwise unbearable responsibilities. Melville, by making Vere's actions of doubtful appropriateness, seems to have been questioning his own earlier artistic strategy for meeting the phenomena of revolt and revolution.

To take these points one at a time, Vere's bookishness, his "unshared studies," had issued in certain *idées fixes* about the human condition that guide his thought during the great upheaval of the French Revolution. Vere opposes the natural rights doctrines of the Revolution not out of class prejudice nor simply from doubts as to their feasibility, but because he sees them "at war with the peace of the world and the true welfare of mankind." [80] Since he denies the view of man's nature implicitly held by the framers of the Declaration of the Rights of Man, by Paine and Anacharsis

Clootz, Vere's respect for the claims of "nature" in his speech to the court must be taken as either unwittingly hypocritical or ironic. Human nature, for Vere as for Burke, is actively dangerous and always deceptive. The speech to the court, with its astonishing parallels to Ivan Karamazov's "poem" of the Grand Inquisitor, is in part a disquisition on the psychological needs of the "People" which extends and amplifies Burke by its exposition of the value of ritual, including ritual punishment, the very evil which in the form of flogging aroused the indignation and fear of White Jacket and "horrified" Billy Budd. Vere's image of the political norm of mankind, neither as good as Billy nor as depraved as Claggart, dictates his judgment.

The framework of Vere's action, the result of a disposition so pronounced that he calls Billy "Fated boy!" immediately after the blow which kills Claggart, is tragic. He instantly must place Billy's discrete, specific, non-treasonous act in the widest possible frame of understanding, maximalizing the philosophical dimension of the problem with which he is confronted so that he will be able to withstand his otherwise intolerable reluctance to doing his "duty." Critical discussion has tended to revolve around the humanity and correctness of that position, but I think that a clearer understanding of Vere's case may be possible if one realizes that Melville is concerned not only with the abstract question of justice but with the practical and fictionally dynamic one of historical judgment.

Because of the Nore and the danger of mutiny "a sense of the urgency of the case overruled in Captain Vere every other consideration." [81] Vere's assessment of "conditions in the Navy" is not a *donnée* of the story but the most important of his decisions, and, as Melville makes clear, the most crucial factor in leading the members of the court-martial (who "dissented from some points" of Vere's legal and philosophical argument) to accede to the conviction and execution. In short, an evaluation of Vere must rest to a large extent on the wisdom of his judgment that a failure to execute Billy would provoke mutinous unrest. The crew or "the people" of His Majesty's Navy and the *Bellipotent* become —even in their indeterminacy—the key motive factor of the tale.

Interestingly, the only light Melville sheds on the actual state of feeling on the ship—other than the instinctive outrage of "the people" at the execution—is the affair of Billy and the afterguardsman. Whether the afterguardsman was suborned to play tempter by Claggart, as one is apparently to infer, or not, Billy's reactions to his advances tend to indicate that for Billy, at least, there is no sense of a dangerous disaffection on the *Bellipotent*. When tempted, Billy is able, after a struggle, to find his tongue— as he was unable to do when threatened by Redwhiskers and Claggart. Furthermore, Billy deliberately suppresses information on the afterguardsman during the court-martial, evidence not only of class loyalty but of an informed belief that the situation is not as Vere imagines; that is, that "the people" are basically loyal to the King's buttons which they wear. To Billy's "erring sense of uninstructed honor" the idea of mutiny is more bewildering than actively threatening. The central question is not which view of the situation is "right," since either one could have been, and since Melville repeatedly cautions against abuse of historical hindsight. The question is why Vere drew from an historical situation which obviously admitted of a variety of opinions the categorical imperative which doomed Billy Budd.

The chief objective factor in that historical situation, the Great Mutiny, helps to explain the experience of Captain Vere.[82] As noted earlier, the dominating metaphor of the mutiny is madness. Claggart's "natural depravity," his rational-appearing insanity, is the most elaborate extension of the metaphor:

Though the man's even temper and discreet bearing would seem to intimate a mind peculiarly subject to the law of reason, not the less in heart he would seem to riot in complete exemption from that law, having apparently little to do with reason further than to employ it as an ambidexter implement for effecting the irrational. . . . These men are madmen, and of the most dangerous sort, for their lunacy is not continuous, but occasional, evoked by some special object. . . .[83]

For Vere all revolt is an unspeakable madness, given man's corrupt nature, and it is significant that the surgeon calls Vere's own sanity into question while Vere is in the throes of the crisis which seals Billy's fate. The entire historical situation is seen in terms of madness, and a madness less romantic than clinical. Vere himelf comes closest to the "rainbow line" between sanity and insanity while trying to avert a form of dementia which all his studies and experience have led him to believe is imminent.

Vere's insistence upon acting himself and not passing Billy's case on to the Admiral stems directly from his belief in that imminent insanity; and the way he meets that crisis is profoundly instructive on the ethics which derive from a tragic consciousness within the progressive frame. Vere's imagination, as I indicated earlier, is essentially tragic in its cast. The consistency of Vere's actions emerges clearly when one recognizes that he has a tragic apprehension of the case from the moment when he pronounces Billy a "fated boy," through his handling of the murder and trial, his interview with the condemned prisoner (Abraham and Isaac),[84] the execution itself, and its aftermath. Both Vere's compassion and his sense of duty are genuine, and the only "acceptance frame" which can encompass both, given his temperament and cast of mind, is the tragic one. On one level Vere's attitude appears to be an extension of Melville's response to the Civil War. However, a tragic apprehension of the French Revolution is precisely what is advocated by Burke himself:

. . . in events like these our passions instruct our reason; because when kings are hurled from their thrones by the Supreme Director of this great drama, and become the objects of insult to the base, and of pity to the good, we behold such disasters in the moral, as we should behold a miracle in the physical, order of things. We are alarmed into reflection; our minds (as it has long since been observed) are purified by terror and pity; our weak, unthinking pride is humbled under the dispensations of a mysterious wisdom.[85]

To quote Burke is to realize the immense spiritual gulf between his position and Melville's, and further, the extent to which Melville denies himself and the reader of *Billy Budd* the solace of tragic catharsis. Melville, like Robin Molineux, is unable to resolve the messy spectacle of history in the classical manner. The novel is tragic and ironic; Vere's view is tragic, but the novel conveys a sense of injustice which escapes "tragic" resolution, in the case of both Billy and all "the people." This complicated attitude should not be confused with "tragic ambiguity," for the novel's ambiguity is not centered on one's acceptance of Billy, but on the tragic stance itself, as embodied in Vere. Vere's approbation of "forms," often quoted out of context, illustrates the full implications of the tragic frame for Melville:

"With mankind," he would say, "forms, measured forms, are everything; and that is the import couched in the story of Orpheus with the lyre spellbinding the wild denizens of the wood." And this he once applied to the disruption of forms going on across the Channel and the consequences thereof.[86]

Vere's ritual punishment of Billy, acting out the supreme form of tragedy, itself is the result of an essentially bestial view of man's nature. The narrow range of Vere's political and historical vision and his tragic attitude are revealed as props for the humane man in rigid reaction to revolt.

Melville, continuously revising his own social vision, had traveled a long course from the institutional criticism and progressive underwriting of revolt of *White Jacket*. In *Battle-Pieces* he rejects that early embrace of political revolt to find a temporary historical faith in the National Tragedy. In his last great effort to find an imaginative framework for the intolerable progressive dialectic of revolt and authority, he rejects tragedy too. Vere's course may be the best of paths for the individual not lifted by an intact social role above the historical domain of chance and necessity as Nelson was. Yet the imaginative vision of *Billy Budd* is the result not of a striving to resolve that progressive dialectic through tragic acceptance or to escape its pressures through the protective shell of a holistic role, but to free it of necessity through the powers of the historical imagination and transcend it. If Melville's ironic grasp of historical complexity prevents the sense of transcendent escape from being unmistakeably realized, one may attribute this to the quality of Melville's mind, which, like the wind of history in his poem "The Conflict of Convictions," "spins *against* the way it drives." [87]

Chapter Six

TWAIN: THE VARIETIES OF
HISTORY AND *A CONNECTICUT YANKEE*

*I*N 1889, while Melville was composing his last meditation on revolt and revolution, Mark Twain published a novel dominated by revolutionary progressivism, *A Connecticut Yankee in King Arthur's Court*. Twain's novel illustrates the extent to which Melville's is the pivotal sensibility of the nineteenth century, the link between the pre- and post–Civil War writers. The transformation of the structural reference of the historical novel from holist to progressive, in which Melville pioneered among American novelists, finds its conclusion in Twain. *A Connecticut Yankee* not only has a "progressive" historical subject, but it is written from a strong commitment to the values and historical vision of the progressive frame of the social imagination.

The problems of historical progressivism in *A Connecticut Yankee* have received a great deal of intelligent and sympathetic study in recent years, notably in works by Philip S. Foner, Roger B. Salomon, James M. Cox, and Henry Nash Smith.[1] At the same time, the novel has gained increasing appreciation for its central place in Twain's career and as an artistic achievement second only to *Huckleberry Finn*. Though this wealth of recent scholarship and critical commentary provides many valuable insights and has defined many of the relevant issues of the novel, the tendency has been to treat the novel as if the primary critical problem it presents were Twain's ambiguous attitude towards his historical *subject*—namely, "progress." Whatever value this approach has for analyzing discursive prose, it has serious limitations for discussing narrative. As I have said, the forms of the social and historical imagination have an enforcing power of their own in narrative art. It is structure, not the discrete "ideas" of an author, which informs the historical novel. In the case of the artistically uncontrolled historical novel, that structure determines form; "ideas" govern only the details of expression.

When the artist is in conscious command of the implications of his imaginative frame, as Hawthorne was in *The Scarlet Letter*, the question of the author's historical "ideas" never obtrudes itself. Consequently, there has been little critical concern with Hawthorne's historical world-view, though I believe his writing shows evidence of as much unresolved intellectual conflict in his attitudes as does Twain's.[2] When the artist has an uncertain grasp of the implications of his imaginative frame, the ensuing contradictions force themselves upon the attention of the reader —unless he too unconsciously shares that frame.

The question of control, then, is central, for I consider Twain's fundamental incapacity and incoherence in his handling of the materials of history to be responsible for the unsettling and unsettled effect of the book as a whole. Almost all recent critics have found the ambiguous ending of the novel disturbing and vaguely redolent of failure. It has been variously suggested that the tone of the ending is the result of Twain's personal conflict with the Machine (especially his financial debacle with the Paige typesetter), his growing doubts about democracy, and his misgivings about the rising entrepreneurial classes.[3] These are valuable approaches to a novel that is confusing in the very multiplicity of its implications for Twain's life and work, for his views on "progress" and his attitudes towards history. I suggest, however, that to explain the effect and meaning of the ending, one must comprehend Twain's aims in writing the book. It is incorrect, I believe, to see a philosophical or psychological crisis as the sole cause of Twain's formal difficulties, however much knowledge of these crises may increase our understanding of the springs of Twain's creative impulse. In *A Connecticut Yankee in King Arthur's Court* Twain attempted completely to revolutionize the nineteenth-century historical novel and adapt it to the progressive social imagination. It is far from easy to discern whether the cause of his failure was inherent in himself or in his goal.

As Roger Salomon puts it in his study of Twain's changing "image" of history: "Certainly the *Yankee* can be most meaningfully read as a serious attempt by Twain to embody the theme of historical progress in a major novel." [4] At the time Twain wrote this novel he was, and had been for some time, a committed historical progressive. He had also been aware that this stance entailed a complete rejection of the holist frame of the historical imagination, a rejection he was to find easier to express in discursive prose than in fiction.

A significant expression of Twain's rejection of the holist historical novel is his vituperative criticism of both Scott and Cooper. Although the rhetorical and factual proprieties of these critical polemics have been astutely questioned in recent years, Twain's central critical motive has consistently been seen as the resentment of a "realist" for two perniciously popular "romantics." [5] Yet if one accepts these terms—Twain's own (he most notably makes the distinction in reference to Scott in *Life on the Mississippi*)—one is soon entangled in severe problems of definition. There are, after all, too many ways in which Scott and Cooper must be called "realists" and likewise too many aspects of Twain which may only be described as romantic.

Twain attacks the "medievalism" of Scott's novels for its reactionary influence on the Western world in general and the American South in particular. Cooper is taken to task for "offenses" against the craft of fiction: inaccurate observation, defiance of probability, a verbose and imprecise style. The two critiques have this in common: in each case the holist frame has obscured the discrete historical "fact," essential both for Twain's conception of good writing and for the moral judgment necessary to the progressive vision. In Twain's view, through the glamor of ancient associations and the excitement of adventure, Scott and Cooper had forced the burden of historical description upon an imaginative "established system" in the past rather than on the weighted, non-relativistic "fact."

Twain's attitudes towards historical "fact" reflect significant tension in his conception of the proper relationship of a writer to the culture he attempts to portray. In "What Paul Bourget Thinks of Us," Twain speaks of the ideal novelist's almost osmotic absorption of the reality of his native culture, and the intense regionalism and particularization of the insights it can provide him. Cultural truths are not even national, much less universal. Nor did Twain regard this as an inessential aspect of the responsibility of the novelist, but rather as its heart and soul. *Huckleberry Finn* is Twain's richest characterization of some of the strains of nineteenth-century American culture, and one of the most thoroughly local, from the author's claim of strict accuracy in the representation of dialects through Huck's incipient flight from the civilization he has so scathingly anatomized.

Twain's other conception of historical fact breaks down this relativistic holism, and sees "fact" (once it is freed from encumbering associations) as communicating its meaning more or less directly to the imagination. Moreover, when it is History that is to be portrayed rather than Life—the unusual and significant rather than the typical and probable—then "osmosis" becomes a liability, blurring the meaning of events and creating normality out of crises. What is not permissible for a foreign observer (especially if he is not Twain) is the *sine qua non* of the historical artist. In *Life on the Mississippi* Twain sketches life in Vicksburg during the siege, then says:

Those are the materials furnished by history. From them might not almost anybody reproduce for himself the life of that time in Vicksburg? Could you, who did not experience it, come nearer to reproducing it . . . than could a Vicksburger who *did* experience it? It seems impossible; and yet there are reasons why it might not really be.[6]

The advantages of historical distance are considerable; but they are lost unless there is an informed intelligence interpreting as well as chronicling the event. The perspective which is most valuable is the temporal relation of the "fact" to the other salient events. This would help place the "fact" on the scale of progress. In *Life on the Mississippi*, Twain demonstrates the antiquity of the river:

The world and the books are so accustomed to use, and overuse, the word "new" in connection with our country, that we early get and permanently retain the impression that there is nothing old about it. We do of course know that there are several comparatively old dates in American history, but the merest figures convey to our minds no just idea, no distinct realization, of the sketch of time which they represent. To say that De Soto, the first white man who ever saw the Mississippi River, saw it in 1542, is a remark which states a fact without interpreting it: it is something like giving the dimensions of a sunset by astronomical measurements, and cataloguing the colors by their scientific names—as a result, you get the bald fact of the sunset, but you don't see the sunset. It would have been better to paint a picture of it.[7]

Twain then locates De Soto's discovery among other events of the sixteenth century. His picture is not colored in with the "atmosphere" of sixteenth-century paraphernalia of the conquistadores, *à la* Prescott, but shown in its true temporal relationship to the progressive post-steamer era of the nineteenth-century Mississippi. The two apparently incompatible attitudes towards historical "sources" exist side by side in Twain's work. The image of the novelist as native son seems a corollary of holism, but is not necessarily so. Familiarity with a culture does not inevitably carry with it a bias towards representation in terms of a distinct cultural "system." Similarly, the "second-hand" experience of the historical imagination does not always dictate a "progressive" refusal to envision a past culture as a healthy, self-maintaining system. In his "medieval" historical novels, however (*The Prince and the Pauper, Yankee, Joan of Arc*), as opposed to the novels of the antebellum South, Twain committed himself to the "progressive" attitude towards historical fact, a commitment which severely limited what he achieved in them.

A *Connecticut Yankee in King Arthur's Court* is the progressive historical novel *par excellence*. Some of the characteristics of the progressive frame common to A *Connecticut Yankee* and the histories of Bancroft, Macaulay, and Motley are obvious. The juxtaposition of types implicit in the title and the basic scheme of the book signifies Twain's rejection of the idea of holist cultural barriers, which would encourage relativistic standards of judgment. (A classic expression of Twain's penchant for cultural reduction is his essay, "The French and the Comanches," which mocks not only the French but the cultural categories of Parkman.) The action of the novel culminates with the typical progressive event of Revolution and Civil War. Twain attempts to show a "party" of superstition and oppression resisting an upstart "party" of progress and to portray their conflict as the result of historical laws of progressive development. Finally, Twain tries to fashion in his protagonist, Hank Morgan, a genuinely progressive hero.

A mere intellectual commitment to the idea of progress is not the same as embodying the progressive frame in fiction. *The Prince and the Pauper*, written at the same time as Twain's paean to progress in *Life on the Mississippi*, is a very rudimentary progressive historical novel. On a superficial level it shows sixteenth-century England divided into two worlds: a world of splendor, luxury, and sycophancy and a world of poverty and ignorance, oppressed by official cruelty. The idea of progress, however, is only present as an assumption underlying the narrative point of view. Instead of showing a "backward" nation transformed by historical progress, the author can only hint at the possibility of inhuman laws being transformed by a ruler's knowledge of human suffering.

The heart of the novel as an art form is character; and in *The Prince and the Pauper* Twain was little freer of the holist conception of character than was Hawthorne. The dominant conceit of the book is a denial, cast entirely in holist terms, of the holist conception of reality. The costume change of the urchin and the monarch at the outset is based on one of Twain's favorite images, the royalty of monarchs inhering entirely in their clothing.[8] The transferral of roles is accomplished with comparatively little difficulty. Though it takes extreme sympathetic suffering for Edward to drop his imperious attitudes (he only breaks down when the Anabaptists are burnt at the stake), it is absurdly easy to train Tom Canty "up" to princehood—so that soon it becomes automatic for him to spurn his natural mother. No one was less likely than Twain to deny the powerful hold of social roles in facilitating inhumanity and injustice. In *The Prince and the Pauper*, moreover, Twain attempted to reveal these roles as almost entirely devoid of intrinsic merit.

Though challenging the holist concept of roles and of society, and illustrating the injustices of a past age, *The Prince and the Pauper* does not yet portray progress as an inexorable historical law. Role-swapping can only awaken uneducated human goodness, the counterpart to man's "damnable" nature. It cannot *change* history. Thus, Edward reigns with mildness as a child but does not rule as an adult. The question the novel is designed to answer is: "What happens if one changes roles within a given cultural system?" The Twain hero must typically step out of a given role-definition—as Edward does—in order to see the truth about the whole system. Thus far the truths of elementary morality and progress are identical. For example, Huck Finn's "moment of truth," when he tears up the letter informing the Widow

Douglas where her slave is, forces him out of the matrix of thought
of his time and place.

But—and this is essential to Twain's understanding of the sociology of feeling and knowledge—Huck has no alternative structure of thought to replace the codes of his native slave society.
He must accept the "hell" of his culture just as he must reject
the "civilization" of the Mississippi Valley for the freedom of
the "territories." He cannot, according to Twain's intuition, op-
pose to his holistic environment a new social ethic based upon
the particular injustice done to Jim. The genuine progressive must
come from another and more "advanced" era, in cultural terms,
either as narrator (*The Prince and the Pauper*) or as protagonist.
A *Connecticut Yankee* grows directly out of the unresolved conflict of Huck Finn's moral limbo.

In Twain's view, the realization of progress, issuing according
to definite laws of development from historical conflict, can only
be represented in fiction through the medium of an historical
agent, a progressive hero. The figure of Hank Morgan raises two
pertinent questions in the context of this discussion. First, is it
possible to write an historical novel in which a progressive Great
Man—a figure similar to Bancroft's Washington or Motley's
William—plays a leading part? Secondly, can such a figure be
the *protagonist* of a great historical novel?

The answer to the first question is provided in part by the
greatest of historical novels, *War and Peace*. The Russian general Kutuzov is the perfect progressive hero: the silent, patient,
unshakeable summation of the forces protecting Russia. Yet Tolstoy straddled in his masterpiece. He developed the bulk of the
narrative (the Bezukhovs, the Rostovs, the Bolkonskys) according to the holist vision of individuals and families in a rich cultural setting under the doom of a sweeping historical event. Napoleon's duel with Russia, however, is interpreted in terms of
the deterministic historical laws of the progressive frame.[9] Though
holistically conceived characters like Pierre or Andrei Bolkonsky

may have intimations of the inexorable *reality* of the historical process at certain points in their lives, they can never comprehend and master it. And though Kutuzov, the progressive hero, has been portrayed *within the progressive frame*, the novel as a whole is only fitfully cast in those terms.

The second question arises precisely because Twain was daring enough not to straddle, but deliberately to write a progressive historical novel with a progressive. Great Man as its protagonist. Twain employed a loose "science-fiction" framework in order to produce the confrontation with "medieval" ignorance he desired, but it is difficult to see how he could have achieved the confrontation otherwise without long authorial digressions on the philosophy of history such as burden *War and Peace*. The utopian aspect of *A Connecticut Yankee* is extremely important, but the "utopian" premise of the novel was a mere convenience for Twain. Twain cast his progressive historical novel in a mock-utopian form, while Edward Bellamy, writing at the same time, presented *Looking Backward*, a progressive utopian novel, as a mock-historical novel of the year 2000.[10]

Hank Morgan, the nineteenth-century Connecticut Yankee, expresses the progressive's insistence on the possibility of moral judgment on the past and the denial of cultural relativism. As Theodore Parker asserted his right to condemn Cortez, so Twain asserts his prerogatives by sending a critical Hartford mechanic into the medieval world glamorized by Scott. In conventional history, the modern "witness" is sufficient; the progressive historian can convey his interpretation discursively as well as by narration. But in the novel, the corollary to the progressive frame's insistence upon the moral immediacy of the past is that Hank must go beyond satire and criticism to revolution because he *is not distant*. As soon as the progressive hero enters the scene, gifted with the technological, political, and moral enlightenment of the nineteenth century, he must *act out* the verbal violence of a Motley or a Parker.

Hank is an aesthetic and moral judge, like a progressive historian, at the same time that he is an attempted history-maker and revolutionary, or progressive Great Man. Many critics prefer to emphasize one or the other aspect of his characterization. Yet both are essential to the progressive social imagination and to *A Connecticut Yankee*. Implicit in that imaginative form is a moral commitment to action *in the past*. "Action" against past abuses, of course, is an absurdity outside the domain of rhetoric, and this may reveal a covert taste for the status quo in the progressive social imagination. Yet if one postulates the "given" of a "progressive" mentality entering the world of a benighted age of the past—as Twain did—it is equally absurd to imagine that the author will not be drawn into making the character an actor as well as a witness.[11]

The "circus side" of the Boss's nature seems incompatible with his progressive mission, but it is the inevitable consequence of Hank's displacement in time. Unlike Washington or Kutuzov, Hank must *create* the objective conditions for historical change, instead of serving as its human focus. Henry Nash Smith has aptly labeled Twain's typical protagonist a "vernacular hero." But unlike his predecessors, Tom Canty in the Court of St. James or Huck Finn in the household of the "aristocratic" Grangerfords, Hank cannot subtly satirize his surroundings; he must use bold strokes of wit. Progress needs *agents*, and Hank is intended —at least initially—not as the victim but as the cutting edge of history.

Progressivism is the intellectual core of the novel, but Twain does not succeed in creating progressivism as its imaginative core. The implicit cultural values of the progressive frame, which centers on conflict and whose natural subject is revolution, are undermined by Twain's confused methodology for evoking a "medieval" milieu. The modes of the historical imagination operate in fiction in much the same way as do the progressive and holist frames; they dictate entirely distinct ways of representing the historical past to the modern consciousness. Just as the progressive frame may govern the form of the novel as a whole, the modes of the historical imagination will govern the quality of its artistic effect.

A *Connecticut Yankee in King Arthur's Court* must be seen as a highly experimental attempt to make a complete break with the "normative" holist form of the historical novel. In coming to a critical judgment of this novel it is important to appreciate the ambitiousness of Twain's goal before assessing his achievement. Writers do not, after all, set out to write "timeless masterpieces" but to meet the artistic problems that their subject and their literary heritage give them in their time.

The problems and possibilities of A *Connecticut Yankee in King Arthur's Court* are fully implied in the title. Twain intended from the beginning both a lampoon on knight-errantry and a contrast of the Middle Ages with modern civilization "to the advantage of the latter, of course." [12] His strategy was to use King Arthur's court to represent the entire medieval period. This approach was only possible through the progressive frame, in which the stages of social evolution (Savage—Barbarian—Civilized, etc.) were seen as relatively homogeneous within each period, which was located on a "vertical" diachronic time-span. He then faced the problem of evoking this truncated age as fictional material.

It was the most complicated problem Twain ever set himself in his historical fiction. In the Twain sections of *The Gilded Age*, he had been able to adopt a broad, caricaturing, journalistic and morally open-ended approach in capturing an age, and he had been eminently successful. He shared a common moral and historical frame of reference with his audience that made both overt comment and comprehensiveness superfluous.

In *Joan of Arc* he was to evoke the fifteenth century (not very happily) by contrasting an idealized Joan with "the brutalest, the wickedest, the rottenest" century "since the darkest ages." [13] The chief technical fault of that book is its narrator, whose mind, despite some self-conscious attempts by Twain, partakes less of the fifteenth century than it does of Twain at his most Victorian. In this Twain points the way toward the uncharacterized narrator of *The Mysterious Stranger*, his last historical fiction. The language of these narrator figures shows clearly how Twain's final, "chastened" style was in fact merely sterilized.

Twain's strategy for evoking the Middle Ages is potentially a superb one. Hank Morgan, the Yankee, is not only a meaningful vernacular hero, but provides the very historical imagination through which the story would be presented. Together with his intellectual freight of nineteenth-century technology, politics, and economics, Morgan was to bring the imagination of the American "common man" to medieval England. Morgan describes himself as "a Yankee of the Yankees—and practical; yes, and nearly barren of sentiment, I suppose—or poetry, in other words." [14] This self-characterization is the first clue to the Yankee's imagination, and immediately establishes his paradoxical kinship with the dreamer who preceded him, Huck Finn. Huck, one will remember, concludes his magnificently garbled explanation to Jim of the ways of royalty with the observation, "All I say is, kings is kings, and you got to make allowances. Take them all around, they're a mighty ornery lot. It's the way they're raised." [15] By juxtaposing such an unimpressed imagination with the age of kings itself, Twain opened a huge field of comic and moral possibilities. He had also created prodigious difficulties for himself.

Twain's choice of King Arthur's court for his setting has confused many critics. His comic instinct was sure, of course, it being the same impulse that led him to have Huck describe Henry VIII dumping the tea in Boston Harbor and drowning the Duke of Wellington in a butt of malmsey "like a cat." [16] Twain wanted to cast a fresh and "innocent" eye on the familiar, and nothing could have suited his purpose better than Malory's *Morte D'Arthur*, in which both characters and mores would be resonant with meaning. That it was the Middle Ages of literary tradition to which he reverted rather than to an "historical" age, as in *The Prince and the Pauper*, is doubly significant. By undercutting the aesthetic ideal of chivalry first, Twain's concentrated social criticism would have free range on the institutions of feudalism and monarchy. He could not foresee that the choice of a literary tradition and framework would have great implications for the success of his critique.[17]

The chivalry of courtly romance is subjected to the mercilessly realistic eyes of the Yankee in the early chapters of the book: "A noble cavalcade wound its way into view, glorious with plumed helmets and flashing mail and flaunting banners and rich doublets and horse-cloths and gilded spearheads; and through the muck and swine, and naked brats, and joyous dogs, and shabby huts it took its gallant way. . . ." [18] It is the incongruities of the courtly ideal with the miserable and indecorous reality of medieval life, always a favorite theme with Twain, that make the opening chapters so delightfully humorous. The Yankee, barren of sentiment and as provincial as he is American, can observe Queen Guenevere "fling furtive glances at Sir Launcelot that would have got him shot in Arkansas, to a dead certainty." [19] His comments on the indelicacy of authentic courtly language, on the boring repetitions of epics, of the entertainment found in the dogfights and the general lack of sanitation are apt gibes at the unmentioned aspects of the courtly tradition.

Far more significant than this mild debunking, however, is the Yankee's analysis of the medieval mind, for it is here that Twain's reliance on the literary tradition has the greatest results for the evolution of the novel. The Yankee finds that mind superstitious, as unconsciously indelicate as it is unconsciously cruel, and to-

tally devoid of the power of reason. Twain's most telling satire
is directed at the gullibility of the medieval mentality, and here
he refers directly to the epic tradition itself:

. . . they were a childlike and innocent lot, telling lies of the state-
liest pattern with a most gentle and winning naïveté, and ready and
willing to listen to anybody else's lie, and believe it too. It was hard
to associate them with anything cruel or dreadful, and yet they dealt
in tales of blood and suffering with a guileless relish that made me
almost forget to shudder.[20]

When the Yankee criticizes the style of Sandy's tales (drawn,
with some judicious editing by Twain, from *Morte D'Arthur*),
one may recognize literary criticism in one of its higher forms,
as cultural criticism.[21] The apparently senseless repetition, the
meaningless carnage, the rhythm that reminds the Yankee of a
railroad hawker, and the failure to conceptualize the narrated
conflicts make the heroic exploits of the Knights of the Table
Round "pale and noiseless—just ghosts scuffling in a fog." [22]
Twain is here making one of his most valuable comments on
the mentality that can be captivated by these "level Saharas of
fact." [23] The Yankee's remarks are not intended as an effort to
debunk a literary masterpiece and genre. In *Joan of Arc*, for instance, Twain sympathetically portrays a household ecstatically
attending to an impromptu rendition of the whole of *La Chanson
de Roland*.

Twain is attempting to gain historical insight through the literary tradition. The appraisal of the morality of Arthur's court,
for example, embodies a severe criticism of the epic mentality
as viewed by the nineteenth-century Yankee. "The fact is, it is
just a sort of polished up court of Comanches, and there isn't a
squaw in it who doesn't stand ready at the dropping of a hat to
desert to the buck with the biggest string of scalps at his belt." [24]
Twain has drawn from Malory (with some justification) an almost barbaric view of sex. He ignores the courtly tradition of

love—perfect fidelity in often adulterous unions—and the significant duties of the code of chivalry. This deprives Arthur and his court of any trace of sensibility.

King Arthur is the character-motif of this age in the same way that Colonel Sellers is the comic character-motif of *The Gilded Age* and the Paladin serves this function in *Joan of Arc*. Arthur has the nobility and fearlessness of a true knight, as is shown by the scene in the smallpox hut and by his indomitable spirit in captivity. He is also vain, gullible, superstitious, and extremely obtuse on moral questions which transcend the current beliefs of his age—as when he wishes to report the escaped sons of a disease-stricken family, to whom he has just ministered with great tenderness. Arthur's sensibility is as small as his intellect, and as the Boss notes, the king "wasn't a very heavy weight, intellectually." [25]

To illustrate this point further, one may return, in Twain's masterpiece, to where Huck finds himself among the Grangerfords. Twain was mocking the "aristocratic" tradition of the South in the earlier book, and his magnificently satirical portrait was also in large part an attack on a "feudal" literary tradition. In the South, however, the tradition was the Romantic one of Scott rather than the courtly epic of Malory. As in Arthur's world, the "aristocrats" live by a code both cruel and stupid, but again the men themselves are not ignoble. The death of Buck is the result of tragic folly, as is the death of Arthur—which Twain significantly retains in Malory's prose. In *Huck Finn*, Twain directs his satire entirely against the literary and artistic effusions of this aristocratic "civilization." When he parodies the morbid sensibility of Emmeline Grangerford, he gives the episode a satiric dimension that the values of the Colonel alone, with all his deadly absurdity, could not provide. By denying the Round Table a sensibility, Twain denies himself satire and restricts himself to burlesque and lampoon. The core of Malory is left untouched. Twain could undermine the falsely romantic with ease; but the epic is not dependent on an artificial sensibility. The Yankee's shock at the loose and bold talk of the court might impair the image of Ivanhoe and Rowena, but it is only a humorously anachronistic reaction to the frank figures of *Morte D'Arthur*.

Twain's choice of a literary frame of reference for his historical *roman expérimental* has another consequence no less important to his basic interests. The courtly epic by its very nature excluded a complete representation of medieval society. As Erich Auerbach has said:

. . . this ruling class adopted an ethos and an ideal which concealed its real function. And it proceeded to describe its own life in extrahistorical terms, as an absolute aesthetic configuration without practical purpose.[26]

Had Twain been able to bridge this deliberate gap, and show the "great and beautiful characters" of Arthur's court in organic relation to the economic and political system of their time, he would have written a great historical novel.[27] As he had done with the Grangerfords, however, Twain balked at the final imaginative step. He had piercingly portrayed the slave-holding "aristocracy" of the old South, but not essentially *as* slaveholders. This is a minor fault, if one may even give it that name, in *Huckleberry Finn*, because the "aristocracy" is a distinctly minor subject in that book. In the *Yankee*, however, the question of the relation of Arthur's court to the political economy of the age is central, but it is badly obscured.

Hank Morgan leaves the court, in Chapter XI, temporarily bringing his plans for revolutionizing the sixth century to a standstill. It is necessary for the Yankee to leave the court to come into contact with the oppression and injustice of the Middle Ages, which was the chief target of Twain's attack. Twain drops the literary burlesque almost entirely, and takes up a completely new frame of historical reference. Instead of Malory, he relies selectively on the insights of nineteenth-century progressive historiography, particularly that of William Lecky, in order to expose the seamy side of the Dark Ages.[28] Typically, the errors of that society are virtually defined in terms of oppressive and unjust *laws*, through which the nobles prey on the poor. The Yankee lists these laws with withering scorn, the infamous catalogue culminating in *le droit du seigneur*—an institution on which Twain dwells with Victorian lasciviousness.[29] The Yankee's definition of the system through laws and castes, and his failure to treat it as an economic and cultural whole, is properly anachronistic, as it should be, but we are now worlds away from the lampooned idyll. It is hard to recognize King Arthur and the Knights of the Round Table as "this gilded minority . . . [which] had elected itself to be the Nation, and these innumerable clams had permitted it so long that they had come at last to accept it as a truth, and not only that, but to believe it right and as it should be." [30] It is even harder to reconcile *le droit du seigneur* and Sir Galahad.

Hank Morgan's adventures on his quest are largely passive and do nothing to advance his schemes. The Yankee becomes less and less the vernacular hero, rebounding his folk wit off archaic literary conventions, and more and more Twain's mouthpiece. Twain muckrakes the Middle Ages as he had muckraked the Reconstruction era. Although it would seem imperative for Twain to show the root and cause of the oppression, and to bridge the gap between the innocent savages of chivalry and the evil system which supports them, he did not do this. While "training" goes far to explain their lack of consciousness of wrong, Twain rests his *historical* argument squarely on the pernicious role of the Church. The heart of *A Connecticut Yankee* as a progressive historical novel lies in the struggle of the Great Man seeking support from the people as their champion against the central source of their oppression, the Established Church. As a bourgeois "go-as-you-please Protestant" revolutionary, Hank seems to be cut to the pattern of William the Silent—circus side notwithstanding.

Yet Hank never fulfills this role. Given the way in which Twain changes the modes of the historical imagination governing *A Connecticut Yankee,* it is hard to see how he could.

The Yankee's diatribe against the Church as the chief center of evil and reaction is a curious thing in a novel which rarely shows a cleric in any role whatsoever. The Church is a distant, far-off threat, for all the Yankee's stout Protestant railing at it, and the Interdict is as much of a surprise to the reader as it is to Morgan himself. This mechanical sort of historical explanation—never *rendered* in fictional terms—becomes a necessity because of Twain's initial use of the literary tradition. If the nobility cannot be conscious of oppressing the poor, the Church must be. If no one were conscious that the system is unnecessarily oppressive, the book's muckraking thesis would be in danger. Whether he was aware of it or not, Twain was paying the price for his mixture of historical modes.

With the elucidation of the two frames of historical reference, the hitherto anomalous role of science in the book becomes much clearer. When Twain is burlesquing the literary Merlin, Science is merely an efficient and showy "magic." Many critics have been puzzled by the "circus side" of Sir Boss' nature, and especially by his frivolous magic shows. We may now see that these exercises of scientific knowledge are always performed in the context of a spoof on the credulous court. Similarly, the suggestively entrepreneurial magician's rivalry ("Merlin's stock was flat") is entirely within the literary lampoon and the Yankee's initial role as vernacular hero. The role of Science changes with Twain's historical source material. Having arbitrarily made the Church the root and branch of reaction, Twain has the Yankee turn to nineteenth-century Science as a counter to it. To expose the court, it was enough for Twain to use the eye of an "innocent." To expose slavery, he must pose something as strong as the Church itself—Science.

The emergence of Science as Juggernaut has aroused the greatest recent critical controversy about the *Yankee*—perhaps as a reaction to the threat of automation and the bomb. This emergence does not occur in the book, one must notice, until the Boss himself changes from his role as muckraker to his final role as revolutionary. When the Yankee begins to talk of his plans for bringing the world of the nineteenth century to that of the sixth, Twain shows the third phase of the Yankee's—and the author's—historical imagination: the revolutionary-utopian. On first encountering the servility of "freemen," the Yankee says:

The thing that would have best suited the circus side of my nature would have been to resign the Boss-ship and get up an insurrection and turn it into a revolution; but I knew that the Jack Cade or the Wat Tyler who tries such a thing without first educating his materials up to revolution grade is almost absolutely certain to get left.[31]

Instead of talking "blood and revolution" to likely prospects, he sends them to his "man-factory." Obviously, the Yankee has a sophisticated historical over-view, as he demonstrates by likening himself to the adventuring nobles and harlots of history. Yet one of the ironies of the novel is that the Yankee does indeed "get left." The Yankee also observes that "no people in the world ever did achieve their freedom by goody-goody talk and moral suasion. . . . What this folk needed, then, was a Reign of Terror and a guillotine, and I was the wrong man for them." [32] Yet the second irony is that a reign of technocratic terror—and very little else—is exactly what the Yankee brings to the sixth century. The ending of the novel, as mentioned earlier, has been seen as the result of Twain's despair over democracy or of his covert anguish over technological progress. It does imply both of these, of course, pervaded as the novel is throughout with the hardy pessimism of Twain's view of human nature. As the Yankee becomes revolutionist, Twain switches modes once more.

Twain carries on his narrative, probing the consciousness of the oppressed classes of the sixth century by historical analogy

as he had probed that of the ruling classes through the literary
tradition. He makes one of his most imaginative uses of analogy
in plumbing the psychology of the mob of villagers who massacre
their neighbors to avenge the murder of a hated lord. The Yankee
relates this class suicide to the behavior of the poor whites who
gave their lives in the Civil War for the slave system that had
degraded them as well as the blacks. The lengthy episode in
which the Yankee and Arthur are enslaved, and the earlier references to the way in which slavery ossified "what one may call
the superior lobe of human feeling" in the society that allowed
it are also, of course, based on Twain's observation and the memoirs of slaves.[33] Twain is consciously reinterpreting the medieval
past through insights gained in observing the society of his lifetime. The Yankee can thus praise the emerging class-conscious-
ness of the peasant who swears to protect him and conceal his
identity as an agitator.

At this same point in the book, the Mob has made its appearance, and it is as ugly, unreasoning, and cowardly as the mobs of
Huckleberry Finn and *The Mysterious Stranger*. The Yankee is
now the vehicle for Twain's darker philosophy of human nature.
At one moment he affirms that "a man *is* a man at bottom," on
seeing a peasant's ingrained resentment of his lot. At the next
minute, however, after seeing the same peasant demonstrate his
servility and caste-bound pride, he swears, "Well, there are times
when one would like to hang the whole human race and finish
the farce." [34] Twain is now out of the Middle Ages entirely and
making his literally timeless judgments on the cowardly nature
of man. The scene ends, apropriately enough, as the Yankee and
the peasant come upon some children emulating their parents
by lynching a playmate.

The problem of revolutionizing the sixth century, as outlined
by the Yankee, hinges entirely upon the matter of education.
The Yankee's one attempt at personally educating the masses is
set in a conspicuously contemporary mode by Hank's choice of

the Democratic party line of Grover Cleveland as his text. The
Yankee's conception of education consists chiefly of browbeating.
Since the workmen he addresses are incapable of perceiving anything beyond medieval "common sense," the upshot is a brawl,
which results in the enslavement of both Hank and the King.
In these passages Twain is manipulating an historical analogy
with the working class of his own era. It is unclear, however,
whether he meant the fault to lie in the Boss' lack of historical
insight, or in the resistance of men at any time to having their
conventional wisdom disturbed.

The last, incredibly jumbled, and somewhat botched portion
of the book is marked by the anomalous conjunction of all three
of Twain's historical methods. This accounts for much of the
disconcerting tone of the novel as it approaches an ending of such
theatrical quality that one can only call it a finale.

The Yankee's first step in revolutionizing the sixth century is
his attack on knight-errantry. However justified this might appear
in terms of his progressive thesis, Twain has so thoroughly identified the knights-errant with his lampoon on the courtly epic,
and so thoroughly neglected to relate them to the "historical"
oppression of the poor, that even he cannot ignore the disjunc-
ture. He tries to bridge the modal distinction by reviving the old
"commercial" rivalry with Merlin, and through such other burlesque props as pink tights, lariat, and rodeo atmosphere. The
Yankee manages to phrase the whole matter in a challenge of
quixotic utilitarianism: "I was the champion of hard unsenti-
mental common sense and reason. I was entering the lists to
either destroy knight-errantry or be its victim." [35]

Next the Yankee exposes his plants and schools, and makes
a bewildering three-year leap in time. With his commitment
firmly made to Science as Progress, the Yankee reveals his two
programs for transformation: a "go-as-you-please Protestant"
church and a republic. With the arrival of the Interdict Twain
switches to muckraking, his second mode of historical presenta-

tion, with Science confronting the Church. The Death of Arthur is disposed of in cursory fashion, in a hodge-podge of burlesque and Malory. At this point integration of modes becomes impossible.

The idea of nineteenth-century Science as a sinister Nemesis becomes dominant, and, significantly, a return to the method of historical analogy to evoke the past accompanies it. Twain's convictions on the cravenness of man—convictions always latent in the book—emerge. Science is recognized as at best a substitute for the Church, for both act on the most vulnerable side of man's cowardice. The manufactory can only replace sixth-century slaves with their modern equivalents, as Clarence explains to the Yankee:

"Did you think you had educated the superstition out of those people?"

"I certainly did think it."

"Well, then, you may unthink it. They stood every strain easily—until the Interdict. Since then, they merely put on a bold outside—at heart they are quaking. Make up your mind to it—when the armies come, the mask will fall." [36]

And so the Yankee "gets left." It may be that Twain never really conceived of an ending in which his technocracy would have succeeded. He made it obvious, however, that if he had, it would merely have replaced the Church, and that it could not make "men." What is important to recognize is that this dark interpretation of Science is related almost entirely to Twain's views on the eternal nature of man, rather than to his views on Progress in history. It impinges only slightly on his "historical" analysis of the oppression of the Middle Ages, and not at all on the tradition of the courtly epic with which he confronted his Yankee.

Henry Nash Smith has said of the Middle Ages evoked by Twain:

. . . this medieval setting is obviously not meant to represent any actual place or time. It is a backdrop designed to allow a nineteenth-century American industrial genius to show what he can do with an underdeveloped country.[37]

Yet such an interpretation would mean casting away three-fourths of the novel. In fact, as a progressive historical novel *A Connecticut Yankee* is terribly divided against itself; and so it begins in literary satire and only concludes in the suggestively grim utopian atmosphere to which Smith and the other recent commentators refer.

The final image in the novel—of the Yankee dying amid the stench of the unburied chivalry of England—is one of the most striking representations of aborted effort in our literature. It may also stand as a symbol of the cross-currents of historical evocation in *A Connecticut Yankee in King Arthur's Court*—perhaps the most magnificent failure of all American historical fiction.

Chapter Seven

BELLAMY, CABLE, JAMES,
ADAMS, CRANE: TOWARDS
THE RED BADGE OF COURAGE

TEPHEN Crane's *The Red Badge of Courage* marked
the predicament in which the American historical imagination
found itself at the end of the nineteenth century as the result
of the rising influence of naturalism. Understanding the evolution of the genre of the historical novel as a serious art form after
Billy Budd and *A Connecticut Yankee* requires a brief step backwards in chronological sequence. Four novels of the late 1870's
contain the most significant alternatives for the historical novel
in this period and in the era to follow: Edward Bellamy's *The
Duke of Stockbridge*, George W. Cable's *The Grandissimes*,
Henry James' *The Europeans*, and Henry Adams' *Democracy*. A
brief analysis of these novels of the Age of Realism also helps to
relate *The Red Badge of Courage* to its true antecedents and
proper context.

⌐ Bellamy: From History to Utopia

The almost simultaneous appearance of *A Connecticut Yankee*
(1889) and *Looking Backward* (1888) indicates, as often noted,
the strength of the incipient utopianism in Twain's novel. Yet it
has seldom been recognized that *Looking Backward: 2000–1887*,

as proclaimed in the title and explained in the sham Preface, is
cast in the form of an "historical romance." This is superficially
a merely formal device by which Bellamy brings about the confrontation of his utopia with nineteenth-century America. Yet it
is also a recognition that the utopian novel is only the historical
novel inverted—a recognition which is the more significant since
Bellamy's first novel, *The Duke of Stockbridge* (1879), was itself
a highly original experiment in the historical genre. *The Duke of
Stockbridge* is in fact a reverse image of the utopia pictured in
Looking Backward. By dealing with the dynamic problems of
social action the novel uncovers Bellamy's social assumptions and
the genuine psychological basis of his utopian vision to an extent
that is almost impossible to secure by textual analysis of the later
work alone. It also reveals that one's understanding of the form
of the historical novel can improve one's comprehension of the
social philosophy of the author. Bellamy's is the unique case in
this study where the thinker is more interesting than the artist.

That *Looking Backward* is still in need of explication after
more than seventy years of study and influence is clear from the
fact that many objections to the novel among socialists and other
sympathizers with utopian planning—including William Morris
—at the time of its appearance have not abated. Thoughtful ad-
mirers of Bellamy today, such as Erich Fromm and Daniel Aaron,
are still disturbed by the apparent regimentation of the year
2000.[1] Morris' original objection was to the strong emphasis on
coercive statism and the discipline Bellamy seemed to believe
necessary for material production. According to Morris, Bellamy
was over-concerned with "seeking (with obvious failure) some
incentive to replace the fear of starvation, which is at present
our only one, whereas it cannot be too often repeated that the
true incentive to happy and useful labour must be pleasure in the
work itself. . . ."[2] It is beyond doubt that, in fact, Bellamy's
emotional reaction to "productive" labor was extremely negative.
The "industrial army" of the year 2000, unfranchised, driven on-

ward by honorific rewards and threats of solitary confinement, seems to have almost no goal but retirement. For Bellamy life was to begin at forty-five, and it is this genuine "leisure class" which governs the new society. As Dr. Leete puts it:

. . . we all agree in looking forward to the date of our discharge as the time we shall first enter upon the full enjoyment of our birthright, the period when we shall first really attain our majority and become enfranchised from discipline and control, with the fee of our lives vested in ourselves. . . . It is a strange reflection that at forty-five, when we are just entering upon the most enjoyable period of life, you already began to think of growing old and to look backward. With you it was the forenoon, with us it is the afternoon, which is the brighter half of life.[3]

The dichotomizing of life between a very highly disciplined and "repressive" sphere of work and a dream-like sphere of freedom and gratification, the latter associated in the narrative with Julian West's romance with Edith Leete, has been seen by one commentator as a brilliant pre-Freudian insight into the relation between waking and dreaming.[4] Whether one accepts this interpretation or not, it does pinpoint one of Bellamy's central psychological dilemmas in creating his utopia: an overwhelming desire for radical social change combined with an equally overpowering fear of the psychological and social derangement that may accompany such change. In turning to Bellamy's historical novel one may see these preoccupations in full dramatic conflict.

The Duke of Stockbridge was originally published in 1879 in the local newspaper of Great Barrington, Massachusetts, and appeared posthumously in book form in 1901, edited by Francis Bellamy, the author's cousin.[5] Perhaps best described as a proletarian romance of Shays' Rebellion, the novel was the result of extensive historical researches by Bellamy, including talks with the sons and grandsons of the original rebels in his home neighborhood in western Massachusetts. Bellamy's strongly sympathetic portrait of the plight of the farmers during the period between the Revolution and the adoption of the Constitution was markedly opposed to the then-prevailing view of the rebellion as the supreme aberration of the "Critical Period." The novel is also a profound criticism of the possibility of achieving the new society through a revolutionary movement by the oppressed, an equally important theme of Bellamy's thought.

The action begins in a way similar to that of *Looking Backward*, with the return of the protagonist to a home made foreign by historical change. Perez Hamlin (based on an actual rebel leader) returns from the Revolution to find his fellow villagers horribly impoverished, their farms auctioned for debt and taxes, and his own brother dying in jail as a debtor. Hamlin is gradually initiated by a series of shocks into the social crisis of the area, a technique Bellamy later used in modified form to reintroduce Julian West to the Boston of 2000 A.D.

Bellamy dramatizes the difficulty of uncovering the causes of the "hard times" in his realistic presentation of the farmers who discuss the situation among themselves with a mixture of intellectual confusion and keen emotional probing. The semi-feudal structure of Stockbridge, with its mores and theology, is described with great sociological amplitude. It is but one generation removed from the era of its most famous minister, Jonathan Edwards; Joseph Bellamy, Edward's ancestor, was his colleague. Bellamy emphasizes especially the psychological effect on the farmers of the association of wealth and the clergy on one side and poverty and a conviction of original sin on the other. The novel traces Hamlin's rise to leadership of a spontaneous rebellion against the foreclosures and imprisonments, the temporary success of the rebellion, and his reign as virtual dictator of the town of Stockbridge. The period of his rule is epitomized in one scene in which Hamlin prepares to have the "aristocracy" and clergy flogged at the public whipping post for plotting a counter-coup—a symbolic reversal and breaking of taboos. Closely linked with this aborted action is Hamlin's domination over Desire Edwards (Bellamy's choice of name is rather unfortunate but to the point), the granddaughter of the great Jonathan, in a peculiarly frank and perverse love affair.

Two themes stand out in the novel: the first is the literal anarchism of the rebellion, which, like the Regulator movement of colonial North Carolina, finds almost its sole concrete objective in preventing the oppressive courts from sitting. Beyond this simple goal, easily comprehended by the poor farmers, the rebellion has no aims, and worse, no constructive vision of society. Although Bellamy is in full sympathy with the rebels, he underlines the impossibility of positive achievement from such spontaneous lower-class action (perhaps with the recent bloody and abortive strikes of 1877 in mind) by showing the way the rebellion dissipates its energies once resistance is overcome. The other theme is the dangerous and unstable leadership of revolutionary movement, as represented in Hamlin. Hamlin is given a very positive characterization as a "genteel" yeoman hero, yet the disappearance of moral sanctions in the revolution, symbolized by the overthrow of the town's "stewards," leads to his sexual transgressions and finally to an extinction of his revolutionary purpose and self-destruction. The novel ends with the complete emotional exhaustion of Desire Edwards, the death of Hamlin, and the return of the ruling class to power with redoubled strength under an authoritarian and "aristocratic" leader.

While Bellamy's novel of Shays' Rebellion expresses the author's sympathies with the oppressed, it also dramatizes his fears of the dangers of anarchism. Bellamy's lifelong antipathy to the anarchists of his own day is well known, and in *Looking Backward* he has the sage Dr. Leete say of them, "No historical authority nowadays doubts that they were paid by the great monopolies to wave the red flag and talk about burning, sacking, and blowing people up, in order, by alarming the timid, to head off any real reforms." [6]

In *The Duke of Stockbridge* one may find an explanation for the bloodless evolution, the almost providential crystallization of nationalism that is described as having brought about the utopian society of *Looking Backward*. Comparing this process with the extensive violence that inaugurates the new era in Morris' *News From Nowhere* (1891), violence emanating from a spontaneous working-class response to oppression, one may see that Morris and Bellamy differed in more than particulars. The philosopher Martin Buber describes two basic Western eschatological traditions:

the prophetic, which at any given moment sees every person addressed by it as endowed, in a degree not to be determined beforehand, with the power to participate by his decisions and deeds in the preparing of Redemption: and the apocalyptic, in which the redemptive process in all its details, its very hour and course, has been fixed from everlasting and for whose accomplishment human beings are only used as tools, though what is immutably fixed may yet be "unveiled" to them, revealed, and they be assigned their function.[7]

Clearly, with his distrust of man's ability to create the new society through a revolt of the oppressed, Bellamy belongs in the imaginative tradition of the apocalyptic, while Morris, the philosophical revolutionary, has a prophetic vision of social transformation. Bellamy exemplifies the importance for the "apocalyptic" utopian of neutralizing and evading the revolutionary theme. *The Duke of Stockbridge*, like *A Connecticut Yankee in King Arthur's Court*, indicates where that theme was to lead for the American writer: the progressive dream aborted, the impulse for change resulting in catastrophe. "Prophetic" utopian novels like *News From Nowhere*, Ignatius Donnelly's *Caesar's Column*, and Jack London's *The Iron Heel*, written from a standpoint of revolutionary socialism rather than bourgeois progressivism (with the partial exception of Donnelly), exemplify this development perfectly. In each, the heart of the narrative is a description of intense and disastrous violence, while the utopian society of the future is only sketchily rendered and feebly imagined. For example, Morris' future England is a preposterous Pre-Raphaelite

fairyland, and London's "Brotherhood of Man" of the remote
future is never described.

The Duke of Stockbridge also illuminates Bellamy's theory of
the personality. Most of his other early "medicated" fiction was
devoted to experiments in the exorcism of the sense of sin and
guilt from humanity, that may well have been for him a necessary
preliminary to the recreated altruistic man of utopia. Bellamy's
instincts were certainly accurate in discerning a supporting relationship between the sense of original sin inculcated in the popu-
lation by the clergy and the comfortable platitudes of laissez-
faire economics and neo-Spencerian sociology. Yet Bellamy, the
descendant of a long line of Puritan divines, could throw off their
theological sanction, but not their moral imperatives and moral
fervor. For him revolution would destroy the necessary barrier
between repression and free gratification.

Bellamy's regime of complete order, discipline, and control is
the external social sanction that is to replace the repressive internal sense of sin. When this is combined with Bellamy's apocalyptic vision, which denies the operation of free will in history,
one may see from the nature of his utopia that he has been
brought almost full circle to Calvinism again. But not quite: for
in Looking Backward the imperatives of "sin" no longer lie in
God's province but rather in man's nature as a social being and
are given the name of hunger; in his coach metaphor, hunger
drives the coach, no matter who the passengers are. Bellamy cannot escape from this sense, but the authoritarian system of Looking Backward offers a means of controlling it. The problems of
the past can at last find resolution in the future.

⌐ Cable and the Holist Tradition

George W. Cable's The Grandissimes (1880) shows the changes
the holist historical vision underwent in order to remain viable
in the post–Civil War "Age of Realism." Like Cooper's Little-

pages, the Grandissime family is the synecdochic medium for Cable's historical insights into his region's cultural history. The novel bears even stronger affinities with *The House of the Seven Gables*, which probably influenced Cable.[8] Indeed, *The Grandissimes* appears to be the vital link modifying and continuing the tradition of the holist historical novel between *The House of the Seven Gables* and *Absalom, Absalom!* Like these novels—especially the latter—*The Grandissimes* is permeated by incidents of melodrama and an atmosphere of sin. In a sense, *The Grandissimes* is more thoroughly holist than any of the novels I have analyzed, because it is essentially about the multiplicity of relationships possible in a heterogeneous society. Cable anatomizes the magnificent complexity of these relationships in the New Orleans milieu of 1803: relations among generations, families, branches of families, races, nationalities, and regions as well as among the media of social intercourse such as land, money, politics, and language.

The Grandissimes is so packed with incident and carefully drawn characters that it is impossible briefly to synopsize the plot. The structure of the novel is rather like that of an Elizabethan play, with each scene superbly controlled but little attempt made to keep the entire work from sprawling. In essence, the novel tells the story of a multitudinous, ancient, and powerful Creole family at the time of the cession of Louisiana, resolving—and sometimes critically failing to resolve—problems inherited from the near and distant past. Part of that heritage is a long-established rivalry with another Creole family (the "histories" of each clan are given from the seventeenth century) that comes to a conclusion on the comic level of rights, wrongs, and matrimonial alliances. The Grandissimes' traditional Creole truculence and prejudice towards the "Américain" invaders is only partially dispelled, and they begin to pay heavily for their intransigence. Cable ironically alludes to the behavior of the post-Reconstruction South of the late 1870's in discussing this unshakable attitude.[9] On a third, tragic level, the Grandissimes, with one exception, embrace their heritage of racism by violent acts of repression. Except for the "enlightened" Honoré and his half-brother Honoré Grandissime f.m.c. (free man of color), the tribe never becomes conscious of racism as a problem requiring resolution.

Cable saw racism problematically and not as a form of "original sin." It is important to define the problem about which he wrote as racism rather than slavery. Although the "issues" of slavery and racism are inextricable in the novel, especially in the central legend of Bras Coupé, most of the Negro characters in the novel are "free," and Bras Coupé's fate illuminates theirs but does not define it. Unlike Twain, who tried to abstract the institution of slavery from its racist context in A Connecticut Yankee, Cable emphasizes the social psychology of racism and its cultural effects. This emphasis is not only far more "holist" but, since racism did not end with chattel slavery, Cable's historical novel presented a more relevant and dangerous analogy to his contemporaries than did Twain's.

Cable has quite properly been considered Faulkner's literary ancestor for his use of the theme of miscegenation as a scalpel to dissect the racist mind. Charles Bon significantly derives from the racial relationships Cable had explored as a literary subject. The theme of miscegenation, arising from sociological fact, was a literary convention, an eminently holist one, in nineteenth-century America. In The Grandissimes the extent to which the theme governs existing and possible relationships among characters implies that for Cable Louisiana was a slave society, not merely a society in which slavery existed. This distinction must be made, because the imaginative world of the novel is largely determined by it. This holist vision is one of the measures of the distance between Absalom, Absalom! and Margaret Mitchell's best seller, also published in 1936, about a society in which slavery exists—and is charming.

In *The House of the Seven Gables, The Grandissimes,* and *Absalom, Absalom!* the past and the present are in direct and living contact, without the artistic distancing of the past found in *The Scarlet Letter, Billy Budd,* or *A Connecticut Yankee.* " 'I have these facts,' it was Agricola Fusilier's habit to say, 'by family tradition; but you know, sir, h-tradition is much more authentic than history!' " [10] Tradition—especially family tradition—is a counter-history in these works, interior, selective, intensely meaningful. History is cruel and confusing in its transitions and conveys a very uncertain meaning to the various times-present of these novels—Jacksonian Salem, New Orleans in 1803, Mississippi and Cambridge in 1910. The novels are concerned with the transmission of tradition in an era that *appears* to be making this living tradition fabulous. One tension running through each of the books is the question: How much of the tradition—good and evil—will survive?

In *The House of the Seven Gables* "history" is mediated first by the narrator's version of "tradition"; only later does one learn Matthew Maule's pure version of the house's tradition. The Present (1880) exists in *The Grandissimes* only in the narrator's authoritative comments and in his assumption of the prerogatives of a storyteller. Yet Cable's storyteller stance implicitly presents the tale as part of a continuous tradition, constantly renewed and remolded. In *Absalom, Absalom!* "history" is narrated by a counterpoint of eyewitnesses and modern reflectors. The tradition is *found* and recreated. As part of the saga, "time-present" is also the past (1910 seen from 1936), and Quentin's death (in *The Sound and the Fury,* 1929) is already "known" to author and reader. Perhaps this is the most essential truth in which the holist novel of tradition deals: that the Past has a Past.

Joseph Frowenfeld, the German Yankee newcomer, is the "modern" yet involved initiate to the traditions of the Grandissimes, the strangely analogous counterpart to Phoebe Pyncheon and Quentin Compson. His task is to begin at once the perusal of this newly found book, the Community of New Orleans. True, he knew he should find it a difficult task—not only that much of it was in a strange tongue, but that it was a volume whose displaced leaves would have to be lifted tenderly, blown free of much dust, rearranged, some torn fragments laid together again with much painstaking, and even the purport of some pages guessed out. Obviously, the place to commence at was that brightly illuminated title-page, the ladies Nancanou.[11]

The language and metaphor of this passage are extremely Jamesian, as is the theme of an intelligent, "innocent" observer experimentally entering a more complex and subtle culture. It is especially reminiscent of Christopher Newman preparing to plumb the melodramatic depths of the Bellegardes in *The American*, James' romance of these same years. Yet, unlike the typical Jamesian situation, what is discovered has *intrinsic* meaning as well as meaning for the protagonist's vision of the world. This is a difficult distinction to convey in purely formal terms. "Melodramatic" episodes or effects, like the murder concealed by the Bellegardes that Newman discovers, may be used as *counters* for cultural meaning; but the crime in *The American* is not meant as a revelation of the nature of French culture so much as it is designed to provoke a further revelation of Newman's character. The novels of Cable and Faulkner, with a less exclusively psychological purpose, are full of melodramatic and violent action at their very core. The story of Bras Coupé or the killings of Charles Bon and Thomas Sutpen are parables that genuinely illuminate the essence of a culture.

Bras Coupé is mentioned often by different characters before his terrible story is told at the very center of the book, and later related in different places by three separate speakers. This admittedly primitive "preparation" makes the tale the center of "traditional" meaning in the culture as well as the turning point of the lives of several characters. Faulkner, with the same purpose, made "preparation" one of the great triumphs of narrative technique in *Absalom, Absalom!* Bras Coupé's curse, like Maule's in *The House of the Seven Gables*, is finally lifted, but his fable of resistance to culturally endorsed exploitation leaves the past as an equally ambiguous burden for the survivors. As the "black" Honoré Grandissime replies to Frowenfeld's urging to become a leader of his people, "Ah cannod be one Toussaint L'Ouverture. Ah cannod trah to be. Hiv I trah, I h-only s'all soogceed to be one Bras Coupé.[12]

Chingachgook, Pontiac, Charles Bon: there can be rebellion but no successful revolution, no successful overthrow of cultural barriers. The essentially tragic view of the holist imagination prevails despite Cable's search for grounds for progressive hope. In the post–Civil War South, Cable and Faulkner, fulfilling their historical vision through the holist frame, deepened its tragic import.

↶ James' Sense of the Past and *The Europeans*

Henry James' *The Europeans* serves to introduce important aspects of the continuity of the historical novel as a major art form in America. *The Europeans* is remarkable for its revelation of the levels of historical meaning and the values of historical perspective in the post-progressive and twentieth-century historical novel. Its action by internal evidence, takes place between 1841 and 1848. James was born—in New York—in 1843. Thus, like *Huckleberry Finn, The Europeans* has documentary interest as an "historical novel," heightened, in terms of historical imagination, by the fact that it is not in any sense a memoir.

Richard Poirier has commented upon the similarity of tone and intention between *The Europeans* (1878) and James' brilliant critical study of Hawthorne, published the following year.[13] It is an apt association, for *The Europeans* is a fictional evocation of Hawthorne's New England of the 1840's, a sympathetic portrayal of the fruits of that culture in manners and mores just as

James' *Hawthorne* attempted to assess the fruits of that culture in art. Eugenia and Felix do not simply encounter "America," but an American consciousness that in retrospect appeared inconceivably pristine. The America of 1878 was chastened not only by thirty years of "progress," but by the wound of civil war.

The subsidence of that great convulsion has left a different tone from the tone it found, and one may say that the Civil War marks an era in the history of the American mind. It introduced into the national consciousness a certain sense of proportion and relation, of the world being a more complicated place than it had hitherto seemed, the future more treacherous, success more difficult. At the rate at which things are going, it is obvious that good Americans will be more numerous than ever; but the good American, in days to come, will be a more critical person than his complacent and confident grandfather. He has eaten of the tree of knowledge. He will not, I think, be a sceptic, and still less, of course, a cynic; but he will be, without discredit to his well-known capacity for action, an observer. He will remember that the ways of the Lord are inscrutable, and that this is a world in which everything happens; and eventualities, as the late Emperor of the French used to say, will not find him intellectually unprepared. The good American of which Hawthorne was so admirable a specimen was not critical, and it was perhaps for this reason that Franklin Pierce seemed to him a very proper President.[14]

If James did lack the "historical consciousness" he recognizes so freely in Hawthorne, he retains in very large measure Hawthorne's awareness of historical distance separating one era from another. This is perhaps part of the quality T. S. Eliot attempted to define when he said that James had "the sense of the sense" of the past.[15] Culture barriers are created not only by the general laws of development recognized by the holists but by specific historical events that can change the temper of a people within one man's lifetime. *The Europeans* is written from a perspective which sets the author and reader at as great a distance from the Wentworths of New England as their "European" cousins are.

The ruling concern of James' rather rarefied historical imagination is a temporal version of the "international theme": the quality of life in cultures separated by a chasm of unshared experience. This theme offers a way for the novelist to reject the search for the reality of social change in order to concentrate on the consequences. It is also an important element in such disparate twentieth-century novelists as Edith Wharton and Faulkner. James did not formulate his conception of the "historical" imagination until the end of his career, in the unfinished *The Sense of the Past*. In that fragment, he describes Ralph Pendrel's aesthetic awareness of the past-as-experience merged in his demand for intensity in art:

It was when life was framed in death that the picture was really hung up. If his idea in fine was to recover the lost moment, to feel the stopped pulse, it was to do so as experience, in order to be again consciously the creature that *had* been, to breathe as he had breathed and feel the pressure that he had felt. The truth most involved for him, so intent, in the insistent ardour of the artist, was that art was capable of an energy to this end never yet to all appearance fully required of it. With an address less awkward, a wooing less shy, an embrace less weak, it would draw the foregone much closer to its breast.[16]

The work of art that will evoke the past is then *centrally* concerned with the recreation of "atmosphere," an idea in itself in the Jamesian world. The characters of *The Europeans* can, with risk, cross cultural boundaries, and to do so is similar to and often identical with an "intellectual" perception. James shows the reader a Boston omnibus and scattered copies of Emerson's *Essays*, *The North American Review*, and the Boston *Daily Advertiser*, all presented as the suddenly insufficient props of the Old Order, but his technique of historical evocation is basically not that of the miniaturist who lovingly sketches in atmospheric "details." James rather attempts to convey the "sense," at once emotional and intellectual, of an atmosphere through manners. For James an "alternative" civilization can be "past" as well as foreign; the sense of difference, and the meaning of that sense, is all.

Thus James builds on the holist assumptions of Hawthorne

without himself being a holist. For James an attitude towards historical "atmosphere" replaces attitudes towards history. And for James—as for Edith Wharton in *The Age of Innocence*—the atmosphere of the earlier age is revealed as charming but claustrophobic for the artistic temperament. The New England of *The Europeans* is unmarred by the symptoms of exotic decay of *The Bostonians* with its post-bellum *mise en scène*. As Felix says of the Wentworth milieu, "It's primitive; it's patriarchal; it's the *ton* of the golden age." [17] The intensely traditional and tribal atmosphere suggested by this description proclaims a culture that for James failed the crucial test of freedom. Thus, at the end of their encounter with the "Europeans," Gertrude is alone freed from organized guilt, while Charlotte and Mr. Brand, a very definite echo of Hawthorne in his characterization, are awakened to one another if not to themselves. Mr. Wentworth, always surrounded by the holy objects of New England culture, is only shaken by the experience. Robert Acton constantly gazes at the clear, brilliant sky, succeeds in discerning "falsehood" in Eugenia —and dares to look no farther. James' attitude towards this atmosphere, which so hedges the imagination, is conclusive. As the Baroness says, "Europe seems to me so much larger than America." [18]

Superficially a holist historical novel written out of a critical but sympathetic understanding of Hawthorne, *The Europeans* reveals the tendency of the holist historical novel in one of its metamorphoses to become pure surface, with no effort to represent historical forces or movements at all. As we shall see in *The Red Badge of Courage*, it is only a short step from the representation of atmosphere-as-idea to that of war-as-experience.

⌐ *Democracy*: Realities of Power and the Great Man

Democracy by Henry Adams is not an historical novel, but is that rarer phenomenon, the successful historian's novel. It is an historian's novel both in the sense that it was written by a master of the historian's craft, and because Adams successfully dramatizes the dilemma of the historical imagination in the second half of the nineteenth century. His heroine, Mrs. Lightfoot Lee, attempts to plumb the mystery of an historical reality that is increasingly resistant to analysis in either progressive or holistic terms. Though so thoroughly contemporary a novel of the Gilded Age in Washington that it was read at the time as a topical *roman à clef*, Adams consistently forces an historical perspective on the present through the consciousness of Mrs. Lee.

The novel begins as Mrs. Lee, oppressed by the ennui of her barren life after the death of her husband and child five years earlier, departs New York for Washington. An incongruity of tone and subject is apparent even in the first chapter, for while the narrative tone is witty and epigrammatic, and the setting is the salons and drawing rooms of the leisure class, the character of Adams' protagonist is so formidable, and her purpose so intense, that theme and manner seem constantly on the verge of tearing apart from one another. Like *Esther*, Adams' later novel of the conflict between skepticism and faith, *Democracy* is basically a novel of courtship and proposed marriage, the traditional themes of the sentimental novel; but both invoke the romantic muse only to gloomily celebrate incompatibility. Adams' heroines are no Jamesian innocents, but hardy intellectuals, characters of such mettle that they can cry, as does Mrs. Lee at the outset of *Democracy*, "To lose a husband and a baby . . . and keep one's courage and reason, one must become very hard or very soft. I am now pure steel. You may beat my heart with a trip hammer and it will beat the trip hammer back again." [19] The novel is somewhat reminiscent of a feminist version of *The Misanthrope*, or of Ahab wishing to "strike through the mask" in the decorum of a Jamesian drawing room.

Mrs. Lee's quest is an intellectual one, though she is constantly reminded that one cannot significantly change what one knows without changing what one is. Her purpose is described in tones almost deliberately echoing Thoreau's in going to Walden Pond; as Adams tells the reader, "she meant to get all that American life had to offer, good or bad, and to drink it down to the dregs, fully determined that whatever there was in it she would have, and that whatever could be made out of it she would manufacture." [20] Her goal is to pierce the heart of the mystery of stasis and change, seeking the balance of the lines of force in history:

She wanted to see with her own eyes the action of primary forces; to touch with her own hand the massive machinery of society; to measure with her own mind the capacity of the motive power. She was bent on getting to the heart of the great American mystery of democracy and government. . . . What she wished to see, she thought, was the clash of interests, the interests of forty millions of people and a whole continent, centering at Washington; guided, restrained, controlled, or unrestrained and uncontrollable, by men of ordinary mould; the tremendous forces of government, and the machinery of society, at work. What she wanted, was POWER.[21]

Like Ahab, having been struck down by an implacable and seemingly irrational fate, Mrs. Lee desperately seeks to make connections; in this case, the links between motive and consequence in the workings of the American government. When she wins her answer to the mystery, namely that power is its own justification and operates according to its own laws whether in Washington or Bucharest, she is appalled, but gratified intellectually. The answer relates motive and action, but only in terms of the absurd logic of courts the world over, where power is pure means, since its only goal is more power.

The source of Mrs. Lee's enlightenment is her erstwhile suitor, Senator Ratcliffe, the *éminence grise* behind a new Presidential administration, and the answer she learns is not so edifying as the way she learns it. Because her social role, as a young, attractive widow, is constantly entangled at cross purposes with her philosophical quest, and sexual politics are inextricably confused

with national politics, Mrs. Lee is able only by the greatest effort
to avoid becoming the captive of her role. This situation—salutary for her purposes as an investigator, Adams implies—is symptomatic of deep fissures within phenomenal reality. Mrs. Lee
learns from the rationalizations of Ratcliffe that one cannot connect words with actions, from observing the hapless President
that one cannot connect power with position, and from the whole
experience that one cannot connect the government with the will
of the people. This is the deeper message of *Democracy*, that
available means of historical explanation cease to satisfy the most
basic intellectual desires for consistency. The investigator is
thrown back from the search for a new theory of historical reality
onto an examination of her own motives. The quest for reality
becomes a quest for self-knowledge in isolation. At this moment
the historical imagination negates history. Mrs. Lee's closing
words have a wry appropriateness, as she says, "Oh, what a rest
it would be to live in the Great Pyramid and look out for ever
at the polar star!" [22]

Before Mrs. Lee reaches this seemingly determined indeterminacy of knowledge, however, the various schemes of historical
explanation are well-nigh exhausted. Classical progressivism finds
a spokesman in the character of Nathan Gore, suggestively modeled on Adams' friend Motley, whose misadventures in office-
seeking are recounted both here and in *The Education*.[23] The
doctrine Gore propounds is similar to that of Motley's essay on
progress and democracy:

I believe in democracy. I accept it. I will faithfully serve and defend it.
I believe in it because it appears to me an inevitable consequence of
what has gone before it. Democracy asserts the fact that the masses
are now raised to higher intelligence than formerly. All our civilization aims at this mark. We want to do what we can to help it. I myself want to see the result. I grant it is an experiment, but it is the
only direction society can take that is worth taking; the only conception of its duty large enough to satisfy its instincts, the only result that

is worth an effort or a risk. Every other possible step is backward, and I do not care to repeat the past.[24]

As Gore puts the progressive case, power is independent of individuals, and operates as a sovereign evolutionary force. Position may give temporary power to individuals, but they cannot prevail unless the forces of historical change are favorable. At the same time, however, these forces manifest themselves only through individuals, and it is just such a vehicle that Gore recognizes in Senator Ratcliffe, a man he woos as if he were more worthy of veneration than his reputation as a somewhat uncouth corruptionist would seem to justify. Gore's progressivism is balanced in the novel by a stout Old World holist, Baron Jacobi, who professes to see nothing but the corruptionist. For Jacobi, power is a game of courtly skill. It may be flagrant, or it may seek the hypocritical color of morality, but it is an entirely self-sufficient system. Hypocrisy, in fact, makes American power politics a suitable subject for Jacobi's satire, and his estrangement from progressive idealism produces a perspective which includes the holist's dénouement of decline and fall. As the Baron casts his cold eye a hundred years into the future, he foresees that "the United States will then be more corrupt than Rome under Caligula; more corrupt than the Church under Leo X; more corrupt than France under the Regent!" [25]

If Gore is a Motley and Jacobi a Voltaire, the figure of the Southerner, Carrington, is meant to evoke the lost synthesis of republican probity represented by George Washington. Carrington is the survivor of a shattered and defeated society, who looks back through Robert E. Lee to Washington as an exemplar of a kind of holist idealism. For Carrington, Washington was able to embody a national ideal because his life was rooted, in all its concrete details of manner and behavior, in a role which realized that ideal, the citizen statesman. In Washington the spheres of political and personal integrity were not separate, but rather the

General and the President represented the extension of a perfect private life into a public one.

Ratcliffe, the "high priest" of Washington politics, is modeled superficially on the progressive Great Man. Ratcliffe himself has a judicious appreciation of this model. He consistently attempts to present himself to Mrs. Lee as the agent of the National Will, as the selfless savior of the Union during the crises of Civil War and Reconstruction. Though Adams implies that self-aggrandizement is the real spring of the Senator's actions, Ratcliffe's own rationale has a significance independent of its truthfulness. A version of the progressive philosophy, it is laden with implications for the idealist structures of Bancroft and Motley. As Gore/Motley only half humorously observes in regard to the preeminent American Great Man, Washington, "we idolize him. To us he is Morality, Justice, Duty, Truth; half a dozen Roman gods with capital letters. He is austere, solitary, grand; he ought to be deified." [26] Portraying himself in the mold of the selfless savior, Ratcliffe reveals that his self-sacrifice lay in violating his own honor. He succeeds in impressing Mrs. Lee with his tale of saving a crucial election during the Civil War, though it required massive ballot tampering to do it. In his last attempt to exculpate himself from the charge of bribery, he swears that that too was done to save the party that was saving the Union.

Adams seems to be saying that the generation that survived the Civil War has converted an idealized view of progress and its agents into a progressive philosophy of dirty hands. Appalled by power, Adams exposes the paradoxical nature of the idealist progressives' concept of the unviolated agent of impersonal forces. Ratcliffe proclaims his own self-violation, his self-sacrifice being his only claim to exoneration. Mrs. Lee refuses to be so violated, and so, one surmises, Adams rejects the progressive rationale that would permit it.

Democracy proposes a series of historical perspectives on power, in each case seeking a more secure vantage point for viewing the bewildering action of the forces of power in the present. The Civil War is the most immediate point, but as Ratcliffe reveals, it still lends itself too easily to abstract conceptualization in the Grant years, and the impersonal categories by which Ratcliffe is a "protector of the Union" and Carrington is a "traitor" can mystify as well as enlighten. George Washington, as presented by the Virginian Carrington, is a more distant and more reliable angle of reference, by the very continuity of his character from private life to statesman. Washington's pecuniary honesty becomes the standard that Ratcliffe fails to meet in Mrs. Lee's eyes, for to her his improper acceptance of money is concrete and damning, while the appropriation of thousands of people's votes is abstract and forgivable.

Yet this conception of character by itself is unsatisfactory—if Washington is supposed to have been a great man as well as an honest one. Mrs. Lee—and Adams as well—is searching for a synthesis, and even the grandeur of the Founding Fathers is not entirely secure, because of the Adamsian sense, developed at such length in the *History*, that they could not control the power they professed to represent.

Forty years later, Henry Adams' brother Brooks was to link their grandfather John Quincy Adams with Washington, and claim that both statesmen were tapping the prime motor of the universe, that both in some ways represented the existence of a covenant with God. John Quincy Adams had wished, according to Brooks, to become a Representative Man of the Divine Will, himself the embodiment of the working out of an Idealist Law, banishing slavery and war. "In other words," Brooks writes, "he was disappointed because he was not supernatural." [27] In *Democracy*, Henry makes plain, the covenant—if covenant there has been—is broken, and the American government is run according to the laws of self-justifying power, or what Dos Passos was to call Power Superpower. No wonder that with the failure of the synthetic image of the Great Man, Mrs. Lee seeks a firmer his-

torical observation tower in the Pyramids, and Henry Adams
comes to yearn for the Virgin of Chartres.

↵ *The Red Badge of Courage*: The Search for Historical Identity

In style, in method, and in all that is distinctively *not* found in his
books, he is sharply defined, the expression in literary art of certain
enormous repudiations. Was there ever a man before who wrote of
battles so abundantly as he has done, and never had a word, never a
word from first to last, of the purpose and justification of the war? [28]

This passage comes from one of the most just appraisals of
Stephen Crane's literary achievement, H. G. Wells' essay in the
North American Review of 1900. It is especially apposite here,
for as a contemporary Wells could amply appreciate the force of
Crane's "enormous repudiations" of the conventionalized imaginative structures with which previous writers had attempted to
formalize historical apprehension. One need only place beside
The Red Badge of Courage the Civil War tales of Harold Frederic—who had lived through the conflict in upstate New York
—to estimate the extent of the discontinuity Crane represents.
In Frederic's tales, politics, religion, economics, manners, family,
and the moral economy of village life are all as much a part of
the war experience as battle. In the best of the tales, such as
"The Copperhead" and "The Deserter," the purpose and justification of the war are not only mentioned but brilliantly explored
and dramatized.[29]

This of course is the traditional distinction between the "realist" and the "naturalist." The designation of Crane as a "naturalist" has quite understandably irritated some critics by the loose-
ness of the label as applied to him and has driven others to
apologetics for, and new definitions of, that literary category. If
one is to be precise, one must admit that Zola is the only major

"naturalist" writer and that even Flaubert is an incipient romantic realist; while Americans like Crane, Norris, and Dreiser are hopelessly eclectic in their aesthetics. The distinguishing characteristic of the finer American craftsmen—James, Crane, Hemingway—has always been in the direction of purity of method rather than philosophical consistency. "Naturalisms" are in fact almost as diffuse as the "romanticisms" catalogued by Arthur O. Lovejoy.[30] Despite Crane's lack of philosophical clarity and precision, however, I believe there is adequate justification for calling the representation of man in the fictive world of *The Red Badge of Courage* naturalistic.

Crane's vision of reality, ironically conveyed through the consciousness of Henry Fleming, is limited to surfaces without essence, perceived by the protagonist in only the most egocentric way. Fleming apprehends war phenomenologically, and its significance is entirely subjective. The elaborate, nervously alive personalization of armies, death, war, weapons, and objects is a salient manifestation of this relationship of the protagonist to his surroundings. Henry Fleming is basically a "type," a being limited to extreme and profound "primary" emotions. His world is elaborately rendered but *only in detail,* and he has no ability to generalize rationally. Even when his perception of reality is not so animistic as to be extremely unreliable from the point of view of narrator and reader (since the battle—very deliberately—is not "rationalized"), the details inevitably *appear* in the form of personalizations. This is very important because this threatening distortion of the total reality is as much a consequence of the disintegration of conventional historical rationalizations of that reality as it is evidence of the projection of Henry Fleming's emotions onto his world. Crane called himself an "impressionist" and did indeed use a technique analogous to that of the French painters: the discrete details cannot remain separate, but *must* regroup themselves, both for Henry and for the reader. Consequently the objective vision of war is precise in details, but appears in sum not as a mosaic but as a blurred vision of monstrous, inexplicable forces.

Perhaps, again, one must finally beg the precise definition of terms like "naturalist" and "impressionist" that imply that the writer has a "philosophy" of life or history or aesthetics that he then applies to his artistic subject. Writers do have such philosophies and they offer enormous insights into their work. They are ultimately significant for fiction, however, only as embodied in narrative structure: plot, character, values, attitudes, incident, imagery, diction, the representation of "objective reality." The central nexus of meaning in *The Red Badge of Courage* entails a view of reality—naturalism—and the relevance of that view to a value cherished in the fictive world of the novel, namely heroism. The value is *philosophically* incompatible with the view of reality, yet in the structure of Crane's imaginative vision their relation is not only possible but necessary.

Crane maintains the superb tension of this paradox of heroism in a naturalistic world within an imaginative frame that is nether holist nor progressive but is the successor of both structures. As Edward Garnett, another contemporary with a sense of Crane's radical departure from previous writers of fiction, put it:

. . . of course, his art is strictly limited. We would define him by saying he is the perfect artist and interpreter of the surfaces of life. And that explains why he so swiftly attained his peculiar power, and what is the realm his art commands, and his limitations.[31]

The Europeans, in the light of *The Red Badge of Courage*, reveals how far the holist novel could go towards the representation of the historical past through surfaces. For Crane the surfaces have *become* reality, and the elaborate assumed world of relationships that justified the presentation of historical reality through manners no longer exists. Though the matrix of relationships essential to the holist frame is either shattered or masked, the dominance of fatal necessity in the author's attitude towards his subject persists, together with the character "types" that are as limited in their way as the role-bound characters of holist fiction.

In another sense, *The Red Badge of Courage* is the ultimate progressive historical novel, the result of a dialectical development parallel to that which led to *A Connecticut Yankee*. The progressive master concept of a predetermined law that in its optimistic and idealist aspect leads from the Whiggish attitudes of Motley and Twain to utopianism, leads just as ineluctably, in its materialist and "scientific" aspect, towards naturalism. The radical discontinuity of phenomena in Crane's vision of the historical past reveals *The Red Badge of Courage* as the heir to the revolution of the historical imagination most amply recorded in the writings of Henry Adams.

I earlier characterized Henry Fleming as a "type." By this I do not mean that he is intended to represent the "average." As Wells wrote, in agreement with George Wyndham:

. . . the hero of the *Red Badge* is, and is intended to be, altogether a more sensitive and imaginative person than the ordinary man. He is the idealist, the dreamer of boastful things brought suddenly to the test of danger and swift occasions and the presence of death.[32]

Henry Fleming is *a* type, just as the "loud," "cheery," "tall," and "tattered" soldiers are other types. Like the "types" of other naturalists—and especially of Brooks Adams—he is obsessively guided by certain dominant instincts, the most crucial of which are fear and self-esteem. Crane locates Henry Fleming in nature on a scale which defines the values governing the novel. I refer not merely to the hidden conflict with a seemingly implacable Nature, much of the explicitness of which Crane apparently excised before the first edition, but to the way in which he handles the central term of value itself: "man."

The most affirmative passage in the novel comes in its last pages: "He had been to touch the great death, and found that, after all, it was but the great death. He was a man." [33] Crane had deleted from the original manuscript the words "and was for others" after the final "great death." [34] Though suggestive, the sardonic phrase was superfluous. Crane had already delimited the nature of "man" in such a way as to make this ultimate assertion of Fleming's successful "initiation" extremely ironic. Crane's attitude toward "manhood" is crucial, as it is apparently the locus of value in the novel. "Manhood" is not the indestructible unit of moral justice essential to natural rights progressivism, the concept which had elicited from Hank Morgan the cry, "A man *is* a man, at bottom." [35] Nor is "man" role-defined. Surely a naturalistic exploration of citizen-soldiers in civil war is not a very congenial premise for holist treatment.

For Crane "man" is an intensely self-regardful and egocentric being who may alternatively be reduced to the level of an animal or liberated from his sense of self by experience. Animal imagery is too pervasive in the novel to require comment, but the moments of selflessness are rare, even in combat:

But there was a frenzy made from this furious rush. The men, pitching forward insanely, had burst into cheerings, moblike and barbaric, but tuned in strange keys that can arouse the dullard and the stoic. It made a mad enthusiasm that, it seemed, would be incapable of checking itself before granite and brass. There was the delirium that encounters despair and death, and is heedless and blind to the odds. It is a temporary but sublime absence of selfishness. And because it was of this order was the reason, perhaps, why the youth wondered, afterward, what reasons he could have had for being there.

Presently the straining pace ate up the energies of the men. As if by agreement, the leaders began to slacken their speed. The volleys directed against them had had a seeming windlike effect. The regiment snorted and blew. Among some stolid trees it began to falter and hesitate. The men, staring intently, began to wait for some of the distant walls of smoke to move and disclose to them the scene. Since much of their strength and their breath had vanished, they returned to caution. They were become men again.[36]

"Men again"—selfish, weak and frightened. The soldiers return to the consciousness of "men":

They looked wild-eyed, as if amazed at this furious disturbance they had stirred. In the storm there was an ironical expression of their importance. The faces of the men, too, showed a lack of a certain feeling of responsibility for being there. It was as if they had been driven. It was the dominant animal failing to remember in the supreme moments the forceful causes of various superficial qualities. The whole affair seemed incomprehensible to many of them.[37]

The condition of man as expressed in Henry Fleming is an uneasy suspension between the "dominant animal" and the rare "enthusiasm of unselfishness." To be a "man," to exist between the two in man's obsessive state of self-regard, he needs above all a social identity, a name. The ironic red badge of courage Henry "wins" behind the lines is only one example of his compulsive search for a name, a label of acceptation that he can wear. Since "man" defines himself neither by essence nor by role but by name, Henry seeks "a poignant retaliation upon the officer who had said 'mule drivers,' and later 'mud diggers,' for in all the wild graspings of his mind for a unit responsible for his sufferings and commotions he always seized upon the man who had dubbed him wrongly." [38]

The epic quality of Crane's vision of history is essential to appreciate; history is a great action in which man can achieve his name. Though rational analysis of the content of historic conflict (in this case, the meaning of the American Civil War) is absent, the *idea* of significant historical action remains and is implicit throughout the novel. One must recognize two versions of history in *The Red Badge of Courage*: the narrator's, with which we have so far been concerned, and the historical imagination of Henry

Fleming himself. Many "political" and historical novels assume that the issues and significance of an historical event or conflict are well understood by author and reader even while the author is undercutting the validity of rational analysis; a celebrated instance of this is Stendhal's description of the battle of Waterloo in *The Charterhouse of Parma*. Alternatively, and since Crane, there may be an implicit or proclaimed understanding between author and reader that the "issues" do not have any intrinsic relationship to what occurs on the battlefield, as in *A Farewell to Arms*. In Crane's novel, however, one is presented with a protagonist who has apparently never conceived what issues *might* be. The fantasy life that Crane sketches in for Henry Fleming, so strikingly similar to the girlhood dreams of Flaubert's Emma and the youth Volodia Kozel'tsov in *Sebastopol*, replaces thought. It is worth quoting in full Henry's early contemplation of his participation in "historic" battle, of acting a part in "one of those great affairs of the earth":

He had, of course, dreamed of battles all his life—of vague and bloody conflicts that had thrilled him with their sweep and fire. In visions he had seen himself in many struggles. He had imagined peoples secure in the shadow of his eagle-eyed prowess. But awake he had regarded battles as crimson blotches on the pages of the past. He had put them as things of the bygone with his thought-images of heavy crowns and high castles. There was a portion of the world's history which he had regarded as the time of wars, but it, he thought, had been long gone over the horizon and had disappeared forever.

From his home his youthful eyes had looked upon the war in his own country with distrust. It must be some sort of a play affair. He had long despaired of witnessing a Greeklike struggle. Such would be no more, he had said. Men were better, or more timid. Secular and religious education had effaced the throat-grappling instinct, or else firm finance held in check the passions.

He had burned several times to enlist. Tales of great movements shook the land. They might not be distinctly Homeric, but there seemed to be much glory in them. He had read of marches, sieges, conflicts, and he had longed to see it all. His busy mind had drawn for him large pictures extravagant in color, lurid with breathless deeds.[39]

Henry Fleming's "epic" conception of history is as tawdry as the future Emma Bovary's "romantic" conception of love. His juxtaposition of the "Greeklike," "Homeric," "crimson blotches on the pages of the past" with a Present prosaically dominated by "firm finance" reveals a sense of the Historic which is radically at odds with Crane's apparent reduction of the American epic, the Civil War. Henry appreciates, in his inchoate way, the "otherness" of History and its elevation; the grand abstract "fate" of peoples and cultures; the magnificence of events destined to pass into legend. And Crane shares with Flaubert the painful irony that is the naturalist substitute for tragedy: dreams and ideals can be isolated, typed, and dissected, but despite their shallowness they are still, and must be, the locus of value for the novelist. They are, in the naturalist world, all one has. They cannot be denied without denying all humanity to the protagonist. What can self-definition in such terms mean?

Henry Adams offers, in his *History*, an answer nearer to our purpose than does Flaubert. Adams allows Jefferson to define his task in his own words at the beginning of his administration. The "argument" of the *History* is a "scientific" evaluation of the validity of that self-definition in the face of ascertainable History. This seemingly objective criterion constitutes the "experimental" aspect of both the *History* and *The Red Badge of Courage*. It also constitutes the chief distinction between the "naturalisms" of *The Red Badge* and *Maggie*. History, and especially Henry's image of history—epic battle—offers the possibility of self-realizing action that does not exist in the naturalistic world of the lower depths. The concept of the great historic action of war lends to the battles of *The Red Badge of Courage* a crucial quality of significance absent from the mindless brawls of *Maggie*.

One must distinguish at this point between the two forms of

the reduction of historical reality that takes place in *The Red Badge*. First, there is the narrative reduction of a complicated historical conflict to the phenomena of military life—especially battle. The novel is, as Crane said, an "episode." The second reduction takes place in Henry's consciousness and is not simply due to the impressionistic character of Crane's art but reflects the profound imbalance in his protagonist's mind. Significantly, Henry's attitude towards war appears morbid when he deviates from his "epic" reverence for it. Thus just before he sees his first corpse he apprehends the anticipated battle not in the context of "epic" or "historic" values but in terms of "tragedies—hidden, mysterious, solemn." [40] Alternatively, war loses all social meaning and becomes "the red animal—war, the blood-swollen god." [41]

For Crane, Henry's self-definition can be meaningful only if validated by the conception of History that Henry holds. Thus Henry wishes to be assured that he is "a man of traditional courage." [42] Unlike some holist characters, his self-image and ideal self are not functions of a "tradition" but of an imaginative concept, the idea of a tradition. Crane's paradox of heroism in a naturalistic world raises a further question in this regard. Can a character be "rescued" from the limitations of a naturalistic "type" by the conditions and values of the epic?

It remains to be seen exactly what *kind* of value History has for Fleming, for even during Crane's short career as a writer his attitude towards the ethical and moral content of "historic" battle underwent a change. In *The Red Badge of Courage* Crane chose a protagonist resonant with historical meaning: the untried citizen-soldier, with all his implications for the portrayal of national character and the entrance of the common man on the formerly élite stage of history. Crane seems to depart from this attitude in his later writings, perhaps, as E. R. Hagemann sensibly suggests, as a result of his finally seeing war with his own eyes.[43] In a story of the Spanish-American War, "God Rest Ye, Merry Gentlemen," he describes an undramatic invasion:

It seemed made to prove that the emphatic time of history is not the
emphatic time of the common man, who throughout the change of
nations feels an itch on his shin, a pain in his head, hunger, thirst, a
lack of sleep; the influence of his memory of past firesides, glasses of
beer, girls, theaters, ideals, religions, parents, faces, hurts, joys.[44]

In *The Red Badge of Courage* the historical moment *is* the "emphatic time" and is still remembered as such—candidly—by
Fleming in the 1896 story "The Veteran."

   In Crane's later battle fiction one may see a progression similar
to that in Tolstoy's early works "The Raid" and *Sebastopol*. Beginning with a profound interest in the common soldier and the
"aristocratic" initiate, the narrator's sympathies and primary interest soon transfer themselves to the veteran and then to the
professional soldier. Tolstoy's admiration for the career officer
appears in his treatment of Khlopov of "The Raid" and is later
reaffirmed in his portrait of Kutuzov in *War and Peace*. Crane's
best-known pieces of war writing move towards an ethic more
easily describable as "military" than as "historical." They include
the repudiation of a nationalistic dilettante soldier in "Death and
the Child," the stoic élitism of "The Clan of No-Name," and the
Bierce-like indifference to death of "Marines Signalling Under
Fire at Guantanamo." "The Clan," indeed, comes closer to for-
mulating a soldier's "code" than any of the other stories, and
seems to be strongly influenced by Conrad.

   This late development of a "code" is significant. "Codes"—
like those of Tolstoy, Conrad, and Hemingway—formalize the
impingement of the public domain on private lives that war
brings, and they do so by limiting the historical resonance of war.
The importance of Crane's "code" is difficult to assess because
of the extreme shortness of Crane's career. Tolstoy and Conrad
began to explore this "code" mystique early in their careers and
then in *War and Peace* and *Nostromo*, were able to place it in
full historical perspective as an insight into an isolated form—

though an admirable one—of human behavior. For the historical novel a *central* concern with professional heroism is the antithesis of meaningful historical content. It scarcely needs to be mentioned that Tolstoy and Conrad were forty and fifty, respectively, when they wrote their masterpieces; Crane was twenty-two when he wrote his.

The Red Badge of Courage does not suffer from this final reduction of the meaning of history. It chronicles Henry Fleming's struggle for the "badge" and the place in history he must have as a "man." [45] He is not to define himself in the context of secret, privately meaningful tradition but in that of public, recorded history. Like the Henry Adams of the *Education*, family traditions are no guide—Henry Fleming can realize himself only at the very axis of History.

The battle in which Henry participates acquires its "epic" historical importance for him almost purely through the quality of his commitment to the army with which he fights. Just before he runs from the front Crane describes him as a "pestered animal, a well-meaning cow worried by dogs," and as "a babe being smothered." [46] In any case he is becoming something less than a "man." Incapable of rational thought about the battle, the army, or himself, he must reduce all his fellows to the "natural laws" of his own nature and call them fools. In Crane's ironic study of changing self-images, he shows Henry shedding the social category of "criminal" for the less threatening one of "animal." This phase of his quest, Fleming's brief attempt to find his place in the scheme of Nature without the aid of historic self-approval, comes to a grotesque end with his discovery of a corpse in the woodland Chapel and the death of Jim Conklin.

Fleming reaches the apogee of his flight from History after the death of Conklin, as he begins to hope for a Union defeat so that his own flight will not be a disgrace. This sequence of emotional turmoil can be characterized by the overused word "alienation" —an estrangement from communal ideals unaccompanied by a loss of desire for a purely nominal place in the community. When Henry finally abandons this hope he does so because he remains still an unconscious slave of community ideals:

His education had been that success for that mighty blue machine was certain; that it would make victories as a contrivance turns out buttons. He presently discarded all his speculations in the other direction. He returned to the creed of soldiers.[47]

Only after he has somewhat mindlessly "returned" to this "creed" is he struck in the head, guided back, and reborn as a soldier. Crane's irony is directed towards these polar drives: fear of death and the desire for social acceptance. War provides the highest expression of this tension. History, the human tradition of this tension, sanctifies the red animal, the blood-swollen god, by awarding laurels to those who face him.

Fleming's final apotheosis is achieved when he becomes the flagbearer—an inchoate escape from this primal dilemma.[48] The flag is the great and unique symbol of historical resonance in the novel—the guarantor that Fleming is participating in the "epic" of which he has dreamt rather than the private "tragedy" that he has witnessed and feared:

Within him, as he hurled himself forward, was born a love, a despairing fondness for this flag which was near him. It was a creation of beauty and invulnerability. It was a goddess, radiant, that bended its form with an imperious gesture to him. It was a woman, red and white, hating and loving, that called him with the voice of his hopes. Because no harm could come to it he endowed it with power. He kept near, as if it could be a saver of lives, and an imploring cry went from his mind.[49]

The flag is basically another animate force which he worships— the physical manifestation of the benign and invulnerable collective aura of History. The unconscious effects of education and training, implied in Henry's rejection of the notion of a Union defeat (a rejection profoundly unprophetic of the actual course of the battle, which the Confederates win), are predominant in these crucial moments. Henry is revealed by them as a "man," above the animals and aspiring to the condition of a selfless fanatic. Crane's ultimate irony lies here, perhaps, for man, attempting to define himself by History, recommits himself to the primal dilemma of the red animals versus the laurels, of the heroic ethic in a naturalistic world. Thus he never *defines* himself at all. The History revered in Everyman's consciousness, Crane is saying, offers neither roles nor ideals but rather the primitive enshrined as civilization.

The Red Badge of Courage is not, I think, a great historical novel. It is, however, as profoundly representative of the *fin de siècle* historical imagination as the writings of Henry Adams. The paradox of the validity of heroism in a naturalistic world is as vital as Adams' investigation of the fate—first in Jefferson, then in himself—of rationality in such a world. Whatever the twentieth-century historical novel might concern itself with, it would never entirely free itself of the vision of the human predicament in a world of power without a master.

Chapter Eight

THE CHANGING FORMS
OF THE HISTORICAL IMAGINATION
IN THE TWENTIETH CENTURY

*T*HE persistence of the progressive and holist frames of the historical imagination in American fiction after the cul-de-sac of *The Red Badge of Courage* can be attributed at least in part to the fact that novelists who emerged between Crane's last years and World War I did not see themselves as formal innovators. Only in an atmosphere of theoretical quiescence can one imagine the composition of works as vigorous in their epic certitude as Theodore Dreiser's Cowperwood Trilogy or as confidently polished as Edith Wharton's narratives of old New York. Dreiser and Wharton, wishing to investigate the imaginative possibilities of history, did not continue the naturalistic nihilism of Crane and wrote as if there were a knowable reality in the past that they could recreate in a unique way.

The cataclysm of World War I threw all the conceptual assumptions of Western culture open to question. The emerging modernist revolution in fiction sought its meaning in exploring the problematic nature of reality. From this post–World War I perspective, the reductionism of Crane's technique, which had erased conventional patterns, seemed to have cleared the decks for a literary art that would regard the past as well as the present as infinitely malleable.

Nineteenth-century American writers found cause for hope in their belief that American history represented a new start, discontinuous from the European past. In the twentieth century, writers as diverse as Henry Adams, Dos Passos, and Cather were concerned with a break within American history itself, dividing the troubling present from the more promising tradition of the earlier years. The present seemed to them, as to the naturalists before them, to be charged with a multiplicity of forces and to lack a feeling of organic unity that would enable an observer to establish a reliable chain of causality between one event or phenomenon and the next. Yet, despite this sense of discontinuities in both American history and the American present, twentieth-century writers perceive the passage of historical time as a continuum moving from the past through the present and on into the future in a way that nineteenth-century writers did not.

Working from an idealized vision of the American past, John Dos Passos presented the society of his era as divided into two nations, hopelessly alienated from one another and their common past. Three highly disparate writers, Willa Cather, Hart Crane, and William Faulkner, through willful idealist reconstruction, attempted to convert history into myth. This development, reflecting in part the shattering impact of the war on attitudes that Dreiser and Wharton worked with, did not result in abandonment of the holist and progressive frames. Indeed, Faulkner, testing the limits of historical idealism through multiple narrators, expressed the tension between the holist and progressive frames in a new form.

⌐ Character and Culture: Dreiser's Progressive Great Man

Confidence in the old imaginative frames is amply displayed in the work of Dreiser and of Wharton, the respective heirs of the progressive and holist schemes for historical narrative. Dreiser's affinity for the progressive mode in his Trilogy of Desire (*The Financier*, 1912, *The Titan*, 1914, *The Stoic*, 1947—published posthumously) is appropriate to his subject, the life and times of a financier. Dreiser modeled his hero on the traction magnate Charles Yerkes, and hence on an individual playing a crucial role in the economic revolution of late-nineteenth-century America. Dreiser's research on Yerkes was of notable dimensions, and, since he wrote in the era of political Progressivism, one would expect a fictional treatment of a notorious financial manipulator inevitably to have the flavor of historical muckraking. Only three years before the publication of *The Financier*, in fact, the socialist Bouck White had written a fictional "autobiography" of Uncle Dan Drew of Erie Railroad and gold conspiracy fame, replaying the old stock-waterer's machinations with immense detail and Twain-like earthy humor.[1] The idea of muckraking is important to Dreiser's trilogy, but his stake in detailed exposure is different from White's. Dreiser lays bare the demi-world of speculators, political bosses, and houses of assignation not to court the indignation of his middle-class audience but to confound it. For the massive documentation of the peculations, subornations, and amours of Frank A. Cowperwood could shock only if they were given a moral reality. Similarly, in *Sister Carrie*, the heroine's unpunished fall from virtue had eluded the middle-class ethical categories of the turn of the century. In the trilogy it is impossible to sit in judgment on the past, as Twain had on monarchy, because Dreiser's mountain of detail only reminds the reader that the "facts" are not the moral truth about a man, but only notes on a myriad of transactions too abstractly naked for moral content.

Dreiser's vision of history has two sides. One is the calculus of the transactions on the stock market and in the boudoir that measures the net change in society. The other is the shadowy world of fathomless motives that people bring to those transactions and the indecipherable consequences that issue from them in ways beyond prediction. Dreiser constantly reminds the reader that Cowperwood is not a mere calculator but is passionately serving an ideal self-image. And for all the apparent determinism of the trilogy, in the world of the novels the student of life may grasp its laws only when it is turned into a controlled game with its own rules. Young Frank at the fish market tank can tot up all the qualities and advantages of the deadly game between squid and lobster, just as he can later in his financial and love affairs where he holds all the cards. Yet the events that crucially change his life—a fire in Chicago, the sudden collapse of a great banking house, a whimsical trip to a provincial bordello, a sudden surge of civic-minded wrath—all are unpredictable and "catastrophic" in their consequences for him. All suggest an historical dialectic that evades the most careful scientific analysis.

The mysteriousness of historical force is surprising at first, for the trilogy, unlike *The Red Badge of Courage*, is built around the impingement of history not on the victim of limited illusions, but on his naturalistic opposite, the superman of unlimited desires. A grasp of the laws of historical change is beyond Crane's Henry Fleming. He consciously perceives only the illusion, and everything else pertaining to the historical situation of war and his instinctive responses to it is experienced only as monstrous and confusing forces within and without. Cowperwood can manage the game of action, but only within his area of security and competence, an area that cannot be protected from the historical juncture of forces that send him to jail in Philadelphia and frustrate his mature ambition in Chicago.

Robert Penn Warren has noted that Hank Morgan, in *A Connecticut Yankee in King Arthur's Court*, is a precursor of Cowperwood as a businessman hero.[2] Morgan and Cowperwood are also comparable as progressive Great Men, each at the controls of a vast game whose rules only they seem to understand completely. And each of these demigods sustains a crucial flaw or treasured illusion that blinds him to the complexity of his historical situation and almost levels him with Henry Fleming. The comparison reminds one of the degree to which the pure progressive idea of the Great Man is modified in these heroes so that force becomes a personal attribute, not a social or historical one. Thus, instead of containing within themselves the forces that will change history, they are only in a position to read history correctly—and there is no guarantee that they will indeed read it aright. The result of miscalculation is humiliation and grotesqueries: Twain's images of electrocuted knights, or the master of men and money blinded by a convict's hood in *The Financier,* or Cowperwood's end in *The Stoic*—his corpse smuggled into the lavish mansion he could not live in, the monument to his determination that shortly will be frittered away in petty litigation.

One of the most striking defects of Cowperwood as a hero of tragic stature is the banality of his speech; he frames his loftiest aspirations and his most ambitious seductions in terms blunt enough for the market floor. Cowperwood's mind is blinkered, so that he invests the conventionally prosaic—finance—with romance, and is immune to the tunes of glory that are the background music of the conventional historical imagination. Thus, during the Civil War, he can only watch with amazed detachment when a Henry Fleming-like workman is seduced by a brass band into unexpectedly joining a recruiting parade. Cowperwood does not seek with avidity the glory of a self-image reflected flatteringly back by the approval of society, the eminently holistic accolade. Nor does he, like the progressive Great Man, serve an advanced idea that is beyond social approval. For Dreiser, as for every naturalistic writer, there is a split between the realm of laws of matter and the realm of illusions and ideas, and the master of the laws of matter ceases to serve anything but himself. Hence Cowperwood's credo: "*I satisfy myself.*" [3] Though he may act in history, history cannot guarantee Cowperwood the possibility of significant action. Like Adams' Jefferson, he may only set his own goals and measure his success by self-derived standards.

Yet it is Dreiser's achievement that even Cowperwood's banality masks a mystery of character as profound as the forces of historical change and indeed part of the same process. Cowperwood is not simply the progressive superman, a vacuum in motion, a vessel in which the vectors of historical force meet. Dreiser's naturalistic perspective requires that even the superman be a type, and Warren properly emphasizes how, for Dreiser, Yerkes "exemplifies the class 'financier,' the class 'titan.' " [4] As a consequence, Dreiser develops Cowperwood's character as a complete *Gestalt*, integrally relating his orientation to finance, success, defeat, politics, social change, the pace of urban life, houses, possessions, art, women. Even when every detail is known and mastered, the essence of the type is still an enigmatic function of character, and thus the type retains the mysteriousness of the progressive Great Man.

In searching for an analogy to Dreiser's sense of Cowperwood's character, one must add to Hank Morgan and Jack London's Martin Eden, D. H. Lawrence's Gerald Crich, the doomed industrialist of *Women in Love*. Crich is uncannily like Cowperwood in his organizational genius, physical force, will to dominate, outer conventionality, anti-democratic social engineering, and acquisitive sexuality. It is appropriate that Dreiser and Lawrence, outsiders to the world of wealth and business, should both have been fascinated on the eve of the Great War by the character formation of the captain of industry. Both Dreiser and Lawrence deny that the role of the business entrepreneur is merely a shell emptied of content by the cultural decay so dear to the holist imagination. Instead there is an unexpected congruence of Dreiser's naturalistic compilation in Cowperwood and Lawrence's expressive form in Crich. Both reify the external role of the business giant in order to expose internal contradictions of will, illusion, and sexuality. These contradictions authenticate the character of this new version of the progressive Great Man. At the same time, they lay

bare the nature of the new culture that these characters represent
and do much to create.

⤳ Edith Wharton: The Constriction of Character by Holistic Cultural Roles

Edith Wharton's *The Age of Innocence* (1920) seems at first
doubly a museum-piece, presenting in measured tones a way of
life—indeed a class—long dead and reviving the holistic comedy
of manners as an artistic strategy. The familiar themes of the
holistic imagination all appear in this drama of New York society in 1870. Moreover, it was written approximately fifty years
after the time it portrays, a period, according to Scott, of ideal
distance for historical fiction; in his greatest series of novels, Scott
wrote about a period of Scottish history distant enough for the
personalities to have died, yet close enough to reconstruct around
cultural issues that were still resonantly alive. There is, in *The
Age of Innocence*, a Scott-like attempt to locate the source of
life of a particular culture, locked in time and space, through an
accurate portrayal of manners and mores rather than a search for
abstract beliefs. The strategy of culture contrast embodied in the
protagonist's choice between the female avatars of cosmopolitan
Europe and provincial New York is in the classic holist tradition,
traceable back through James and Cooper to Scott himself. The
elegiac note of decline and fall sounded in the title is struck repeatedly by witnesses to the disintegration of New York's tight-
knit social élite. Finally, the role-defined personality, the source
of whatever psychological richness the holist novel may lay claim
to, is unequivocally the center of the novel's drama.

Yet for all these formal similarities to classic holist historical
fiction, there is something ghastly about the revival, as if the author had indeed breathed fresh life back into a corpse. Certainly
Edith Wharton is not merely a pallid and faithful imitator of
Henry James. In her historical imagination there is a character-

istic view of human possibility and limitation that is all her own. Her novel revolves around Newton Archer, one of the best of his New York brownstone society, a man who is full of the passionate intensity of a lover, yet seemingly lacks the conviction to become one. His impulses to action are all self-frustrated. No scene in the novel is more revealing than that in which Archer, after having arranged a meeting in a deserted cottage with the exciting Countess Olenska that a less ingenuous age would call a tryst, waits for her to seduce him:

He spoke without shifting his position, without even turning to look at her: if the thing was to happen, it was to happen in this way, with the whole width of the room between them and his eyes still fixed on the outer snow.

For a long moment she was silent; and in that moment Archer imagined her, almost heard her, stealing up behind him to throw her light arms around his neck. While he waited, soul and body throbbing with the miracle to come, his eyes mechanically received the image of a heavily coated man with his fur collar turned up who was advancing along the path to the house. . . .[5]

The scene is repeated again and again through the novel, of Archer willing his passive seduction, only to accept the dashing of his hopes at the hands of one improbable *deus ex machina* or another with an alacrity and a joy in his own disappointment that suggests Edith Wharton is adding a new dimension of perversity to the deviousness of the role-dominated personality.

This motif of self-frustration is especially striking if one keeps in mind *The Europeans,* so clearly the forty-year-old ancestor of *The Age of Innocence.* In that novel the cosmopolitan native son, Robert Acton, had ambivalently admired his Baroness, but instead of renouncing his passion had cannily rejected her with her "infinitely larger" but troubling possibilities in order to marry a "particularly nice" girl from home.[6] James' novel had sustained the idea of action, however blind, narrow-minded and culturally determined. One may be appalled by the cultural barrenness of the right-thinking New Englanders of the 1840's, the novel seems to say, but one cannot deny them the ability to execute their wills. Archer, of course, never plays out his passion, and never even enjoys the dubious pleasures of renunciation. His part is to acquiesce at last in the determinations of his wife and would-be mistress and the collective will of the tribe of New York society.

Surfaces contain essence in *The Age of Innocence,* and they are described with all Edith Wharton's skill as a student of society and, not irrelevantly, as a pioneer interior decorator. In *The Red Badge of Courage,* the surface impressions of reality had seemed to prevent Henry Fleming from acting rationally. Surfaces that impinge upon Newton Archer prevent him from acting meaningfully at all, for in his crisis he can no longer read them nor control them. The line from Hawthorne through James to Wharton has been a steady diminution of the possibilities of meaningful action in favor of demonstrating the claustrophobic constriction that cultural roles produce. *The Age of Innocence* may prove the point too well, and raises the question of whether a literature of frustrated half-gestures does justice to psychological reality any more than Cooper's tales of para-military adventure.

Inevitably, the work of Edith Wharton, as surely as that of Dreiser, prompts questions about the source of the novel's drama. The shrinking of moral potentialities at the heart of the novel affects the relativity of cultural judgments so essential to the holistic historical imagination. *The Europeans* itself is a superb example of such relativism in its pure form. Its two most significant commentators, F. R. Leavis and Richard Poirier do not disagree that the central drama of the book issues from the contrast between cultures. Yet they so far differ that Leavis emphasizes the defeat of Eugenia (and Europe) while Poirier sees the sharpest edge of James' criticism reserved for the narrowness of the American culture in which she could not find a place.[7] In *The Age of Innocence,* however, the issue is not Ellen Olenska versus May Welland, for that would necessitate a state of consciousness capable of choice. The contrast between the New York society of the provincial Manson Mingotts and the Europe of the depraved Count Olenski is finely drawn. Yet Edith Wharton is so far from finding anything to praise in either that the issue moves from the viability of antithetical cultures to the question of how best to assess cultural values and the value of culture.

For this reason the greatest tension of the novel, the source of the special quality that makes *The Age of Innocence* the minor masterpiece it is, is that between the novelist and her protagonist. Archer presents the sole narrative point of view in a way of which Henry James' and Edith Wharton's friend Percy Lubbock, author of the influential *The Craft of Fiction*, would approve.[8] He strives with his role-blinkered perception for greater sight. Yet he is constantly under implicit judgment by the author, whose satirical purpose is masked in the objective language of the progressive science of cultural anthropology. Edith Wharton has risen out of the limited vision of her class, but since she has only borrowed the judgmental qualities of the progressive imagination, without subscribing to the myth of progress, her judgment on Archer and the society that produced him constantly threatens to lose the force of a controlling satiric purpose and become mere ambivalent nostalgia.

ᕫ Dos Passos: The Progressive Depressed by the Present

A tension between satiric purpose and nostalgia is not unique to Edith Wharton. John Dos Passos' *U.S.A.* (1938), bearing the same terminal relation to the classic progressive imagination as *The Age of Innocence* does to the holist, similarly attempts an objectivity that only succeeds in making the stance of the author more problematic. Logically, the satiric historical imagination would work from a fixed and well-understood point in time with a well-defined historical attitude, like that of Mark Twain's Hank Morgan. Northrop Frye has made a useful distinction between the allied modes of satire and irony, characterizing satire as "militant irony" in which the stance and standards of the narrator are clear. But he notes that "whenever a reader is not sure what the author's attitude is or what his own is supposed to be, we have irony with very little satire." [9] This distinction has a particular pertinence in U.S.A. for Dos Passos employs a satirical perspective only fitfully, directing it primarily at characters trying to climb the mythical American success ladder to money and power. But with regard to characters who, like himself, reject these values and seek progressive change he maintains an ironic distance that leaves the reader uncertain of his meaning. Dos Passos writes as a progressive profoundly depressed by the present, rendering history as banal as the private lives of his characters. For them the creation of selfhood through significant action is impossible, as all their action is rendered pathetic by Dos Passos' ironic distance. Nor can the sense of historical significance lift them out of themselves as it does Henry Fleming as flagbearer. In this twilight of historical significance, the realistic portrayal of heroes and victims alike can only emphasize their banality.

Thus Dos Passos' narrative techniques largely work somewhat sardonic variations on the terms of the progressive frame, especially his Biographies of the Great, most of whom are rather ordinary people who have been the vehicles for important ideas, but who do not "transcend" the limitations of their historical appearance in the old Idealist progressive sense.[10] Beyond the biographies there is the *roman fleuve* quality of the work as a whole, emphasizing the genetic flow of history, the role-lessness and mobility of the characters of the narrative sections, and, above all, the sense that Dos Passos' vision of society is working towards the classic progressive image of "two nations." This is trenchantly conveyed in one of the final autobiographical "Camera Eye" sections which records his reaction to the execution of Sacco and Vanzetti:

America our nation has been beaten by strangers who have turned
our language inside out who have taken the clean words our fathers
spoke and made them slimy and foul

their hired men sit on the judge's bench they sit back with their
feet on the tables under the dome of the State House they are igno-
rant of our beliefs they have the dollars the guns the armed forces
the powerplants

they have built the electricchair and hired the executioner to throw
the switch

all right we are two nations[11]

And it is echoed in the stark concluding image of the homeless
Vag thumbing his way down a highway while the wealthy vomit
their too-rich dinners in a luxury airplane above his head.

Yet *U.S.A.* contradicts the classic progressive attitude towards
the past by denying the two possible progressive attitudes towards present and future. It denies the future-oriented attitude,
for, however ample the justification, there is no hope held out for
revolution; the nation has not divided in preparation for the final
conflict but has rather frozen into permanently alienated spheres.
Even less can one discover the more complacent of the two progressive beliefs, which maintains, at least formally, that the past
culminates happily in the present moment.

The implications of progressivism without progress are revealed
most forcefully in the narratives of the characters' lives. When
Jean-Paul Sartre, in the most celebrated appreciation of Dos
Passos, declared that the time of *U.S.A.* was neither "fictional"
nor "narrative," but "historical time," he was insisting on Dos
Passos' superb rhetorical strategy for denying his characters' actions causality and potentiality.[12] Rather, they are reduced to the
kind of pure unconnected sequentiality which Henry Adams increasingly insisted upon as the only knowable thing in history,
with linked narrative replaced by "the jerky unreeling of a rough
and uneven memory, which sums up a period of several years in
a few words only to dwell languidly over a minute fact." [13]

This negation of potentiality is an extension of the banality of Dreiser's trilogy, for now history threatens to become as banal as the private lives of the characters. For unlike Cowperwood, the characters of *U.S.A.* are only victims with more or less imagination, who cannot create their selfhood through meaningful action, since all their action is rendered pathetic by Dos Passos' satiric distance. A sense of historical significance may lift them out of themselves for a moment as it did for Henry Fleming as flagbearer, but Dos Passos never spares them or the reader the let-down which follows such elation.

The *locus classicus* of this "hopeless" progressivism is, as indicated earlier, the works of Henry and Brooks Adams. In his memoirs Dos Passos recalls debating with E. E. Cummings in the early twenties over the value of *The Degradation of the Democratic Dogma*[14] and his strong dislike for it "because it went against the Walt Whitman-narodnik optimism about people I've never quite lived down." [15] One should note that Dos Passos' optimism was reserved for people, not for historical forces, of which the Adams brothers take an apocalyptic view in that volume.

Without an optimism about "people," Dos Passos would not have been able to eschew an Adams-like irony for the satiric tone of *U.S.A.*; but it is indisputable that the destruction of the nineteenth-century view of progress embodied in the works of Henry and Brooks Adams left a decisive mark on Dos Passos' historical imagination. There is the same ironic distrust of the "POWER" that Mrs. Lightfoot Lee went to Washington to seek,[16] combined with a dogged recognition that power and the laws of historical development could not be ignored. (Dos Passos' last hostile Biography in *U.S.A.*, that of the stock swindler Insull, is called, ironically, "POWER SUPERPOWER.")

Dos Passos also shares with Henry Adams a tortured belief that America's past tradition of progressive growth has been arrested. Though some of the technical experiments of *U.S.A.* may be attempts to imitate the "multiplicity" that Adams felt characterized twentieth-century America, the real similarity is the sense of usurpation they shared about the political and social leadership of the nation. Adams called it Caesarism. When Dos Passos, in "The Camera Eye" quoted earlier, indicts the "strangers" who have executed Sacco and Vanzetti and robbed us of "our storybook democracy," the effect is similar. There is no freedom in the present or potentiality in the future because any authentic and organic connection with the past has been ruptured.

The break in the progressive tradition finds its analogues everywhere in *U.S.A.*, and points the way to an understanding of the problematically aloof tone of the narratives. For Dos Passos' radical individualism, his anarchism, is a function of his demonstration of alienation in modern life in all its range of meanings, from the classic Marxian alienation of characters pursuing the big money rather than meaningful work to the Sartrean sense, in which they are alienated from their own past actions. Dos Passos' satire comes not simply out of a desire to judge and "correct" history after the progressive fashion, but to try, via pity and contempt, to bridge the gap of humanity in a world in which the atomistic multiplicity of Henry Adams threatens the idea of *human* history itself. As Dos Passos noted in 1937 about the work of the great German satirist, George Grosz:

A satirist is a man whose flesh creeps so at the ugly and the savage and the incongruous aspects of society that he has to express them as brutally and nakedly as possible to get relief. He seeks to put his grisly obsession into expressive form the way a bacteriologist seeks to isolate a virus. Until that has been done no steps can be taken to cure the disease. Looking at Grosz's drawings you are more likely to feel a grin of pain than to burst out laughing. Instead of letting you be the superior bystander laughing in an Olympian way at something absurd, Grosz makes you identify yourself with the sordid and pitiful object. His satire hurts.[17]

For Dos Passos, as for Edith Wharton, the sense of discontinuity that became dominant in the naturalist period and is best recorded in the work of Henry Adams and Stephen Crane has undermined the confident assumptions which underlay the old frames. The touchstone for both is Thorstein Veblen, who is in fact represented in *U.S.A.* by one of the most insightful and moving of the Biographies. Edith Wharton had absorbed Veblen's satirical use of the tactics of cultural anthropology and applied them to the holist belief that a culture may be apprehended by observing its surfaces. The satirical techniques of deflation by scientific description that Wharton explores in *The Custom of the Country*[18] acquire the historical dimension in *The Age of Innocence*.

Dos Passos' satire is also Veblen-like, but not because of a fondness for the master's rhetorical tropes. It is rather Veblen's radical insight, coupled with despair for the individual, that moves Dos Passos. Yet Veblen taught that there is a freedom that the threatening discontinuity of historical appearance can imply for the individual chronically alienated from a conventional society. Such an individual, said Veblen, "becomes a disturber of the intellectual peace, but only at the cost of becoming an intellectual wayfaring man, a wanderer in the intellectual no-man's-land, seeking another place to rest, farther along the road, somewhere over the horizon." [19] Such an acceptance of alienation by Dos Passos, who was often to characterize himself as a Seeker in later years, provides the extraordinary energy to the despair that sustains the satire of *U.S.A.*

↜ Concepts of Idealist Reconstruction

A resurgence of the historical imagination in American literature did occur—in the work of Willa Cather and, especially, in that of William Faulkner. What distinguishes these novelists from the naturalists may best be understood through consideration of the analogous development in historical theory. The Italian philosopher-historian Benedetto Croce and his English follower and popularizer R. G. Collingwood articulated a new idealist emphasis.[20] Their thinking derived from F. H. Bradley's earlier recognition that history is primarily a matter of critical interpretation. Hart Crane's poem *The Bridge*, a deliberate effort to create a myth from the materials of American history and culture, reflects this new idealist current.[21]

Both Crane's poem and the idealist concepts of these philosophers of history signalize an effort to free the historical imagination from the scientism of the naturalistic perspective by proposing history, in its spirit, methods, and concerns, as an antidote to science. History was to be redefined in such a way as to evade the seeming blind alley of either the fact accumulation or system-building associated with science—the result of the intrusion of a materialist basis in the previously idealist progressive tradition.

The idealist philosophers of history contributed a special emphasis to a central proposition, namely, that true history is not "out there," but is a function of the consciousness of the historian. This idealist historical strain has American roots going back to Ralph Waldo Emerson, who wrote, "We are always coming up with the emphatic facts of history in our private experience and verifying them here. All history becomes subjective; in other words there is properly no history, only biography." [22] F. H. Bradley insisted in 1874 that the historian could only infer cause and effect in history by analogy with his contemporary experience, and at the same time could only be freed of the seemingly whimsical subjectivity of such a proceeding by his awareness of what he was doing. It is not unlikely, by the way, that Bradley's thought had a direct impact on the development of the historical imagination in American literature between the wars; for T. S. Eliot, whose *The Waste Land* (1922) epitomized a whole generation of works of the poetic consciousness in history—including Ezra Pound's *The Cantos*, William Carlos Williams' *Paterson*, and *The Bridge*—had written his doctoral dissertation on Bradley.[23]

Benedetto Croce put the case succinctly by radically distinguishing "chronicle" from history, maintaining that history could only be written when the past event was entirely relived in the imagination:

Do you wish to understand the true history of a neolithic Ligurian or Sicilian? Try, if you can, to become a neolithic Ligurian or Sicilian in your mind. If you cannot do that, or do not care to, content yourself with describing and arranging in series the skulls, implements, and drawings which have been found belonging to these neolithic peoples.[24]

R. G. Collingwood, attempting to simplify the idealist view of historical reconstruction still further in a programmatic way, insisted on the non-progressive and eternally repeatable nature of human thought. To the earlier idealist philosophers' insistence that rethinking the thoughts of the past was *all* history could be, Collingwood added the confident assurance that the thoughts were available for rethinking, that historical knowledge, in the only meaningful sense of the term, was within grasp.

Hart Crane: Idealist Myth-Making Through Language

Idealist reconstruction as an explicit reaction to scientific naturalism may be seen in Crane's *The Bridge* (1930), a poem that is not so much an attempt to rethink the past (except in certain sections, like "The Dance") as it is an attempt to develop an idealist counter-myth to the reductionism of the naturalistic method. Crane sought in his poem to create a "mystical synthesis" of "the Myth of America." Rejecting what he called the "viewpoint in any history primer," he explained, "What I am after is an assimilation of this experience, a more organic panorama, showing the continuous and living evidence of the past in the inmost vital substance of the present." [25]

This idealist impulse is essentially willful, for the counter-myth cannot simply be recognized as a pattern inherent in the past, but must be deliberately created, or read into it. The implications behind this notion become clearer if one compares it with the quasi-scientific detachment of the narrative voice in the work of Dreiser, Wharton, and Dos Passos. For them, the narrative mission is presented as one of discernment and recording, rather than creation; they are to be praised for how much they know. With the writers who recast the old frames in an idealist mold, like Willa Cather and William Faulkner, the narrative energy is concentrated not in how much, but in *how* the narrator knows the past.

Crane said in an essay that *The Bridge* was written in defense of science, that rather than being an attempt to negate the machine, it was an effort to acclimatize and absorb it. Yet the poem is also "beyond all sesames of science," [26] because the crucial aspect of the scientific historical consciousness for Crane was not its technology (in Adamsian terms, the dynamo) but the acceptance of discontinuity as an absolute that that technology seemed to represent. The willfully "transcendent" aspect of Crane's ambition grows out of this concept.

Explicitly, he set out to create a myth to counter what he felt was the "negation" represented by *The Waste Land*. It is as if he were sending the shade of John Roebling, the designer of the Brooklyn Bridge, to do battle with the equally Teutonic spirit of Oswald Spengler. Yet, instead of creating a myth of technological progress as his answer to an image of spiritual decline, Crane shifts the locus of his work to the plane of language in order to transvalue perceptible decline by the very symbols of technological progress. Like the Russian mystic Ouspensky,[27] he affirms the "broken world" [28] of discontinuous phenomena in order to find a "spiritual" unity higher than the debased "general laws" of naturalism.[29] In this way he creates an historical myth from the impedimenta of technology—Brooklyn Bridge, the airplane, the subway. The transformation at which Crane aims is not to be resolved in terms of a new philosophical theory of history, but on the level of language, and one's assessment of the success or failure of *The Bridge* depends largely on how well one believes Crane's language experiment to have succeeded.

↶ Willa Cather: Idealist Transcendence of Conflict

After World War I, Willa Cather, like Edith Wharton, turned towards historical subjects, most notably in *Death Comes for the Archbishop* (1927), *My Ántonia* (1918), *Shadows on the Rock* (1931), and *Sapphira and the Slave Girl* (1940). In her work one may see the implications of idealism seized as an antidote to historical scientism, rather than as the key to the science of history as it had been in the old progressive frame of Bancroft, Motley, Twain, and the Whig historians. Willa Cather writes within a basically holist tradition; she is concerned in *Death Comes for the Archbishop* with the clash of races and cultures, the cultural shadings separating Spanish, Indians, and Anglo-Americans. Yet it is a small society as a whole unit that most deeply engages her (this is also true of *Shadows on the Rock*, a novel of seventeenth-century Quebec), and her attention is lavished on all the peculiarities of custom and behavior that mark off an encapsulated time as unlike time-present. She is most deliberate in joining the traditional holistic belief in the absolute barriers between one era and another with the catastrophic note of Henry Adams. "The world broke in two in 1922 or thereabouts," she wrote, and her books clearly project a past from which she is separated by an unbridgeable chasm.[30]

Implicitly accepting Adams' polarization of history into the unified reign of the Virgin and the discontinuous multiplicity of the age of the Dynamo,[31] both *Death Comes for the Archbishop* and *Shadows on the Rock* appropriately have a Catholic orientation. Not only are the principal characters Roman Catholics— in *Death Comes for the Archbishop* they are missionary clerics —but there is an attempt to achieve the sense of stillness and unconcern for historical change that marks the great masterpiece of Catholic historical fiction, Manzoni's *The Betrothed.* While a strong historical sense plays a role in all of Willa Cather's work, *Death Comes for the Archbishop* constitutes her purest attempt to reimagine a past that is not only usable but desirable.

Death Comes for the Archbishop is the story, conveyed through ten anecdote-like installments, of two Catholic missionaries in the American Southwest in the mid nineteenth century. The aristocratic, intellectual Father Latour and the warm, earthy Father Vaillant come to know their new parishioners in these tales as they carry on busy careers till their deaths—each an archbishop by now—in a West which they have done much to Europeanize, if not to civilize. The characters are most attractive, and the descriptions of New Mexico are superb in a painterly way; yet the tale of men cultivating a civilization in the semi-wilderness is told too much like *The Swiss Family Robinson* and not enough like *Robinson Crusoe.* The priests fit their roles too well; there are no conflicts between them, and none within, other than those which their roles dictate as commendable; and even these are resolved in too exemplary a manner. Thus, *Death Comes for the Archbishop* gives the unfortunate appearance of marrying the worst features of the Catholic hagiography and the Protestant success story.

This is a severe judgment, but it is important to understand what brought such a finely perceptive writer to such a pass in her most ambitious work. In part, the strength of all Willa Cather's fiction is to be found in her graphic detail, a description of people and things which is not so much holistic as it is the detail of interior decorating, of landscaping, or portraiture; a description of discrete beings, not of relationships. Because the original holist imagination was quintessentially a study of relationships, even at its most conservative it could not ignore the tendency of human relationships to alter according to their own dynamics. In those changing relations and in the threat of change lies the heart of the historical artist's drama.

Perhaps the best critique of the naturalistic form of the historical imagination is that of Georg Lukács in speaking of *Sa-lammbô*, Willa Cather's favorite novel by Flaubert, whom she admired deeply:

What then can art take from a past conceived in this way? This past appears, more so even than the present, as a gigantic iridescent chaos. Nothing is really objectively and organically connected with the objective character of the present; and for this reason a freely roaming subjectivity can fasten where and how it likes. And since history has been deprived of its real inner greatness—the dialectic of contradictory development, which has been abstracted intellectually—all that remains for the artists of this period is a pictorial and decorative grandeur. History becomes a collection of exotic anecdotes.[32]

And yet *Death Comes for the Archbishop* has a particular quality which is valuable and unique in American literature. The novel is an historical pastoral that attempts to overcome its unreality by an effort of pure idealist imagination. Near the end there are two crucial passages. Willa Cather identifies the conception of time in the novel in the idealist manner of Bradley and Collingwood:

During those last weeks of the Bishop's life he thought very little about death; it was the past he was leaving. The future would take care of itself. But he had an intellectual curiosity about dying; about the changes that took place in a man's beliefs and scale of values. More and more life seemed to him an experience of the Ego, in no sense the Ego itself. This conviction, he believed, was something apart from his religious life; it was an enlightenment that came to him as a man, a human creature. . . . He was soon to have done with calendared time, and it had already ceased to count for him. He sat in the middle of his own consciousness; none of his former states of mind were lost or outgrown. They were all within reach of his hand, and all comprehensible.[33]

The consciousness does not seek the past, but rather frees itself from time. The Ego separates itself from its own past, as well as the communal past. Latour's whole experience is a frontier one, but more than that it is an essentially repeatable one, as old as the Church or as old as mankind. For Willa Cather the past is close to the present in an entirely new way. The old progressive frame had seen all men as identically gifted in rights, reaction to oppression, desire for liberty and truth. The new historical idealism emphasizes the repeatable nature of thought and detaches it entirely from the notion of conflict and progress generated by the struggle for natural rights. For Cather, the eternal aspects of consciousness are entirely compatible with historical stasis.

The other passage is an anecdote of the appearance of the Holy Family to the famous missionary of the distant and miraculous past, Father Junipero Serra. The Family had manifested itself in the guise of simple peasants. The worldly Father Latour admires the story aesthetically:

There is always something charming in the idea of greatness returning to simplicity—the queen making hay among the country girls—but how much more endearing was the belief that They, after so many centuries of history and glory, should return to play Their first parts, in the persons of a humble Mexican family, the lowliest of the lowly, the poorest of the poor,—in a wilderness at the end of the world, where the angels could scarcely find Them! [34]

The tale projects in little the impulse of the novel as a whole, in which escape from the present is not so much a defect as a frank goal of art. In this sense *Death Comes for the Archbishop* (though not comparable as an artistic achievement) is as willful an attempt to transcend the present through the past as *The Bridge*.

ᴗ Faulkner: An Historically Founded World

The works of William Faulkner constitute the most splendid achievement of the historical imagination in twentieth-century American letters. His collected fictions of the past and present of Yoknapatawpha County embody a countermyth to the scientific progress and literary naturalism that were dominant in the rest of American culture, a countermyth with foundations deeper than those of Crane's *Bridge* and more catholic than Willa Cather's pastoral. The Yoknapatawpha saga surpasses the cumulative works of even Cooper or Hawthorne in creating an historically founded world, because Faulkner is able to make the past function in a much more organic and less rhetorical way in his novels and stories of the present.

Despite all his emphasis on the social and individual past and his experimentation with the presentation of memory and the passage of time through structural and stylistic means, only four of his novels (leaving aside some short stories and segments of others) significantly trespass into the unremembered past of the nineteenth century, that past which must be imagined afresh if it is to exist at all in the present. Two of them, *The Unvanquished* and *Go Down, Moses*, are amalgams of short story and novel, products of Faulkner's second great burst of creativity. Together with *The Hamlet*, these works fill in the gaps in the background of Yoknapatawpha—especially *Go Down, Moses*, in which Faulkner chronicles the relations of white and black to each other and to the land through the history of the McCaslin family from the eighteenth century to World War II.

⤳ The Leap of Inference

The cornerstone of Faulkner's historical edifice, however, is *Absalom, Absalom!* (1936). In this novel written at the height of his powers, Faulkner investigated the nature of historical narrative with an intensity unmatched by any other American work. Depending on a leap of inference rather than the proof of laws based on accumulated data, Faulkner attempts to create a countermyth through the idealist imagination. He also reflects critically on historical idealism at the very time he appears to be embracing it. Faulkner uses multiple narrators in his reconstruction of the career of Thomas Sutpen and his descendants, in part to test the restorative and therapeutic powers of historical idealism. Thus while Crane attempted an idealist transcendence of an inimical historical reality and Cather sought to create a timeless realm, Faulkner subjects the efforts of his narrators—his surrogate historians—to a searching and occasionally ironic critique. The two greatest American historical novels, *The Scarlet Letter* and *Absalom, Absalom!*, are so in part because they embody to the fullest degree a tension among the possibilities of the historical imagination of a given time. The tension between the holist and progressive frames, maintained with such architectural symmetry in *The Scarlet Letter*, is present in a new form in Faulkner's masterpiece. Faulkner adds an inquiry into the nature of the historical understanding that probes at its psychological roots.

Faulkner is truly one of the twentieth-century masters in the self-reflexiveness of his major fiction, and in *Absalom, Absalom!* the relationship between the tale told and the manner of telling is of inescapable importance. The tale is that of Thomas Sutpen, his wives and children, and those who are vitally affected by him. The telling is performed directly by Rosa Coldfield, sister of his second wife, by Mr. Compson, by Quentin Compson, and by Quentin's college roommate, Shreve McCannon. At one or more removes, parts of the story are also told by Quentin's grandfather, General Compson, and by Sutpen himself. Tale and telling seem to have little in common except an atmosphere of violence and an unresolved stress that produces the impression of hysteria.

⌐ Faulkner's Holist Social Imagination

To look at the tale first. Faulkner has a distinctly holist social imagination. He values the culture of the South even while he despairs of it. Race, tradition, custom, and personal and moral style are the important referents for his social sense, just as culture clash is often his main drama and decline and fall his dominant

theme. It is usually mores, not institutions or ideas as such, that
critically affect moral choices in his work. As in Cable's *The
Grandissimes*, it is racism, not slavery, that corrupts the consciousness of Sutpen and the other characters. Sutpen is a discordant figure largely because he is outside the holist web of culture—even the rather primitive frontier culture of antebellum
Mississippi—and some of the most lively critical disagreements
have arisen over the degree to which Sutpen is representative of
the culture he seems to dominate, awe, and defy. The threat of
renegadism hangs around many of Faulkner's most vital creations
—Popeye, Joe Christmas, Flem Snopes, Lucas Beauchamp, Ike
McCaslin—and much of Faulkner's power of characterization has
always depended on this traditional resource of the holist writer.

In Faulkner's work the theme of renegadism is often associated
with racial false consciousness, as it was for the great nineteenth-
century writers. In Melville's *Benito Cereno*, for example, Captain Delano perceives Cereno as a renegade as long as Delano is
under the holist illusion of slavery as a harmonious system. This
racial false consciousness is destroyed in the pivotal scene when
the slave Babo leaps knife-in-hand after Don Benito. This dramatic dropping of the masks forces Delano to recognize the merciless dialectic of domination that is slavery, a dialectic that can
be adequately understood only in progressive terms.

In Faulkner's image of Southern history, the fact of race is the
reality that outrages progressive idealism and upsets holistic structures of cultural identity. In *Light in August*, for example, the
ambiguous fact of Joe Christmas' existence endangers the false
ideals of all the characters. Heirs of the progressive revolutionary
world-view, their ideals are byproducts of Calvinist ideology. For
Hightower it is the heroic ideal that is violated; for McEachern
the ideal of a just God; for Byron Bunch the ideal of innocence;
for Joanna the ideals of social uplift; for Percy Grimm the fascistic
ideal of social order; and for Gavin Stevens the ideal of reason.

Even the two characters who are less dominated by an ideal

than by a belief in the cursed nature of the blacks are tormented by reality. Joanna Burden's grandfather believed that the blacks were a curse to be borne by the whites, while the grandfather of her lover Joe Christmas believed they were a curse to be exterminated. The ideals of both violent ancestors negate black people as not fully human. This root concept, the essence of the false consciousness Faulkner analyzes, renders the actual human existence of the blacks a potent outrage to all these ideals.

In this holistically conceived society, Sutpen is that progressive anomaly, the self-made man, the stuff from which Faulkner's countermyth is fashioned by his narrator-historians. Social mobility is in a sense characteristic of the frontier society in which Sutpen arrives, but Faulkner makes it very clear that the nature of his rise offends the community's sense of values. He endures years of distrust and humiliation, such as his arrest or the assault on his wife on their wedding night, before he can achieve the eminence of an elected commanding officer in the Civil War. The self-made man as a type is of course a contradiction, as has been seen with Hank Morgan and Frank Cowperwood, for the image denotes a man created by his own exertions but to another's model. Classically, it has designated the bourgeois who gains the wealth to ape the aristocrat. Unlike the Scottian or Cooperian middle-of-the-road hero, the self-made man in historical fiction tries by sheer will to create the social and psychological security that the middle-of-the-road hero gains after proof of courage and loyalty. As Mr. Compson observed:

yes, he was underbred. It showed like this always, your grandfather said, in all his formal contacts with people. He was like John L. Sullivan having taught himself painfully and tediously to do the schottische, having drilled himself and drilled himself in secret until he now believed it no longer necessary to count the music's beat, say. He may have believed that your grandfather or Judge Benbow might have done it a little more effortlessly than he, but he would not have believed that anyone could have beat him in knowing when to do it and how.[35]

It is the hollowness of Sutpen's performance and career that seems to cause him anguish, for he is as much of a role-seeker as Hawthorne's Tobias or Dimmesdale. He differs from them chiefly in having a plan, a program. David Minter has written about Sutpen's Gatsby-like qualities;[36] like Gatsby, Fitzgerald's social climber, he is an idealist whose problem, according to General Compson, is "innocence." For Sutpen the role of gentleman is conceived in material terms—lands, a great house, slaves, a male heir, and "—incidentally of course, a wife" [37]—but it is presented as an heroic ideal. It cannot be realized in material terms alone, for the security he seeks is less economic than psychological. As Sutpen explained to General Compson shortly before precipitating his final disaster:

> either I destroy my design with my own hand, which will happen if I am forced to play my last trump card, or do nothing, let matters take the course which I know they will take and see my design complete itself quite normally and naturally and successfully to the public eye, yet to my own in such fashion as to be a mockery and a betrayal of that little boy who approached that door fifty years ago and was turned away, for whose vindication the whole plan was conceived and carried forward to the moment of this choice, this second choice devolving out of that first one. . . .[38]

Sutpen is neither a born gentleman like Sartoris nor a squatter like Wash Jones. Like the progressive Great Man, he is not the representative of a class but the extrapolation of the possibilities of a class, in this case the class of Wash Jones moving in the direction of heroic acquisitiveness. For a poor white in the world of *Absalom, Absalom!*, there are only two directions to take to resist negation by the wealthy and the self-hate that that negation brings. One may attack the blacks as an available symbol of oppression, as when Sutpen's father joins in beating the slave of a wealthy and hated planter. The other course—Sutpen's—is to become one of the oppressors. It is ironic but appropriate that Sutpen goes to General Compson to ask where the "mistake" [39] had been in his design—as if the kind of man he had tried to copy in externals could advise him on a question of self-ordained identity.

There is a puzzle, then, at the base of the novel, for Faulkner's analysis demands that Sutpen be interpreted as a representative figure, while at the same time making him expressive not of unity but of paradox. Miss Rosa is the first to attempt to interpret him. She sees him as a "demon" agent of the moral flaw of the South, the "moral brigandage" [40]—Mr. Compson's term—that explains "why God let us lose the War." [41] This echoes the theme of blind acquisitiveness, the expression on a larger scale of the "two hundred years of oppression and exploitation" that General Compson refers to.[42] At the time *Absalom, Absalom!* was published, books as varied as *Gone With the Wind* (1936) and W. J. Cash's *Mind of the South* (1941) were also developing the same Beardian theme of the Second American Revolution: that having been defeated at the hands of the industrialized North, the New South would grow out of bourgeois seeds in the Old. Miss Rosa sees as far as any into the countermyth, though she lacks the factual information to verify it.

⌐ The Two Major Actions and Their Interpretation

It is left to the novel's other narrators to find an alternative to the Lost Cause myth of the Old South and test the limits of historical understanding. There are two major actions that they must interpret. The first is the appearance, rise, and fall of Thomas Sutpen. The second is a murder: the killing of Charles Bon by Henry Sutpen at Sutpen's Hundred at the close of the Civil War. As in *The Brothers Karamazov*, the murder lies at the very center of the novel. Sutpen's career is fairly well documented, although crucial revelations are delayed. We have the testimony of two eyewitnesses to his progress, and his own view of his life, as given on two occasions to General Compson. The problem is to understand him through the design which, like Adams' Jefferson, Twain's Morgan, and Dreiser's Cowperwood, he projects as his life program. In this interpretive effort judgment focuses on the qualities of insight and blindness that have gone into the framing of Sutpen's plan and the skill, courage, and ruthlessness with which the plan is executed.

The interpretation of the murder is substantially different. Instead of creating a new, complex paradigm—the progressive career in a holistically conceived society—the narrators develop a pattern of interpretation that works towards the banishment of complexity, towards unitary truth. As several critics have remarked, *Absalom, Absalom!* is a detective story, though the question that consumes the last part of the book almost exclusively is not whodunit but why. The identities of the murderer and the victim are well established; only the motive is lacking. The search for a motive gains significance because in a holistically conceived society there is never any question of motives, since characters seek to meet the demands of their roles. As Natty Bumppo puts it, Iroquois and Delaware kill each other to satisfy "natur." Instead of defining the contours of a role, the narrators—and especially Quentin and Shreve—attempt to isolate a single motive, to establish a dialectic of Sutpen's will and the resistance of his children to the destiny he has designed.

As Ilse Dusoir Lind has noted, the nature of Sutpen's "trump card," upon which hangs the motive for Henry's act, is the central mystery of the novel.[43] The reader moves from Miss Rosa's perplexed inability to understand what whim of Sutpen's could have canceled the marriage of Bon and Judith to narrators who possess more information. Mr. Compson uncertainly suggests Bon's marriage to his black mistress in New Orleans as an adequate insult to Henry. With additional information—supplied by Quentin after actually talking to Clytemnestra and Henry— Mr. Compson is then able to elaborate on the idea that it was the threat of incest involved in the proposed marriage that prompted Sutpen's—and Henry's—action. Finally, Quentin and Shreve together imagine how Henry would react to the knowledge that Bon is his brother.

Finally, two surmises knit the story together: the first, that Bon knows his relationship to Sutpen, and the second, that the reason Sutpen put aside his first wife was that she was part black. Both surmises have a high degree of aesthetic and historical probability, but neither is documented, and a strong case could be made against either. For example, Quentin says that "nobody ever did know if Bon ever knew Sutpen was his father or not." [44] When Shreve and Quentin embroider the story in such a way that he would have *had* to know, they are led by their sense of probability, not by new knowledge. The same is true for Bon's Negro blood—it is a probable motive for Sutpen to have set aside his wife, but illegitimate birth would have been, too.

Cleanth Brooks has argued vigorously for the certainty of the information about Bon's Negro blood.[45] Brooks points out that on the night of his visit to Sutpen's Hundred, Quentin has learned new information that, when added to his father's knowledge, changes the elder Compson's explanation of Sutpen's and Henry's motives. Yet there is no indication that Mr. Compson knew race to be the difficulty, for he specifically refers only to the knowledge that Bon is Sutpen's son. It is farfetched to imagine that if Quentin learned that Bon was part black from Henry or Clytie, he would have withheld that information alone from his father. In a dramatic narrative spoken by neither, Shreve and Quentin realize together that Sutpen's "trump card" was telling Henry that Bon's mother is part Negro. They perform this ultimate act of historical reasoning together, and afterwards their lines of thought diverge.

The allusions within the tale to the stories of the House of David and the House of Agamemnon become clearer when one follows the steps of thought that lead to the motive for murder. In the Biblical legend of David there is incest, fratricide, adultery, and the rebellion of a son against his father. The sins of the father are juxtaposed with those of the son. In the Agamemnon tale as recounted in the Oresteia, there is infanticide, adultery, regicide, and matricide. Both tales are set against a background of war and test the most basic taboos of their respective cultures. The author of the Book of Samuel and Aeschylus attempt to balance taboos against one another for the respective weight they should have as cultural imperatives. The search for a motive in *Absalom, Absalom!* is a similar quest, with the young historians acting as cultural anthropologists sifting Southern mores in order to comprehend an act of passionate premeditation.

This then is the problem: "What would impel a man to kill the brother whom he loves?" Given a situation in which Henry could have been outraged by the threat of either bigamy, incest, or miscegenation, which constitutes the motive? For a Henry holistically conceived, the demands of his role—his honor—might have forced him to act for any of these reasons or *all three at once*. Yet Shreve and Quentin, in detective-story fashion, seek to isolate one.

The Detective Story and Idealism

The detective story analogy, which was R. G. Collingwood's most effective example of historical idealism, has especial relevance to the kind of thinking that Shreve and Quentin engage in and invites closer scrutiny.[46] The detective story has two classic forms. The first is the typically British whodunit set in a situation of country-house normality, in which a motive within the "normal" range leads to violence. The goal is, of course, discovery of the perpetrator by deductive reasoning. The American variant, as practiced by the *Black Mask* magazine writers and such contemporaries of Faulkner as Dashiell Hammett and Raymond Chandler, is the hard-boiled thriller.[47] Its action takes place within an eccentric, violent, cynical world, and the motivations of the characters are adapted to this setting. It is to this latter genre that *Absalom, Absalom!* has the greater affinity.

The hard-boiled story, urban and urbane in contrast to the country-house ambiance of the whodunit, takes place in a night-time world where anything can happen and for almost any reason. The hard-boiled protagonist searches for the root cause of a sequence of apparently random and inexplicable violence only to find at bottom something that is less a cause or a motive than a profound symptom of social malaise. The act that sets everything in motion need not be rational at all, merely an appropriate aberration. Thus in the hard-boiled thriller there is almost always an absurd disparity between ultimate cause and effect. Almost inevitably the attention is moved sharply from the motive behind the crime to the motive of the investigator.

For example, in Dashiell Hammett's classic of the genre, *The Maltese Falcon*, the murder of Sam Spade's partner is a natural outgrowth of machinations to which the partner was merely incidental. In his attempts to uncover the killer Spade seeks a delicate balance of involvement and professional detachment. The significant action of the novel is not the murder at all, but, rather, Spade's choice of the woman he loves as the one who must "take the fall" for the crime. The rigorous logic with which he redefines his role, his responsibilities, and his identity reinforces the legal assignment of guilt. The killer's motives are unimportant—they are merely part of a world of avarice and violence.

As an idealist detective story, *Absalom, Absalom!* focuses on the motives of Quentin, not Henry, because it is Quentin's role that wants definition. For Henry any or all of the proposed motives might do. Only by finding Henry's motive can Quentin begin to objectify his own attitude towards his family and culture, because clarification of Henry's motive would allow Quentin to begin to deal with them. That he cannot do this is made clear by Shreve's last question: "Why do you hate the South?" [48] The clarification has not taken place.

Indeed, for Quentin this search cannot clarify. The difficulty lies not in Quentin's courage or imaginative grasp, but in the very nature of the historical inquiry on which he embarks. As I mentioned earlier, in the hard-boiled detective story there is an almost absurd disparity between cause and effect. For Quentin, the solving of the riddle of a man's murder of his beloved brother leads in the direction of the most arbitrary culture-bound reason. (Quentin and Shreve imagine Bon saying to Henry, "So it's the miscegenation, not the incest, you can't bear." [49]) I do not mean to suggest that racism is an irrelevant motive for murder in Henry's time and place, far from it. Rather, that motive is never shown—or more properly, *imagined*—to have anything *personally* to do with Henry. It is not Henry who wishes to strike out at the "balloon face" of the blacks that his father sees; rather, he is imagined by Miss Rosa—who knew him—to be literally nauseated by the spectacle of his father asserting the dominance of his will over his slaves with his bare knuckles.

In other words, the novel is in part an attempt to establish a context for cultural judgment in which the act of judgment usually delegated to Pallas Athene takes place within the individual consciousness. The motive at which Shreve and Quentin arrive by a series of imaginative leaps makes sense finally only in terms of what one knows about Henry's world, not in terms of anything the reader knows about Henry.

For Quentin—given what one knows of him from *The Sound and the Fury*—has deduced the motive that should seem least threatening to himself. There is thus an opposition between the intolerable fable of the Sutpens and the attempt to isolate a single bearable motive from that fable. One must never forget that it is Quentin who pushes Shreve towards the single motive, for Quentin alone holds all available parts of the fable.

Bigamy as a motive for murder would have unsettling implications for Quentin, as the Faulkner reader would know from *The Sound and the Fury*. Caddy, Quentin's beloved sister, is to torment him within a few months by marrying one man while carrying another's child. Quentin's obsession with Caddy makes the incest motive an even more potent psychological threat. In his racial attitudes, however, Quentin is patronizing in the manner of the conventional Southern gentleman. Of all his roles, it is the one in which he feels most at ease. Thus it should be comparatively comforting for Quentin to bestow upon Henry the status of a man quixotically defending sectional prejudice and honor.

If one examines the character Sutpen for the holistic cause of his tragic fall, one finds, instead of a role, a system-building innocent. When one attempts to discover what transgressed taboo would explain Henry's murder of Bon, the holist should find an historical categorical imperative, a three-in-one knot of bigamy, incest, and miscegenation. Instead, we have an idealist construction by our narrator historians. This is the root contradiction expressed in the novel.

⤻ Use of the Progressive Frame

Shreve and Quentin try to erect a hedge against the fable of Sutpen and his children. They believe that they can, by extrapolation from the known, reconstruct a train of thought. Their method is not only idealist but progressive, for their attempt to understand the fable is also an attempt to control or even negate the power of the culture that produced it. The wintry dormitory room in which Shreve and Quentin recreate the past is described by Faulkner as

dedicated to that best of ratiocination which after all was a good deal like Sutpen's morality and Miss Coldfield's demonizing—this room not only dedicated to it but set aside for it and suitably so since it would be here above any other place that it (the logic and the morality) could do the least amount of harm—the two of them back to back as though at the last ditch, saying No to Quentin's Mississippi shade who in life had acted and reacted to the minimum of logic and morality, who dying had escaped it completely, who dead remained not only indifferent but impervious to it, somehow a thousand times more potent and alive.[50]

The progressive quality of the inquiry is nowhere more marked than in the attempt to isolate a single motive for Bon's murder. The progressive frame characteristically selects one factor in a given historical situation as the agent of change, the engine or cutting edge of history. It may be the power of an idea or religion, or the struggle of opposing races, economic groups, or social classes. This has broad implications for Quentin's ordeal if one looks at the reflections of the Sutpen fable in still another mirror, that of Southern history and the causes of the Civil War. One is encouraged to make this relation by Miss Rosa herself, who, trained in Protestant allegorizing by her father, sees in Sutpen's life the explanation for the Southern loss of the war.

Viewed as an historical allegory, the murder of Bon by Henry is the war itself, the fratricidal conflict. The search for a motive becomes the search for the cause of the Civil War. The taboos, as they are probed to ever deeper levels, then appear as ways of rationalizing the conflict. Bigamy, of course, is a question of legal definition, of a relationship defined by society. Its natural analogue among the recognized sequences that led to the Civil War is the Constitutional conflict over states' rights and the Union. Incest as a motive has an analogue as well, in the dispute of North and South over the "virgin land" of the West, in which each section wished to keep the unoccupied territories inviolate from its rapacious sibling. Miscegenation as an historical explanation refers to the complex of racial fears that affects the whites of both sections, rather than to slavery. As a result of these fears, a situation of racial equality is a phenomenon that Southerners wish to inflict on the North, and that the North wishes to maintain as the exclusive "punishment" of the South.

Faulkner is not simply leading the reader to an acceptance of the unitary proposition that the Civil War was caused by the racism endemic throughout American society. In peeling away levels of taboo, seeking for the most basic motives, the existence of deeper levels does not negate the more "superficial," that by themselves may be the proximate causes of action. What does happen is that the emotional implications of the action become deepened and complicated. At the same time the reader is constantly aware of the consciousness of the four narrators as allegorists, each reading out of the tale a meaning that "pleases"— as Henry Adams would say—themselves. The allegory is that created by the narrators. Yet Faulkner is not truly an allegorist, and it is foolish to attempt to reduce his work to an allegory. Since the atmosphere of the fable is made up entirely of brutality, violence, and sensational events, history would remain only a chaotic and inchoate sequence if motive and direction were not finally separable. The narrator historians seek to pierce the confusion, the sound and the fury of the historical past, in order to reclaim the timeless thought and feeling of an earlier man or woman. It is this idealist hope that relates Faulkner to Cather. Yet the effect of Cather's work is towards peace, while Faulkner's great novel, when the meaning of the fable is "clear" to Quentin, reaches a peak of hysterical intensity as sharp as that in the obscure, "gothic" version of Miss Rosa. Why should this be?

⌐ Holistic Tragedy: Quentin's Inability To Free Himself

In trying to find the root cause of the tragic fable, Quentin and Shreve decide in effect that it is the abiding presence of two races that distinguishes the South and that states' rights and the old *Drang nach Westen* were comparatively ephemeral as culturally determining characteristics. (From the perspective of 1910, before the great migration of black people to the North, this reasoning has a great deal of cogency.) To complete the line of historical thinking, however, the isolated engine of historical change should have a part in an emerging historical dialectic. Shreve does push on—however perversely and facetiously—on the very last page of the novel. He proposes that the Jim Bonds—the black Sutpens—will take over the earth at last. Because Bond is a half-wit, critics have usually dismissed this suggestion as merely grotesque and callow. Yet Quentin cannot see the suggestion as only grotesque; after all, his brother Benjamin is far more mentally deficient than Jim Bond.

Shreve's conclusion is genuinely inescapable, for the fratricidal act was also an act of race war. If race war is not to be the future as well as the past of American society, Shreve suggests, there must be a new synthesis, sexually, socially, culturally. The taboo that is the peculiar product of American historical experience, the color bar, must be erased if the most basic relationships—of brothers to sisters, of parents to children, of one human being to another—are to be preserved with integrity.

The attempt to exorcise the fable of Sutpen by progressive dialectic requires this last step. Without it the entire cycle repeats itself, and the isolated racial factor once more enforces the web of holistic tragedy instead of being the progressive key to the nightmare's end. It is a step, however, that Quentin cannot take, for he cannot free himself from his culture's thralldom.

Quentin's memory of his last conversation with Henry is an obsessionally repetitive pattern like the "nevermore of peace" that he incants to himself. The hidden joker in progressive thought, the awareness that the present itself embodies the contradictions of change, is as intolerable for Quentin as the fable. Shreve senses that Quentin's efforts to free himself have given him a tool of liberation he dares not use, and that his Herculean ordeal of the imagination has collapsed into the phantasmagorical web of the flawed culture from which it sprang. The question and response that end the novel measure the degree of that failure:

"And so do you know what I think?" Now he did expect an answer, and now he got one.

"No," Quentin said.

"Do you want to know what I think?"

"No," Quentin said.

"Then I'll tell you. I think that in time the Jim Bonds are going to conquer the Western hemisphere. Of course it won't quite be in our time and of course as they spread toward the poles they will bleach out again like the rabbits and the birds do, so they won't show up so sharp against the snow. But it will still be Jim Bond; and so in a few thousand years, I who regard you will also have sprung from the loins of African kings. Now I want you to tell me just one thing more. Why do you hate the South?"

"I don't hate it," Quentin said, quickly, at once, immediately; "I dont hate it," he said. *I dont hate it* he thought, panting in the cold air, the iron New England dark; *I dont. I dont! I dont hate it! I dont hate it!* [51]

Chapter Nine

LIBERAL CONSCIENCE AND
APOCALYPTIC PARODY

I
N the period since World War II, the most pronounced division among significant novels of the historical imagination has not been between holist and progressive, but between novels of the liberal conscience and those of apocalyptic parody. The first group includes most notably Robert Penn Warren, Bernard Malamud, and William Styron, and typically finds its form in a first-person narrative (or a third-person narrative rendered from a single actor's point of view) in which an individual grapples with the psychological and ethical dimensions of an historical crisis. The second, identified by R. W. B. Lewis as a major strain in contemporary American fiction, made its greatest impact in the early 1960's and is represented in the work of John Barth and Thomas Pynchon.[1] Their novels parody not only fictional forms but the historical assumptions underlying both progressive and holistic frames. They also flirt with the idea of an apocalyptic Day of Doom, an end to history that is foreshadowed by the exhaustion of the historical imagination that their parody signifies. Finally, there are two writers who combine the apocalyptic perspective with a probingly personal voice, intent on establishing the individual consciousness as a field spacious enough to accommodate even the spectacle of annihilation. This paradoxical

and complex vision belongs to Ralph Ellison's *Invisible Man* and the work of Norman Mailer in the late 1960's.

➷ *All the King's Men:* Ironic Acquiescence in Historical Change

Of all Robert Penn Warren's excursions into history, as biographer, historical essayist, journalist, critic, poet, and novelist, none crystallizes more completely his attitude of ironic acquiescence in historical change better than his most famous novel, *All the King's Men* (1946). Based on the career of Huey Long, it is an attempt to redefine the idea of the Great Man for fiction.

It is instructive to read in sequence the three successive attempts by important twentieth-century novelists to come to terms with the story of Long: Sinclair Lewis' *It Can't Happen Here* (1935), John Dos Passos' *Number One* (1943), and Warren's novel of 1946. Lewis' tale of a dystopian fascist nightmare is not so different in its attitude towards history from what might have been written by a conservative Bellamy or London. Although Lewis fears rather than welcomes the possibility of a break in the historical continuum (as is evident from the title), and thus stands in contrast to American writers from Crèvecoeur through Bellamy and Twain, his focus on such a break is central to his imaginative conception of the story.

Warren's novel somewhat resembles that of Dos Passos in its superficial form, since it tells the story of the Great Man from the viewpoint of his flunky, on the theory that no man is a hero to his valet. Dos Passos' novel is the debunking exposé of an opportunist, in which the flunky's service to the Long figure is simply the objective correlative for his self-contempt. *All the King's Men* moves towards an image of greatness that the flunky sees only when he is shaken free by tragedy—the Great Man is not an opportunist, but an incarnation of popular will:

I saw the face. Enormous. Bigger than a billboard. The forelock
shagged down like a mane. The big jaw. The heavy lips laid together
like masonry. The eyes burning and bulging powerfully.

Funny, I had never seen it before. Not really.[2]

The significance of Warren lies in his conservative hopefulness
in a redemptive meaning to be drawn from the chaos of change.
The conservatism lies in the violence and destruction his work
sees attending History, with the dead and maimed strewn across
his stage at the end like the dénouement of a Jacobean tragedy.
The hopefulness emerges in the narrator's ability to give a sense
that entering that chaos and accepting his role in it have been
steps in his moral growth.

It is as if Warren had grafted Scott onto Faulkner to produce
an idealist detective story that is at the same time a parable of
maturity forged in the heat of historical change. His narrator-
protagonist Jack Burden makes two excursions into the past. The
first is a doctoral dissertation on Cass Mastern, a distant relative
and nineteenth-century youth who was tortured by a sense of
responsibility for the consequences of a passionate love affair.
Unable because of his arrested development to imitate, in the
Collingwood sense, either the passion or the sense of responsibility of Mastern, Jack is stymied, and cannot translate the facts
into a dissertation. The second is more directly in the vein of
the tough detective story of Hammett and Chandler, with Burden
running down leads on a sordid bit of graft in the past of a
prominent judge. The significance of the new set of facts belongs
more to the neo-Freudian private-eye yarns of Ross Macdonald
than to R. G. Collingwood, however, for the discovered judge, who
commits suicide to avoid exposure, is Burden's father.

But these revelations do not shatter a tortured psyche further,
as happens to Quentin in *Absalom, Absalom!*; instead, Burden
seems to follow the injunction of E. M. Forster: "Only connect. . . ." As Burden says, "And all times are one time, and all
those dead in the past never lived before our definition gives them

life, and out of the shadow their eyes implore us." [3] Each new connection, no matter what its apparent consequences, promotes Burden's reintegration and health. Like the Scottian hero, Jack Burden is the wavering and uncommitted protagonist whose maturity and identity is a gift bestowed upon him by historical strife, but the seal is set upon that maturity by his ability to frame the narrative that is the novel.

As *All the King's Men* moves towards its conclusion, the voice of the narrator becomes more and more openly meditative, assigning—somewhat too explicitly—significance to the people and events of the tale in a kind of historical allegory. Because he can at last accept what he "learns" from history, the therapy that failed him earlier (when he was unable to complete his study of Cass Mastern) and that Quentin Compson had been unable to carry through, gives his voice authority. It may be asked whether the authority of Warren's protagonist depends more on rhetoric than on the kind of dialectical passion that sustains the heightened tone of Faulkner's great novel. The sureness of that voice depends on the reader's acceptance of the proposition that maturity is the recognition of responsibility, and that Jack Burden is prepared to shoulder the weight of his all too portentous name in a complex and problematic world. As he concludes, "soon now we shall go out of the house and go into the convulsion of the world, out of history into history and the awful responsibility of Time." [4]

⌐ *The Fixer* and *The Confessions of Nat Turner*: The Individual Conscience in Crisis

Responsibility has remained the key word in that significant stream of the historical imagination in which the drama is concentrated on the individual conscience in crisis. Outstanding among such novels have been Bernard Malamud's *The Fixer* (1966) and William Styron's *The Confessions of Nat Turner*

(1967). Like Warren's novel, these works are prone to moralize
in the guise of philosophy and they strive to prescribe, directly
or by implication, a viable set of principles by which one may
triumph over intolerable conditions or chaotic change.

Malamud's and Styron's works were very widely read, *The
Confessions of Nat Turner* even provoking an extended controversy over Styron's portrayal of the leader of the most significant of all American slave revolts. These novels appeared in the
midst of a sharpened debate in American historiography; the two
camps were labeled by Richard Hofstadter "consensus" and "conflict." [5] On one side, the old guard, proponents of a holistic
perspective on the American past, emphasized a kind of functional pluralism in which violent disagreement and change in
American history are seen as superficial in the face of a fundamentally shared set of social and cultural assumptions. The in-
surgent scholars took up a classically progressive position, in which
conflicts in the American past—of sections, classes and races—
were seen as fundamental to an understanding of the past.
Throughout this debate there has been a quite explicit awareness
of historical interpretation as a form of allegorical commentary
on the present. Historians nurtured during the cold war celebration of the American way of life—even when critical, like Hofstadter, of aspects of that way of life—are found in the school
of consensus, while those more affected by the radical social criticism of the sixties tended to emphasize underlying conflicts.

An effort to strike a new balance between conflict and consensus, progressivism and holism, appeared twenty years after Warren's novel in *The Fixer* and *The Confessions of Nat Turner*.
As in *All the King's Men*, history is perceived as a test of individual conscience and maturity. Each novel is the story of a man
in prison for an offense that carries tremendous political consequences; he relives the past from his cell and contemplates the
future. Malamud's Yakov Bok, a Jew accused of ritual murder

of a Christian child in Tsarist Russia, is aware that his conviction would bring about a vast pogrom. Styron's Turner reflects on the slave revolt he has led in the Virginia of 1831, which in its defeat catalyzed a devastatingly oppressive reaction within the slave states.

Parallels between the novels abound and are worth noting because, together, these two works exemplify most of the merits as well as the limitations of this variety of historical fiction. For example, in both novels the protagonist cannot accept his role as a member of an oppressed minority within a dominant society. Yakov Bok is unable to accept the traditional confinement within the Jewish shtetl. Nat Turner's rejection of his role stems more from his unwillingness to accept the defined relationship of the races within slave society. Each in turn becomes in effect a renegade; Bok by leaving the Pale and attempting to pass for a Gentile craftsman, Turner by learning to read and consciously alienating his manner of thought from that of his people. Most significant for Styron's purpose is his protagonist's obsession with a white woman. In this regard Turner is as conventional a holist creation as Cooper's Magua.

What makes these novels more adventurous than this pattern would suggest is the authors' attempt to see their characters from within. For each, the development of this classically holistic relation of character to culture is only a prelude, since once emancipated from their roles, neither character sees his own or the larger dominant culture as a seamless web. They gain the power to use the freedom of the renegade through a covenant suggested by the religious tradition of each. Turner forms a pact with God because God has given him a vision, and he embarks on his mission after the visitation of an angel. While Styron's Turner attempts to become a history-*maker* as an agent of God, Bok makes his covenant as an existential gesture that will give meaning to his passive endurance of history:

So what can Yakov Bok do about it? All he can do is not make things
worse. He's half a Jew himself, yet enough of one to protect them.
After all, he knows the people; and he believes in their right to be
Jews and live in the world like men. He is against those who are
against them. He will protect them to the extent that he can. This is
his covenant with himself. If God's not a man he has to be.[6]

The result of the covenant is progressive transcendence of roles
—including that of the renegade. Yakov Bok and Nat Turner
come to conceptualize the oppressive society as a totalitarian
camp rather than a cultural matrix sanctified by tradition. Both
fictions recreate the historical transition of their protagonists from
a holistic to a progressive perspective; the protagonist passes from
a hated role through alienation to a commitment to struggle
against oppression.

It is an interesting sidelight that both novels attracted heavy
criticism upon publication for "distorting" history. Malamud was
criticized in the Eastern European press for inappropriately imi-
tating Arthur Koestler's A Darkness at Noon and for presenting
Jews and Gentiles in the old Russian Empire as two warring
camps. In brief, The Fixer was blamed for being the progressive
version of history. The Confessions of Nat Turner was vigorously
attacked by black intellectuals and some white Marxist historians,
such as Herbert Aptheker, for explaining the slave revolt as a
psychopathic aberration that reflected the maiming effects of
slavery rather than as a clear-eyed blow for freedom.[7] In other
words, Styron was blamed for treating the revolt in too holistic
a fashion.

Both works exemplify the present-mindedness that keeps the
historical imagination vital. Though Styron disclaimed direct inspiration from the black rebellions of the 1960's, his novel gained
force from analogies in the minds of his readers with the upris-
ings of black people in Watts, Harlem, Detroit, Newark, New
Haven, and other cities, just as the Jewish holocaust is clearly
close to the thoughts of both author and reader in The Fixer.

The two novels may be seen as a Janus-like portrait of the contemporary liberal amidst renewed conflict within American society. Malamud's hero offers a reproachful glare at those who
shirk all social responsibility, whereas Styron creates in his violent
revolutionary a cautionary figure to encourage a moderate pace
of social change. Conflict may become the setting for an even
greater liberal consensus, and to achieve it Malamud turns the
victimized Jew into a hero, while Styron turns the black hero into
the psychologically warped victim of a racist society.

⌐ *The Sot-Weed Factor* and V.: Imperialism and the Apocalypse

The present-mindedness of John Barth's *The Sot-Weed Factor*
(1960) and Thomas Pynchon's V. (1963) does not depend on
analogy between times of historical crisis and an idealist recreation of the dilemma of an individual consciousness. Whatever
his disclaimers of intent, William Styron has in effect tried to
rethink the thoughts of an early-nineteenth-century rebel slave
leader. Barth and Pynchon take off rather from the kind of sustained uncertainty about the meaning of the past that Faulkner
explored so brilliantly in *Absalom, Absalom!* This uncertainty
reflects an anxiety about both the immediate future and the ultimate direction of historical change. As was true in other novels
of the early sixties—especially William Burroughs' *Naked Lunch*
and Joseph Heller's *Catch 22*—the years of cold war threats of
massive retaliation produced a vision that distrustfully scrutinized
the bland, affluent fifties for telltale signs of an annihilating catastrophe.

Though this distrust of historical reality had a clear topical
source in the shadow of the bomb, it also had distinguished antecedents. There is something of the skepticism of Henry Adams
in the chapter title of *The Sot-Weed Factor* in which "The Poet
Wonders Whether the Course of Human History is a Progress,

a Drama, a Retrogression, a Cycle, an Undulation, a Vortex, a
Right- or Left-Handed Spiral, a Mere Continuum, or What Have
You. Certain Evidence Is Brought Forward, but of an Ambiguous and Inconclusive Nature." [8] There is more than skepticism
in V., in which Pynchon seems to be writing a novel in the spirit
of Adams' controversial late essays "A Letter to American Teach-
ers of History" and "The Rule of Phase in History" in which the
historian attempted to draw from physics a formula that would
illuminate the phenomenon of historical change.[9]

This radical skepticism is reflected in the formal characteristics
of the two novels. Both are packed with incident, rapid shifts of
scene, and a multitude of rather flat characters and attempt to
mimic by the illusion of formlessness the confusing shifts and
changes of history itself. This abundance of sheer narrative vigor
is alluded to by one of Barth's characters, who says, "we swim
in an ocean of story, but a tumblerful slakes our thirst." [10] The
Ocean of Story, the novel of pure incident, mocks one of Henry
Adams' most ambitious efforts, that of composing his *History of
the United States* in order to see "whether, by the severest process of stating, with the least possible comment, such facts as
seemed sure, in such order as seemed rigorously consequent, he
could fix for a familiar moment a necessary sequence of human
movement." [11] Adams based his emphasis on pure sequentiality
out of a distrust of the available theories of causality. Barth shares
the distrust, as we have seen, but is all too aware of the danger
of "slaking the thirst" of his readers with anecdote alone. He
seeks refuge in the sanctuary of time-hallowed form, creating a
plot of coincidence and resolution that profits from the eighteenth-century models it parodies.

For Pynchon the problem of causality is not resolved so easily.
It is true that his plot parodies—in this case such a classic thriller
as Eric Ambler's *A Coffin for Dimitrios*, in which the search for
an archetypal figure of intrigue and violence becomes a search
for the clue to the decadence of contemporary Western culture.
A passage from the Ambler novel is representative of both:

Latimer stared at the corpse. So this was Dimitrios. This was the man who had, perhaps, slit the throat of Sholem, the Jew turned Moslem. This was the man who had connived at assassinations, who had spied for France. This was the man who had trafficked in drugs, who had given a gun to a Croat terrorist and who, in the end, had himself died by violence. This putty-coloured bulk was the end of an Odyssey. Dimitrios had returned at last to the country whence he had set out so many years before.

So many years. Europe in labour had through its pain seen for an instant a new glory, and then had collapsed to welter again in the agonies of war and fear. Governments had risen and fallen; men and women had worked, had starved, had made speeches, had fought, had been tortured, had died. Hope had come and gone, a fugitive in the scented bosom of illusion. Men had learned to sniff the heady dream-stuff of the soul and wait impassively while the lathes turned the guns for their destruction. And through those years, Dimitrios had lived and breathed and come to terms with his strange gods.[12]

For Pynchon, historical reality in the twentieth century presents itself as a chaotic mass of catastrophic events. When the events are arranged sequentially, the only pattern to emerge—at least from those selected by Ambler and Pynchon—is that of an accelerating breakdown of a decadent civilization on the verge of total loss of control. As noted earlier, in regard to *Absalom, Absalom!*, the hard-boiled detective novel searches for a cause, only to find a symptom. The spy-thriller part of Pynchon's novel, which portrays the search for the mysterious femme fatale V., shares this characteristic, for V. (or Dimitrios) is not herself the cause of escalating calamity, but is a definitive and representative symbol of the ominous syndrome of events.

Each incident is representative of some profound law of motion, signalled by tremors of catastrophe and fears of a triumph of "the Inanimate" over humanity that is strikingly reminiscent of Henry Adams' application of the Second Law of Thermodynamics to human life. The radical discontinuity of phenomena in Pynchon's novel is an invitation to the reader to ponder the mystery of causality in a period of history increasingly difficult

to analyze in terms of the idealist belief that individual consciousness is the central stage of historical action.

↖ The Uses of Roles and Types

Despite some formal similarities, Barth and Pynchon are as far
apart in historical imagination as the holist and progressive
frames. This is especially clear in characterization. Barth's parody
of the classical historical novel is a happy marriage of his own
pet theory of personality with a form providing that theory with
enormous scope and validity. Barth had long been fascinated by
the notion of role-playing as the sole thing that preserves people
from a state of total vacuous indeterminacy—that of "a shocked,
drooling animal," as he puts it in his first novel, *The Floating
Opera*. Roles are as crucial to him as to Cooper or Scott, but he
employs them with critical self-consciousness. His protagonist in
The Sot-Weed Factor, Ebenezer Cooke, preserves himself from
inanition by assuming a role, namely that of "Virgin and Poet
Laureate of Maryland." It is not long before he begins to lose
proper title to the name of poet laureate by dint of his unfortunate adventures in his new home, and as for his style as Virgin,
a would-be seductress observes to him late in the novel that "this
precious Innocence you cling to hath been picked at and pecked
at till you've scarce a meager tit-bit of't left." [13]

The loss of the role and the loss of Innocence are one, and
necessary for Barth's purpose. Cooke first responds to his new
sense of self in a brutal manner, attempting to rape and then
betraying the woman who loves him. Having achieved his identity beyond roles, he is prepared for acts of selflessness strangely
reminiscent of Warren's Jack Burden and Malamud's Yakov Bok.
In refusing to save himself at the expense of his companions
when all are captured by rebellious blacks and Indians, he honors
the same notion he had earlier violated: "How's that for a pathway, John McEvoy? I'Christ, 'tis a *grande avenue*, a *camino real*,

a very boulevard; at one end lies your Slough of False Integrity
—to call it by its name on the Map of Truth—and at the other
stands the storied Town . . . where Responsibility rears her
golden towers." [14] Again keeping the faith he had trampled before, he later consummates his marriage with Joan Toast, the
diseased ex-prostitute who loves him, precisely because he has
betrayed her.

Ebenezer's mentor, Henry Burlingame, is a Chillingworth to
his Dimmesdale, a madcap role-player to Ebenezer the role-seeker.
Thus he turns up in a vast number of different guises, explaining
his protean role-playing by his orphan status. Having no father,
he has no link with the past and hence no fixed identity. With
no natural bond to the world he can engender nothing. In the
relativistic universe of *The Sot-Weed Factor,* he is a seeker of
relations, even developing an elaborate theory of the significance
of twins because they are a relative phenomenon. Only after
establishing his identity by confronting his father can he beget
a child with Ebenezer's sister. Thus while Ebenezer proves that
roles alone are inadequate to sustain identity, it would seem that
the fable of Henry Burlingame is intended to show that even the
most active man cannot be fulfilled without the sense of relation
that roles—son and father in this case—provide.

Pynchon also has two major protagonists, shaped much to the
same purpose as Barth's. There is an ingenuous bumbler, Benny
Profane, designated a "schlemihl and yoyo," who endures a long
and uncertain pilgrimage towards identity much like Ebenezer
Cooke. There is a quester like Burlingame—Herbert Stencil, who
calls himself at one point "He who looks for V.," and who seeks
to unravel the mystery of his father's end through solving the
puzzle of contemporary history. Burlingame's quest meant uncovering a document that on one side had the key to the in-
trigues plaguing Maryland at the end of the century and, on the
other, his grandfather's secret diary of the campaigns of John
Smith. For Stencil, world history and his own past are contained

in the person of the mysterious woman V. The resemblances with Barth's work end there, however, for Pynchon's characters are not created in terms of the cultural roles of the holist imagination. Rather, they are progressive types like those described by Henry and Brooks Adams. Benny Profane is a schlemihl by essence, not circumstance, and he is doomed to suffer without understanding just as Stencil is doomed to seek without finding.

The two novels reverberate to different myths of place. Ebenezer Cooke sets out for a glorious New World—to be a Virgin in Virgin land—only to discover the same lesson that Crèvecoeur's farmer learned, that his pastoral Eden has been invaded by all the vices of the Old World and in fact was only "poor shitten Maryland." Yet he passes through the stage of bitter Jeremiad too, at last accepting his adopted home as neither better nor worse than his old, but blessed with the philosophic liberty that is the result of having a short past.

Where Barth turns the mythology of the New World into a message of moderation, Pynchon signifies the depth of the historical crisis by inverting the traditional roles of Europe and America. In V., although its scenes range all over the globe, New York comes to represent the greatest sink of decadence, the city of philosopher dentists, mad plastic surgeons, a robust sewer life, and "The Whole Sick Crew." The sanctuary from this chaos is in one of the oldest parts of the Old World—Malta. In the center of the Mediterranean, Malta is symbolically at the center of the earth, and its history has been largely that of the imperial powers who have occupied it as a vital strategic stronghold. A Maltese writer describes the attitude of Maltese children during the World War II siege towards the rise and fall of these empires:

A wheel, this diagram: Fortune's wheel. Spin as it might the basic arrangement was constant. Stroboscopic effects could change the apparent number of spokes; direction could change; but the hub still held the spokes in place and the meeting-place of the spokes still defined the hub. The old cyclic idea of history had taught only the rim, to which princes and serfs alike were lashed; that wheel was oriented vertical; one rose and fell. But the children's wheel was dead-level, its own rim only that of the sea's horizon—so sensuous, so "visual" a race are we Maltese.[15]

Although a crossroads of history, Malta also promises—however fitfully—an escape from the vicissitudes of inexorable change. The rock at the center may be a refuge or the hope of a rebirth, an escape from history into sacred eternal time such as the "eternal return" of which Mircea Eliade writes.[16] While the rock has some of this power for Fausto Maijstral and his daughter Paola, it fails the two major protagonists drastically. Stencil arrives at Malta seeking the truth about the past and leaves on a wild goose chase. Profane's confrontation with the island seems to be only a prelude to suicide. It is desperation, not moderation, that Pynchon teaches.

⌐ Barth's Holistic Resolution and Pynchon's No Way Out

The apocalyptic historical imagination, as R. W. B. Lewis has shown, unites such diverse novels as Joseph Heller's *Catch-22*, Nathanael West's *The Day of the Locust*, and Ralph Ellison's *Invisible Man*.[17] In *The Sot-Weed Factor* and *V.*, Barth and Pynchon invoke the Day of Wrath with a difference characteristic of distinctions already noted. Yet, for both, the engine of destruction is, significantly, the struggle attendant upon imperialist exploitation.

The ultimate menace in Barth's tumultuous colonial Maryland is an uprising of Indians allied with escaped slaves in a last-ditch effort to sweep the white man into the sea. Holism and the conventions of its most appropriate form, the classical historical novel of Scott and Cooper, provide Barth with his resolution to the menacing dialectic of imperialist violence and the resistance of darker races who face genocide and slavery. Ebenezer Cooke, when confronted with the reality of the plan of revolt by the

blacks and Indians, admits the justice of their cause, but later acts
to foil their plan. In his mood of mature moderation, he places
in one pan of the scale of Justice the actual dispossession of the
Indians and the murderous slave trade. In the other he places the
fancied danger of violent revolt—and takes the middle course of
preventing the revolt. As Cooke says, " 'tis not the English case I
plead: 'tis the case of humankind, of Civilization *versus* the Abyss
of salvagery." [18]

Barth then draws upon all the conventions of the Scottian novel
to resolve the issue—including the timely interposition of the
Great Man, Governor Nicholson, a conservative and a pragmatist
—in order to sort out the affairs of Maryland and help the hero
win his estate. Barth uses convention in witty fashion to under-
line the same kind of moderate liberal moral pointed out with
less ingenuity by Malamud and Styron.

Pynchon refers to the points of imperialist tension running
from the scramble for Africa by European powers in the late
nineteenth and early twentieth centuries through two world wars
to the present time of the novel, the Suez crisis of 1956. Two ex-
amples indicate his conclusions from this synoptic view of modern times. The first point of imminent explosion is the Fashoda
crisis, in which the simultaneous attempts of the English to bisect Africa from north to south, and of the French to bisect it
from east to west, demonstrate with geometrical precision the inevitability of their sparking the powderkeg of world imperialism.
The second is a chapter of stunning brilliance in which an atmosphere of Weimar decadence provides an evocative entry into
the genocidal extermination of blacks in German South East
Africa in 1904. Parody disappears from Pynchon's tone as he portrays the fusing of imperialist lust for dominance with the pervading apotheosis of the Inanimate.

In V., Pynchon refuses to posit civilization and savagery as absolutes, after the holist fashion. He insists on seeing both as locked
in our time in the dialectic of imperialism, an escalating coil of

destruction without the means, conventional or otherwise, to cheat the Apocalypse.

Through Pynchon and Barth the historical imagination has returned to its nineteenth-century roots, however modern the black humor guise of each. Barth shows the return to convention itself, the need for moderation, the impropriety of judging the past by contemporary standards—in fact the impropriety of judging the morality of civilizations at all. Pynchon does judge the twentieth century, and from the perspective of the future.

Like Adams a progressive pessimist, Pynchon concludes that if the future of modern man is his further development along the lines of nineteenth- and twentieth-century history, there is no escape from an apocalyptic conclusion, be it nuclear bang or inanimate whimper. Like the progressively optimistic Marx, Pynchon judges the past and present from the viewpoint of the most probable future, not from the viewpoint of the eternal status quo of the idealist progressives. He deviates from the revolutionary materialists in offering no moralistic suggestions on how to exist meaningfully in such a world. And, unlike the classical progressives, his judgment is reserved for contemporary civilization alone, not for those who endure its travail. The watchword of one of his most positive characters, "keep cool but care," [19] pleads for a kind of dignified passivity in the face of the Apocalypse.

⌐ Ellison: The Defining Choices of the Individual

Although the structures of the historical imagination have undergone metamorphoses, largely as a result of new order being imposed on old facts rather than of new historical subject matter, the most striking quality of the historical imagination in the postwar period would seem to be a sense of pressing analogy, a desire to "place" the present in terms of an imaginable, pertinent past. This is reflected both in conventional historiography and in the historical novel, as noted earlier with regard to *The Fixer* and *The Con-*

fessions of Nat Turner. The crucial work in this regard is Ralph Ellison's *Invisible Man* (1947), the first-person narrative of a black man in every sense anonymous—a self-told history of the consciousness of a people, or "autogenography" that is at the same time intensely personal.

In interviews Ellison has related his indebtedness to André Malraux, whose *Man's Fate* (1934) he carried with him constantly during the years when he first experimented with the uses of history in fiction; one of his 1941 *New Masses* stories concerns two black youngsters who invent a history to serve their purposes. Malraux centered attention on the choices that determine the identity of an individual through his actions in history; such choices have become the focal point of modern historical consciousness in the novel. In his highly political novel *Man's Fate* the way characters choose to die defines the meaning they give their lives. Who they were, what they did or had done to them fade into insignificance before that historical choice. One of Malraux's characters, Ch'en, confronting the emptiness of his existence, gives to death "the meaning that others give to life." [20] Both Ellison and Norman Mailer, post-World War II American ironists, focus their concern on the hero's individual responsibility for his historical role—his self-defining choices of action. In *Invisible Man* Ellison's nameless black protagonist, though defeated and detached, asserts that he still considers history as a means to action, a guide to securing full human rights.

What gives *Invisible Man* its special quality is that its tensions arise from the author's knowledge of black Americans whose "invisible" lives are peculiarly dominated, if not immobilized, by the past. Where Barth's Ebenezer Cooke can select his role as virgin and poet, the invisible man finds that his role was selected for him by the white man long before his birth. As a result of its restrictions, which demean him and deny his humanity, he is thrust into a progressive search for a role that will permit some satisfying identity.

In dealing with the concept of the unity of mankind despite racial diversity, Ellison combines Bancroft's concern with the scientific laws of history, Hawthorne's sharp focus on the unbearable demands that the holistic role makes on the human spirit, and Melville's fascination with violent revolt. The struggle of Ellison's protagonist becomes a progressive effort to break a mold formed in the past. Black Americans are, to use the phrase recurring throughout the novel, "outside history," which means, in the sense in which Ellison uses it, that they are not the decision-makers and influencers of the actions that make history. To be "inside history" is one of the goals of the protagonist because such participation provides a sense of identity. But it also means, for the protagonist, a break with the confining past. Thus Ellison's book focuses on the choices his hero must make as he encounters historic attitudes and roles that are either forced on him or that he himself seeks.

On one level, *Invisible Man* is an elaborate and ironic *roman à clef*. At the time the book appeared, its hidden identities excited critics, with the Founder being recognized as Booker T. Washington and Dr. Bledsoe as his follower, Emerson as the rich white Jeffersonian liberal, the Brotherhood as the Communist Party, and Ras as a Garvey-type nationalist. Significant characters are given pun-names, like Bledsoe, Wrestrum, Trueblood, always suggesting a different meaning and story than the one ostensibly being told. This aspect of the novel served to distract attention from the quality of Ellison's historical imagination.

At a deeper level, *Invisible Man* may be read as the story of Everyman. The nameless narrator points out that his invisibility is not "exactly a matter of a bio-chemical accident to my epidermis" and concludes in the last line of the book: "Who knows but that, on the lower frequencies, I speak for you?" [21] Nevetheless, the story he recounts is that of a black Odysseus traveling through the warring conflicts of the American past and present. In his title Ellison created a transcendent organizing image that is instantly recognizable as describing the role of black people in American society—and yet it could speak more broadly for all poor and powerless people.

His hero resembles the desperate Odysseus who responds to the one-eyed, man-eating Kyklops' demand for his identity by asserting he is "Nohbdy" and thus escapes.[22] In the end, this is what Ellison's protagonist does—escaping the raging fires of history, personal and objective, to hibernate in a coal cellar. Like Ezra Pound's "man of no fortune and with a name to come" [23] he asserts that his hibernation is a "covert preparation for a more overt action," [24] and promises to come out of the coal hole and seek his place in history.

In revealing the lives of black people, Ellison abandoned the naturalism that had been dominant in American literature in the depression years because it could not adequately express a vision of reality that encompassed social and psychological attitudes and images drawn from dreams, myths, symbols, and folk themes that made the historic black past part of the present. In drawing upon black folklore, Ellison explored a unique store of history that is neither institutionalized culture nor counter-culture, but truly independent in its roots. Traditionally oral, it is expressive of emotional essences and flavored by wisdom gained from experiences not known by whites; "we were older than they," as the narrator puts it.[25]

If at times Ellison's narrator is unreliable and inconsistent in character, it is because he speaks in two voices which are never completely separate. One is that of a trusting, innocent, anxious, and conforming Southern black boy. The other is that of an ironic, disillusioned, and detached intellectual who sees history as a guide to action but, distrusting his own feelings, cannot commit himself to any course; they all "boomerang," he complains.

The hero is introduced as a deferential, scholarship-winning black boy who wants to do good, be good, and then do better. Like Saul Bellow's protagonist in *The Adventures of Augie March*, he tries only to please others; even belatedly in the coal cellar, he sees himself as responsible to others—not to himself. He is bookish, earnest, white-believing. Yet, despite his passivity and innocence, the protagonist represents a potentially progressive character. The prime, continuing question of the novel is: can he break out of the holistic mold?

His threat to expose Dr. Bledsoe is a progressive note that echoes one part of his grandfather's ambiguous deathbed declaration. In that final testament, the grandfather, once a slave, denounces his own meekness and asserts: ". . . our life is a war and I have been a traitor all my born days, a spy in the enemy's country ever since I give up my gun back in the Reconstruction. . . ." [26] This passage is the progressive counter-theme of the book, returned to again and again in guilt-ridden memories of his grandfather evoked by the hero's humiliating conformity in role-playing.

This contrasts sharply with the dominant holistic motif also sounded in the grandfather's deathbed statement: "Live with your head in the lion's mouth. I want you to overcome 'em with yeses, undermine 'em with grins, agree 'em to death and destruction, let 'em swoller you till they vomit or bust wide open." [27]

It is tempting to interpret *Invisible Man* as a picaresque novel like *Huckleberry Finn* or *The Adventures of Augie March*. However, the novel begins and ends with the protagonist underground; its refrain—"the end is the beginning and lies far ahead"—echoes the opening and closing lines of T. S. Eliot's poem *East Coker*,[28] which deals with his feelings on returning to the origins of his family in England. This line signals the circular structure of the novel as a whole and of each episode within it. Each episode goes through a cycle of unmasking the pretensions of the historic social forces that promise to solve the dilemma of black people in America, such as education, industrialization, nationalism, and socialism. With these cycles repeated again and again, there is virtually no progress. Instead there is a mounting intensity of frustration and rage that builds towards the final apocalyptic riot. This circular structure helps to explain Ellison's anxious, often spectacular inventiveness, which keeps the intensity rising.

Each major cycle presents the protagonist with a model who has found a role that provides a satisfying identity. The first significant model is Dr. Bledsoe, president of the black college the narrator attends. Dr. Bledsoe frankly uses a "burr-head" holist mask in his dealings with whites to conceal his true interest in power. He is enraged by the hero's naiveté in taking a white liberal trustee to the sites of local scandals merely because the trustee wanted to go there: "Why, the dumbest black bastard in the cotton patch knows that the only way to please a white man is to tell him a lie! What kind of education are you getting around here?" [29]

Indeed, Dr. Bledsoe seems to conceive of education as a mask. He unhesitatingly sacrifices black political and human rights to gain, in limited areas, a gratifying personal power over both blacks and whites. As he puts it:

The white folk tell everybody what to think—except men like me. I tell *them*; that's my life, telling white folk how to think about the things I know about. . . . It's a nasty deal and I don't always like it myself . . . I didn't make it, and I know that I can't change it. But I've made my place in it and I'll have every Negro in the country hanging on tree limbs by morning if it means staying where I am.[30]

Bledsoe expels the protagonist as a fool who has endangered the school. Still revering the college president, the protagonist accepts his expulsion with its promise of reinstatement and ultimate Bledsoe-like power; he wants to hurry north, work hard, and return to win a place in Dr. Bledsoe's scheme of things. Only when he discovers in New York that the letters of introduction provided by Dr. Bledsoe read, in effect, *Keep this nigger running,* does he become enraged at Bledsoe's ruthless fraudulence and yearns to destroy him. So ends his admiration of Bledsoe and his illusions of finding a place through education.

In the next cycle he is confronted with the bewildering choices of any migrant black from the South. He gets a job in a paint factory, a setting that provides Ellison the symbolist with rich opportunities for irony and satire. Liberty Paints, for example, specializes in white, advertising "If It's Optic White, It's the Right White" [31]—which sets off the black protagonist's childhood memory: "If you're white, you're right." [32] His job is to add ten drops of black goo to make each bucket of white paint whiter—and he fails at it. Finally he's assigned to assist an old and crazy black man deep in the bowels of the plant who, significantly, operates its basic power machinery. The old man is proud of having helped work out the advertising slogan. And, like Bledsoe, the old man enjoys hidden power through his knowledge of the plant's buried pipes and innards; *"we the machines inside the machine,"* [33] he says. Ultimately the old man, apparently out of fear of being displaced by young men, permits the factory to blow up rather than show the protagonist how to operate it. As a model the old man is rejected, because he is a mad relic of the past—an "old-fashioned, slavery-time, mammy-made, handkerchief-headed bastard." [34]

The explosion, opening a new episode that bitterly satirizes the medical care given black people by white professionals, lands the protagonist in a *"factory* hospital." [35] There he is used as a guinea pig for an electric lobotomy that relieves him of his Southern identity. As the lobotomizing surgeon proudly puts it, "He'll experience no major conflict of motives, and what is even better, society will suffer no traumata on his account." [36] The protagonist discovers his memory is gone, that he no longer has the capacity to become angry and no longer expects anything from "important men" like the college trustees. For the first time he is aware of his lack of identity: "When I discover who I am, I'll be free," he says.[37]

Thus prepared, he is confronted in Harlem with a new choice of roles. Models for these roles appear almost simultaneously.

They are Ras the nationalist, who is "not afraid to be black," and
Jack and Tod of the socialist Brotherhood. Much later, in the
final pages of the book, another model, Rinehart the imposter,
appears. Each represents a different response to the black American's historic confinement to limited participation in the nation's
life.

Ras, a West Indian black nationalist, speaks directly and eloquently to the emotional experiences of being black in white-con-
trolled America. Calling for exclusion of whites from Harlem and
establishment of a black society, Ras expresses black people's resentment of their degradation and celebrates black identity:
"Don't deny you'self! It took a billion gallons of black blood to
make you. Recognize you'self inside and you wan the king among
men! . . . You black and beautiful—don't let 'em tell you different!" [38]
Despite Ras' strong emotional appeal, the protagonist rejects
the nationalist movement. Intellectually, he recognizes that an attempt to build a black world without white allies "will get you
lost in the backwash of history." [39] He sees Ras as short-sighted,
"outside history," and unable to achieve power because, as another character puts it, he turns his back on history.

The role the protagonist accepts is that offered by Jack, the
dominating white leader of the Brotherhood, the anonym Ellison assigns the Communist Party. Jack becomes a significant model
for the protagonist in the longest, most critical cycle of the book.
It is also the only cycle which Ellison writes with unrestrained
bitterness, perhaps because the Party's program was initially so
attractive and his ultimate disappointment correspondingly great.
The Brotherhood preaches a "brotherly" integrative approach to
human problems, promising to bring black Americans "inside
history" to share in influence, power, and dignity. This approach
would assure the end of the holistic mold into which black Americans are born and expresses the idealist progressive concept of

man's movement through history towards Liberty and Equality on a measurable scale.

Initially, Ellison's hero finds his Brotherhood role as spokesman for the Harlem district enormously satisfying. He is given a new name—a new identity—and recognized for his oratorical ability to express the discontent of the black community. His deepest gratification, however, springs from the feeling that he is helping his people in their struggle against oppression and from the new ties he makes in the black community. In a mass meeting he transfixes the audience with an account of how he feels about Brotherhood membership, a conversion speech reminiscent of religious revivals: "*Something strange and miraculous and transforming is taking place in me right now. . . .* I feel suddenly that I have become *more human. . . .* I feel that I've found my true family!" [40]

Why did he say he found himself "more human," he later asks himself. What was so fulfilling? The answer, a reassertion of the progressive theme, is that he found in the Brotherhood

a way that didn't lead through the back door, a way not limited by black and white . . . [that] could lead to the highest possible rewards . . . a way to have a part in making the big decisions, of seeing through the mystery of how the country, the world, really operated . . . the possibility of being more than a member of a race.[41]

This passage is reminiscent of Mrs. Lightfoot Lee's search for the roots of power in Henry Adams' *Democracy.*

His personal satisfaction in his role, however, is not what interests the Brotherhood leaders; they intend to mold him to serve their organization's needs. They criticize his "more human" speech as lacking in the Brotherhood's "scientific" view of history. To discipline him, the Brotherhood leadership committee sends him out of Harlem, thus destroying his identification and ties with black people. The sacrifice of these relationships seriously threatens the protagonist's view of himself and his role. At a

crucial point Jack, the Brotherhood leader, reveals that he too has
made a sacrifice in fulfilling his duty to the Brotherhood. To
dramatize that sacrifice, Jack removes his glass eye and contrasts
his own sense of discipline with the "personal responsibility" that
the protagonist espouses. That's what discipline means, says Jack,
"sacrifice, *sacrifice*, SACRIFICE!" [42] Ellison often writes on several
levels simultaneously. On a symbolic level Jack's sacrifice has
transformed him into a kyklops, Homer's monstrous man-eater.
The basic complaint of the protagonist is that the Brotherhood
sees him as a tool, not as a human being.

On being ordered back to Harlem from his "discipline" tour,
the protagonist finds himself out of touch with its people. They
are uncertain of him and the Brotherhood. Unbeknownst to him,
the Brotherhood has abandoned the struggles in Harlem to "protect our gains" nationally and internationally.[43] The protagonist
thus finds that he is only a shallow bit-player, without human
identity, literally a mouthpiece "hired to talk," and remote from
decision-making committees. It is a shattering, disillusioning discovery. For a while, though, the protagonist continues in the
Brotherhood, feeling he will never be the same yet hoping to get
revenge on its leaders.

Many other black members have quit the Brotherhood out of
disillusionment. The most significant is Tod Clifton, a dedicated
activist, who emerges at this juncture as a significant model. Tod
Clifton has disappeared; to replace him the Brotherhood leadership has summoned the protagonist back to Harlem. He finds Tod
(whose name means "death" in German) peddling paper Sambo
dancing dolls, symbols of a servile past; such behavior is inexplicable to the protagonist. He then sees Tod deliberately provoke
a policeman, who shoots him dead. Like a Malraux character, Tod
chooses death as though, by this sacrifice, he may redeem his own
association with the Brotherhood in misleading the people of
Harlem. Although the protagonist feels that a part of him dies
with Tod Clifton, he realizes that Tod's redemptive sacrifice is

a Ras-like plunge outside history and he continues in his determination to destroy the Brotherhood from within.

Appearing belatedly and mysteriously, negatively defined by the
assumptions of others and never seen in person, Rinehart the
imposter is a unique model. Rinehart does not represent, as
Bledsoe, Jack, Ras, and others do, a well-recognized, institutionalized, societal form of expression. Instead he is the cynical ex-
ploiter of *any* of the needs of urban black people at any level.
Where others, such as Bledsoe or Jack, want to reorganize and
control society according to their lights, Rinehart simply exploits
its chaos. He is more passive, more individual than the other role
models, playing many different parts with different people. Rinehart is a pimp, a gambler, a minister, a parasitical racketeer, a
lover, and a scoundrel. Nothing matters to him but the opportunity of the moment; he is the consummate confidence man.

Such a role fascinates and attracts the protagonist. Disillusioned
and enraged by the Brotherhood's abandonment of the cause of
black people, he discovers his own invisibility and decides to "do
a Rinehart" within the Brotherhood. He thus hopes to destroy
the Brotherhood leadership by providing them with information
that is false but satisfies their ideological beliefs, justifying this
with his grandfather's advice to "overcome 'em with yeses." "You
don't have to worry about the people," he tells himself. "If they
tolerate Rinehart, then they will forget it and even with them
you are invisible." [44] He shocks even himself with this lapse of
conscience.

The test of his cynicism comes during the explosion of the
apocalyptic riot that arises from the unresolved fury of Harlem
people over the police killing of Tod Clifton. The protagonist
comes to a new understanding and acceptance of himself: "I was
my experiences and my experiences were me." [45] He sees that by
doing "a Rinehart" [46] with the Brotherhood leadership, seeming
to agree with them, he shares responsibility for their schemes. In
a confrontation with Ras, who is trying to transform the riot into

a shooting war against the whites, he tries both to stop Ras and to expose the Brotherhood. In a paranoid rage about the Brotherhood, he denounces it for creating the riot and assails Ras as a "destroyer" whose call for war will only result in more black people dying. Ras orders his followers to hang the protagonist as a traitor. Rather than sacrifice his life uselessly, he flees, plunging "outside history" into the coal cellar where the book finds him in its opening and leaves him at its end.

By diving into the coal cellar the protagonist completes his rejection of the role models, in all of which Ellison has related identity to power; without power there is no identity—and no satisfaction. The invisible man comes to the end of his Odyssey unable to find a role endowed with power that his conscience and his feelings will accept.

The most critical scene in the book in terms of the protagonist's quest for self-definition in history is the eviction scene, which occurs immediately after he has lost his Southern identity by lobotomy in the "factory" hospital. Unemployed, bewildered by what has happened to him, taken in off the streets by a motherly Harlem woman, the protagonist is strikingly human and no longer "ashamed of the things I had always loved." [47]

In this receptive state he encounters an aged black husband and wife being evicted from their home by white city marshals. Their shabby belongings clutter the Harlem street while a sullen, angry crowd gathers. A feeling of outrage wells up in him. In the dirty white snow he sees the "free papers" of an ancestor of one of the old folks. After reading it, he feels "as though I myself was being dispossessed of some painful yet precious thing which I could not bear to lose. . . ." [48]

The strength of his indignation frees him to act. In a short, spontaneous speech he demands the right for all to pray in the emptied apartment. When this is denied, the aroused crowd pushes aside the marshals and restores the old couple and their belongings to their home.

This is the most significant individual action that the hero takes. His speech unites the past and present in an assertion of black human rights. Guided for once by his feelings, he surmounts his anxious need to please others and frees himself from his passive, dependent, and role-conscious pattern. Breaking the holist mold, he achieves an identity and power. He is the man others turn to, seek out, praise, and about whom the newspapers write. Yet this progressive development, which arises from his unanalyzed and unintellectualized human feelings, is not continued. Instead, the speech brings him to the attention of the Brotherhood, which sees him as material for a special kind of role—its mouthpiece—and once again he falls into a role created by others.

The coal cellar in which the protagonist ends up establishes, from the first pages of *Invisible Man*, the symbolic motif of the "underground" man (a descendant of Dostoevsky's paradoxicalist), which suggests hidden identities about to emerge, unseen realities, the infinite possibilities of a man in a hole. The expectations aroused by the invisible man's continual promises of action endow the novel with an unusual degree of tension. (It also should not be overlooked that in 1952, when *Invisible Man* appeared, the idea of the "underground" had an additional connotation of heroism from the memory of the underground fighters, many of whom were intellectuals, against the Nazi armies of occupation.) From the beginning, action against the tyranny that denies the protagonist his humanity seems just about to begin.

But it never comes. Ellison's invisible man, sunk in passivity and sorry for himself because of his self-critical "honesty," is incapable of action, forever intellectually undermining whatever scheme or emotion might commit him to some liberating action. Thus immobilized, he celebrates the "freedom" of the cellar. Ellison leaves unanswered the question of whether his freedom is real or perverse, or whether, as in Dostoevsky's equation—the freedom to say $2 \times 2 = 5$—perverse freedom is the only real kind. Reality itself seems at stake in the coal hole; the invisible protagonist needs 1369 light bulbs to reassure himself of his real existence. While his passivity in the cellar has provided him a refuge, he has known no peace. His constant intellectualizing paralyzes and torments him.

Consequently his efforts at self-confrontation inevitably fail. "But what do I really want, I've asked myself. Certainly not the freedom of a Rinehart or the power of a Jack, nor simply the freedom not to run. No, but the next step I couldn't make, so I've remained in the hole." [49] His fear that his feelings cannot be trusted to guide him because they are "absurd" and "boomerang" prevents the emotional identification with his past that would thrust him into action, as happened for a moment when he spoke out at the eviction scene.

Instead he seeks the lesson of his life by writing it all down, thus creating the novel. But as he puts it all down, "the old fascination with playing a role returns" [50]—and a role is always determined by others in *Invisible Man*, never by the protagonist. Trying to achieve a balanced understanding of all the characters in his experiences, Ellison's invisible man identifies with all of them. The very act of writing, he reveals, "has confused me and negated some of the anger and some of the bitterness. . . . in spite of all I find that I love. In order to get some of it down I *have* to love. . . ." [51] His effort to discover a guide to action in his own history thus fails, because he only finds himself locked more deeply into the confused ambivalence that has characterized his life.

In the epilogue the protagonist tries anew to decide what his grandfather's deathbed declaration really meant and concludes—leaving much undefined—that the old man "*must* have meant the principle, that we were to affirm the principle on which the country was built and not the men, or at least not the men who did the violence." [52] Presumably the violence was done to black people, and the principle means egalitarian democracy and liberty.

In all this, his intellectuality is no help. At best he moves towards an uncertain, vague pluralism, saying only: "America is woven of many strands; I would recognize them and let it so remain. . . . Our fate is to become one, yet many. . . ." [53] He is not really able to define the course that can reconcile America's ideals and its racial diversity. That Ellison sees this to be white America's problem is made clear by his choice of a quote from Melville's *Benito Cereno* for an epigraph to his novel: "What has cast such a shadow upon you?"

Ellison's protagonist is in marked contrast to the hero of that other novel of political disillusionment, Warren's *All the King's Men*, who matures through his struggles and becomes increasingly able to act alone "in the awful responsibility of Time." [54] Ostensibly recognizing his failure, Ellison's protagonist still promises action, asserting the "possibility that even an invisible man has a socially responsible role to play." [55] Yet the question that Ellison, circling back again, asks in the last lines of the novel reflects the protagonist's paralyzing inability to identify with his own history and expresses the fear that that is the case for all Americans—that despite their democratic history they are unable to act in the face of the denial of humanity to black people. "And it is this which frightens me: Who knows but that, on the lower frequencies, I speak for you?" [56] Whatever the affirmative accents of the epilogue, the alternatives for the individual of conscience could hardly be more frightening.

⤳ Mailer: Participating Guest Star in the History of the Present

In a way different from Ellison's, Norman Mailer's novels of the late 1960's maintain a perilous balance between the individual conscience so central to Warren, Malamud, and Styron and the pending annihilation of the individual by history that obsesses Barth and Pynchon. The cracks in the nineteenth-century structures that began to show in the works of Adams and Crane have widened into drastically changed attitudes towards history: history as both the story of the past and the artistic means of creating and telling the story. The resistance to accepting the present as a qualitative continuum with the past, so troubling to Crèvecoeur and typical of the historical novel in the nineteenth century, has weakened considerably in the twentieth. Indeed, partly as a consequence, the historical novel has aggrandized "contemporary history" as virtually fresh subject matter. The sense of history "happening" has penetrated contemporary literary realism and no longer belongs exclusively to the past. *The Armies of the Night* (1968) epitomizes the twentieth-century tendency to view the present moment as history. The book's subtitle, "History as a Novel, The Novel as History," underlines Mailer's insistence on history *now*. Yet Mailer, whose roots are in naturalism, holds a view of history not unrelated to that of Stephen Crane. Mailer, like Crane's hero, recognized and joined a historical struggle in a self-conscious effort to gain a place for himself in history—presenting it in Crane-like terms as a primal struggle for manhood.

The Armies of the Night is an example of the so-called new journalism, highly personalized, as though subjectivity were a means towards greater objectivity. Henry Adams provides the model for this sort of autobiographic history. In the era of the omnipresent TV camera, the media participate in history and history becomes a media event. Like Burroughs in *The Naked Lunch*, Mailer diagnoses the modern disease as communication control, as he attempts to ape mass media techniques. He begins and ends his novel with extracts from a news magazine, *Time*, which represents for him the threat to literature in an age like the present, when the integrity of the work of art, and the word itself, is in danger. Mailer exposes the contradictions of this condition while himself embodying them. In a speech during the weekend of demonstrations, Mailer denounces reporters as "the silent assassins of the Republic." [57] Yet he concludes Book One with the admission that he has composed it under the same pressures of deadline that plague the news writer: "he wrote of necessity at a rate faster than he had ever written before, as if the accelerating history of the country forbade deliberation." [58]

Mailer divides his account of the anti-war demonstrations at the Pentagon in the fall of 1967 into two parts: one called "history," the other "novel." In Book One, "History as a Novel: The Steps of the Pentagon," Mailer—his opinions on everyone and everything, his motives and hesitations—is at center stage. Like the hero of the classic historical novel as defined by Lukács, Mailer is at the fringe of the main events, which he records only insofar as they impinge upon his experience. In Book Two, "The Novel as History: The Battle of the Pentagon," the personality of the narrator is submerged in a well-researched account of what went on without Mailer. The designation of the personal account as a "history" and the objective account as a "novel" may appear paradoxical, but it is highly revelatory of Mailer's conception of historical writing. Book One, as Mailer puts it, is "history in the guise or dress or manifest of a novel" because it was written "to the best of the author's memory scrupulous to facts and therefore a document. . . ." [59] Mailer insists that there is something mysterious about the collective events described in Book Two and that "only the instincts of the novelist" can provide an explanation. Existential history, that is, can only be a novel, for

the difficulty is that the history is interior—no documents can give sufficient intimation: the novel must replace history at precisely that point where experience is sufficiently emotional, spiritual, psychical, moral, existential, or supernatural to expose the fact that the historian in pursuing the experience would be obliged to quit the clearly demarcated limits of historic inquiry. [60]

His commentary on American manners and his appreciation of nuance notwithstanding, Mailer is basically a progressive. His comic hero, the narrator, is not a role-player, but a self-created man. Mailer's creation of himself as a persona begins in *Advertisements for Myself* (1959) and continues throughout his books of the 1960's—*The Presidential Papers, Cannibals and Christians, The Armies of the Night, Why Are We in Vietnam?* and *Miami and the Siege of Chicago.* Referring with some irony to the feelings which compel him to be where the action is, Mailer dubs himself the "Participant" in *The Armies of the Night.* Barth's Ebenezer Cooke begins his existence with the choice of a role; Mailer's persona is recreated by each of his thousands of choices. His uniqueness and egotism are all-important. He is, however, not meant to be idiosyncratic, but is an attempt to deal expressively with the *whole* meaning of experience. As with the Great Men of Bancroft's progressive history, where there is most personality there is least individuality. Like Bancroft's Washington, Mailer's persona is characterized by a kind of "negative capability." The artist *can be* one with the statesman. Quoting Jean Malaquais, Mailer claims he can pierce any mind—except that of a superior novelist.[61] In *Why Are We in Vietnam?* Mailer enters the soul of Texas in Vietnam; and he has essayed the same feat in every book since *The Naked and the Dead,* always in flight from his origins as the nice Jewish boy from Brooklyn.

In contrast to *The Sot-Weed Factor,* where the revolutionary question is an incidental way of flirting with the apocalypse, this question is central to *The Armies of the Night.* Mailer's novel works *away from* the sense of elaborate and articulated social relations with which it begins. In the early scenes conversations are enormously pregnant with suggestion, but little is said. The book works towards a revelation of American society in the progressive's terms of two opposing sides, two cultures—middle-class counter-culture and working-class authoritarianism—as well as two sets of ideas.

Mailer conceives of struggle between the two sides in terms of confrontation: Mailer versus the Nazi, the young demonstrators versus the troops. Progressivism poses a dilemma for Mailer: the danger of the confrontation is that it will empty an encounter of content. Mailer and the Nazi could eyeball one another in a bar-room fight over anything.

Confrontation holds real meaning only in "The Novel as History" in the clash between troops and kids, the "Armies of the Night." Despite the bloodshed, their confrontation is symbolic and is itself all in all. It need not (and does not) ever end in domination or possession of the source of power. Every brick, every step of the Pentagon contributes to its freight of symbolic meaning—the architectural expression of totalitarianism in its corporate liberal phase. The demonstrators cannot make the Pentagon levitate, nor can they even penetrate it. This is the crisis, for even if they did succeed in getting past the outer halls, the building is "undifferentiated as a jelly fish" and they would not be able to discover its power center:

it was impossible to locate the symbolic loins of the building—para-digm of the modern world indeed, they could explore every inch of their foe and know nothing about him; the twentieth century was in the process of removing the last of man's power from his senses in order to store power in piled banks of coded knowledge. The essence of coded knowledge was that it could be made available to all because only a few had the code to comprehend it.[62]

In *Why Are We in Vietnam?* Mailer probes the psychology of the American warmakers, hunters who render the hunt unfair by their technology of overkill.[63] The title of that book is an his-torical question, and Mailer frames the answer in terms of the classic American literary tradition from *Moby Dick* to *The Bear*. The title is a deliberate joke. Yet Mailer's intent is serious: he seeks a usable past in the literary tradition, a guide to a sane and viable historical consciousness of the present in the poetic con-sciousness of the past.

There is a deep ambiguity in Mailer's progressivism. Ostensibly he wants to disrupt the totalitarian expression of a totalitarian war. The Pentagon demonstration of *The Armies of the Night*, however, attracts him by its very unpredictability. Though a Marxist heretic at heart, Mailer shares Ellison's distaste for the Old Left's "sound-as-brickwork-logic-of-the-next-step." [64] The Yippies' invocation of magical assistance and ancient lore seems more appropriate to Mailer than Old Left cunning. The "mystery" returns to politics. If he calls the demonstrators an army, it is only to enhance the contrast between them and the government forces. Mailer is filled with both admiration and horror at the spectacle of this new generation of middle-class young people who, united by nothing stronger than their hatred of "the authority," are willing without any military preparations to risk their heads in an assault on the most mighty military establishment in the world. Yet for them, as for Mailer, the confrontation, finally, has only self-reference. The outcome of their action is never closely calculated; at the end they only know better who they are. As for Mailer himself, one is never entirely convinced that he is interested in an army for collective action rather than as an extension of his ego. He is a participant of an odd kind—neither private nor general, but a kind of special guest, the media star. The weekend's climax for the Mailer persona comes with his arrest, "his Rubicon"—to an uncertain future. [65]

AFTERWORD

I T is easy to point to the force of historical analogy permeating many contemporary novels. It is less easy to recognize the extent to which the historical novel is a political act in the case of authors whose own historical experience one does not intimately share. In the case of "classic" American literature, where all sense of "topicality" is lost, criticism has tended to ignore the basic historical relationship, that of the past to the storyteller's present, in order to relate both to patterns of life and art that presumably are eternal.

One can do this more readily with *Invisible Man* than with the background of the Anti-Rent troubles behind the Littlepage trilogy, the analogy between Hawthorne's dark enthusiasts and mid-nineteenth-century Abolitionists, the specter of the compromise of 1877 behind *The Grandissimes*, the strikes of that year behind *The Duke of Stockbridge*, and the Haymarket hangings behind both *A Connecticut Yankee* and *Billy Budd*—all these "non-literary" circumstances are difficult to relate with precision to the texts of the novels as one reads them today. Yet one's sense of those circumstances is as vital to an appreciation of these books as awareness of the structures of the historical imagination is to understanding their form. A deeper assessment of the art of the historical novel will not be attained until the vision of the past created by novelists is itself approached historically.

And it is plain that the varieties of the historical novel that appeared in nineteenth-century America by no means exhaust the possibilities of this form of art. A survey of the French, the Russian, and even the English historical novel over the same years might uncover very different imaginative structures than appeared in America. Certainly the attitudes towards history and the tensions they produce in art would not be the same. This would particularly be true, one suspects, in Russia, where the socialist revolution has completely altered not only the life of the people, but their culture and their consciousness of their history.

These considerations indicate a major field of study and make it clear that it is far too early to propose a universal definition of the form of the historical novel—even in America.

NOTES

Chapter One
INTRODUCTION

1. Lionel Trilling, "Manners, Morals and the Novel," *The Liberal Imagination* (New York: Viking, 1950), p. 213.
2. Richard Chase, *The American Novel and Its Tradition* (Garden City, N.Y.: Doubleday, 1957).
3. Cf. Leo Marx, *The Machine in the Garden* (New York: Oxford University Press, 1964).
4. J. Hector St. John de Crèvecoeur, *Letters from an American Farmer and Sketches of Eighteenth-Century America* (New York: New American Library, 1963), Letter IX, p. 162.
5. *Ibid.*, p. 167.
6. *Ibid.*, pp. 167–68.
7. Henry David Thoreau, *A Week on the Concord and Merrimack Rivers* (New York: Holt, Rinehart and Winston, 1963), "Thursday," pp. 273–74.
8. *Ibid.*, p. 275.
9. *Ibid.*
10. R. G. Collingwood, *The Idea of History* (London: Oxford University Press, 1969). First published by the Clarendon Press, 1946.
11. Claude Lévi-Strauss, "The Structural Study of Myth," in *Structural Anthropology* (New York, London: Basic Books, 1963), p. 209.
12. Roy Harvey Pearce, *Savagism and Civilization* (Baltimore: Johns Hopkins University Press, 1953).
13. Roger B. Salomon, *Twain and the Image of History* (New Haven: Yale University Press, 1961); Henry Nash Smith, *Mark Twain's Fable of Progress* (New Brunswick, N.J.: Rutgers University Press, 1964).

14. David Levin, *In Defense of Historical Literature* (New York: Hill and Wang, 1967), p. 77.
15. For some of the livelier attacks, see John Henrik Clarke, ed., *William Styron's Nat Turner: Ten Black Writers Respond* (Boston: Beacon, 1968). For the defense on grounds of historical "accuracy," see Eugene Genovese's review of the Clarke volume in *The New York Review of Books*, Vol. XI, No. 4 (Sept. 12, 1968).
16. For an interesting effort to relate the techniques of historian and novelist, see Leo Braudy, *Narrative Form in History and Fiction: Hume, Fielding and Gibbon* (Princeton: Princeton University Press, 1970).
17. See Georg Lukács, *The Historical Novel* (Boston: Beacon, 1963), first published in Moscow, translated from the German, 1937. See also his *La Théorie du roman* (Lausanne: Gonthier, 1963), originally published in Germany in 1920, and *Studies in European Realism* (New York: Universal Library, 1964), originally published in Hungary in 1948. On the epic descent of history and the novel, see Robert Scholes and Robert Kellogg, *The Nature of Narrative* (New York: Oxford University Press, 1966).
18. See Chapter VII.
19. Erich Auerbach's analysis of Vico's contribution to the historical appreciation of the uniqueness of cultures is worth quoting extensively. The relevance of this description to the holist frame will, I hope, be clear shortly:

> [Vico's] term *il mondo delle nazioni* includes not only political history in its specific sense, but also the history of expression, of language, of script, of the arts, of religion, of law, of economics, since all these parts of human activity originate from the same conditions, i.e. the specific state of the human mind at a given time. The understanding of one of these parts of human activity at a certain stage of the development necessarily provides the key for the understanding of all the other parts. . . .
>
> According to Vico, this natural course of history has been ordained by Divine Providence which, it is true, works exclusively within history, not from without. Still, it is Divine Providence; each of the stages of historical development is necessary, perfect in itself, and good; the whole of human history is a permanent Platonic state, in spite of the continual change. Vico's form of historical perspectivism is almost exclusively normative and diachronical; he is much less interested in the individual genius of the particular peoples than were his preromantic and romantic successors.

Erich Auerbach, "Vico's Contribution to Literary Criticism," *Gesammelte Aufsätze zur Romanischen Philologie* (Berne and Munich: Francke Verlag, 1967), pp. 259–65. See also his "Vico and Aesthetic Historism,"

Scenes from the Drama of European Literature (New York: Meridian, 1959), pp. 183–98.

The "newness" of the holistic frame becomes doubtful if it is identified with the cyclical view of history—many of whose characteristics it shares. I am concerned here only with its non-cyclical nineteenth-century American manifestation. Cf. Frank Manuel, *Shapes of Philosophical History* (Stanford: Stanford University Press, 1965).

20. Though this structural approach has obvious analogies to the structural anthropology of Claude Lévi-Strauss, the use of structures here was developed quite independently. Lucien Goldmann projects a theory of literary structural analysis derived from Lukács rather than Lévi-Strauss and Roman Jakobson which would have definite affinities to the structural method of this book. See especially his "La Méthode structuraliste génétique en histoire de la littérature," in *Pour une sociologie du roman* (Paris: Gallimard, 1964).

Chapter Two
THE ROMANTIC HISTORIANS

1. E. H. Carr, *What Is History?* (New York: Knopf, 1962).

2. I derive my use of the term "functionalism" here from the writings of Talcott Parsons. My usage of the concept of Gestalt is based on Wolfgang Köhler, and especially his *Gestalt Psychology* (New York: New American Library, 1959). The kinship between holism and such significant post-war trends in the social sciences as pluralism in political science, structuralism in anthropology, and revisionist consensus historiography should be evident. All of these trends are characterized by the belief that the homeostasis of societies is the proper object of study, rather than the conflicts which result in change.

3. See Herbert Butterfield's Rankean critique of this school of history, *The Whig Interpretation of History* (New York: Norton, 1965), originally published in 1931, esp. pp. 95–102, 30–31.

4. See Russel B. Nye, *George Bancroft, Brahmin Rebel* (New York: Knopf, 1944), esp. pp. 1–60, 184–201. Cf. Peter Gay, *A Loss of Mastery: Puritan Historians in Colonial America* (Berkeley and Los Angeles: University of California Press, 1966).

5. George Bancroft, *History of the United States*, Centenary Edition (Boston: Little, Brown, 1876), V, Chapter XLVIII, p. 71.

6. George Bancroft, *History of the United States from Its Discovery* (Boston: Little, Brown, 1834), I, p. 403.

7. Bancroft, *History*, Centenary Edition, IV, p. 317.

8. For an excellent elaboration and discussion of precisely these overtones and the problems they raise for the critic, see Eric Bentley, *A Century of*

Hero-Worship (Boston: Beacon, 1957), second revised edition, especially "Foreword."

9. Bancroft, *History*, Centenary Edition, IV, Chapter XXXVII, pp. 596–98.

10. *Ibid.*, V, Chapter LXX, p. 322.

11. John Lothrop Motley, *Historic Progress and American Democracy* (New York: Charles Scribner, 1869), p. 6.

12. *Ibid.*, p. 28.

13. John Lothrop Motley, *The Rise of the Dutch Republic* (London: Everyman, 1911), III, p. 363. First published in 1855.

14. *Ibid.*, p. 367.

15. David Levin, *History as Romantic Art* (New York: Harbinger, 1963), Chapter III.

16. Cf. Motley, *Historic Progress*, in which he refers to the recent Civil War as the triumph of the Right, p. 71.

17. Pieter Geyl, "Motley and his 'Rise of the Dutch Republic,'" in *Encounters in History* (Cleveland: World, 1961).

18. See Motley, *Rise*, II, pp. 346–47.

19. Cf. Richard Chase, *The American Novel and Its Tradition* (Garden City, N.Y.: Doubleday, 1957), Chapter I and *passim*.

20. William Charvat and Michael Kraus, eds., *William Hickling Prescott* (New York: American Book, 1943), p. xlvii.

21. William Hickling Prescott, *The Conquest of Mexico and the Conquest of Peru* (New York: Random House, The Modern Library, n.d.), "Preface," p. 5. *The Conquest of Mexico* was originally published in 1843; *The Conquest of Peru* in 1847.

22. *Ibid.*

23. See Bentley, *Hero-Worship*, for a discussion of this distinction in Carlyle's own work, pp. 36–37.

24. George Plekhanov, *The Role of the Individual in History* (New York: International Publishers, 1940), p. 43.

25. William Hickling Prescott, *History of the Reign of Ferdinand and Isabella* (Philadelphia: Lippincott, 1872), originally published in 1837, I, pp. 274–75.

26. Cf. Leo Braudy, *Narrative Form in History and Fiction: Hume, Fielding and Gibbon* (Princeton: Princeton University Press, 1970), pp. 253–71, for an appreciation of the ways in which Gibbon, himself a holist historian of the decline and fall of an organic civilization, came to an appreciation of how much the "role" conception of character had meant to his own art.

27. Theodore Parker, *Works*, F. P. Cobbe, ed. (London: n.p., 1863–70), X, p. 217.

28. Lewis Henry Morgan, "Montezuma's Dinner," *North American Review*, CCLI (April, 1876), p. 308. Cf. A. F. A. Bandelier, *On the Social Or-*

ganization and Mode of Government of the Ancient Mexicans (12th Annual Report of the Peabody Museum of American Archaeology and Ethnology, Cambridge, Mass., 1879), pp. 557–699.

29. Morgan's line of progressive inquiry and speculation was most influentially popularized and continued, of course, by Frederick Engels, *The Origin of the Family, Private Property and the State* (1884). See Marvin Harris, *The Rise of Anthropological Theory* (New York: Columbia University Press, 1968), for an appraisal of the contribution of Morgan and Engels and a defense of the progressive structural imagination in anthropology.

30. Charvat and Kraus, *Prescott*, p. lii.

31. Howard Doughty, *Francis Parkman* (New York: Macmillan, 1962), cf. p. 92.

32. See Wilbur R. Jacobs, ed., *The Letters of Francis Parkman* (Norman: University of Oklahoma Press, 1960), I, pp. 190–91.

33. Francis Parkman, *The Conspiracy of Pontiac* (New York: Collier, 1962), p. 169.

34. *Ibid.*, p. 377.

35. *Ibid.*, p. 175.

36. In many ways, just as Hegel stands as the spiritual father of nineteenth-century American progressivism, so does Gibbon seem to have "created" the terms of the holist historical imagination. The theme of decline and fall, the characterization through roles, the relativism of judgment, and the contingency of causality all are typical of the holist frame.

37. Cf. W. J. Eccles, "The History of New France according to Francis Parkman," *William and Mary Quarterly*, XVIII (April, 1961), pp. 163–75. Eccles attacks Parkman for his Whig interpretation, defense of laissez-faire, Great Man theory, and social Darwinism. By imputing all the currently chic labels of historiographical denigration to Parkman—without examining any of his own social assumptions—Eccles has achieved a remarkable feat of the recommission of the sins of the fathers.

38. Francis Parkman, *The Old Regime in Canada*, Centenary Edition (Boston: Little, Brown, 1922), especially pp. 373–79.

39. John Lothrop Motley, *Merrymount: A Romance of the Massachusetts Colony* (Boston: Munroe, 1849), I, p. 3.

40. *Ibid.*, II, pp. 235–36.

41. John Lothrop Motley, "The Novels of Balzac," *North American Review*, LXV (July, 1847), pp. 85–108.

42. *Ibid.*, pp. 91–92.

43. William Hickling Prescott, "Memoir of Charles Brockden Brown, the American Novelist," *Biographical and Critical Miscellanies* (Philadelphia: Lippincott, 1879), p. 47.

44. William Hickling Prescott, "Novel-Writing," *North American Review*, XXV (July, 1827), p. 195.

45. Francis Parkman, "James Fenimore Cooper," *North American Review*, LXXIII (January, 1852).
46. Cf. Henry Adams, *The Education of Henry Adams* (New York: Random House, The Modern Library, 1931), especially Chapter XX. First published in 1918.
47. Brooks Adams, *The Emancipation of Massachusetts* (Cambridge: Harvard University Press, 1887).
48. H. Adams, *Education*, p. 382.
49. Henry Adams, *Mont-Saint-Michel and Chartres* (Garden City, N.Y.: Doubleday, n.d.), originally published 1905; see his one excursion into social and economic history in a pithy description of the lot of the French peasant, p. 259.
50. H. Adams, *Education*, p. 301.
51. Brooks Adams, *The Law of Civilization and Decay* (New York: Vintage, 1943), Chapter X, p. 243. First published in 1895.
52. H. Adams, *Mont-Saint-Michel and Chartres*, p. 422.

Chapter Three
COOPER

1. Francis Parkman, "James Fenimore Cooper," *North American Review*, LXXIII (January, 1852).
2. C. Hugh Holman, "The Influence of Scott and Cooper on Simms," *American Literature*, XXIII (May, 1951), pp. 203–18. See also Donald Davie, *The Hey-Day of Sir Walter Scott* (New York: Barnes and Noble, 1961), and Alexander Welsh, *The Hero of the Waverley Novels* (New York: Atheneum, 1968).
3. Georg Lukács, *The Historical Novel* (Boston: Beacon, 1963), first published in Moscow, translated from the German, 1937, Chapter I. Lukács' identification of Natty Bumppo as such a figure is, I think, an overextension of a good definition. Cf. pp. 64–65.
4. In this study I have omitted one class of Cooper's historical novels from consideration. These are the "nautical" novels (*The Pilot, The Wing and Wing, The Water Witch, The Two Admirals,* and *Mercedes of Castile*), which have been passed over because of their disparateness of theme, uneven quality, and less significant historical subject matter.
5. James Fenimore Cooper, *The Spy* (Philadelphia: Jacobs, n.d.), Chapter XIII, p. 181.
6. *Ibid.*, Chapter XXV, p. 315.
7. Charles A. Brady, "James Fenimore Cooper: Myth-Maker and Christian Romancer," in H. C. Gardiner, ed., *American Classics Reconsidered* (New York: Scribner's, 1958).
8. R. W. B. Lewis has fully delineated this archetype, in another context,

in "Days of Wrath and Laughter," in *Trials of the Word: Essays in Literature and the Humanistic Tradition* (New Haven: Yale University Press, 1965).

9. Constance Rourke, *American Humor* (Garden City, N.Y.: Doubleday, 1931), especially Chapter 1.

10. Cooper, *The Spy*, Chapter XXVII, p. 359.

11. *Ibid.*, Chapter XXIX, p. 369.

12. Cf. Marius Bewley, *The Eccentric Design* (New York: Columbia University Press, 1959), especially Chapter IV.

13. The only comparable project at the time was William Gilmore Simms' chronicles of the Revolution in South Carolina in seven novels. The local theme proved much more successful than Cooper's national designs. The true analogy to Simms' achievement is not *Lionel Lincoln*, of course, but Cooper's novels of New York colony and state.

14. In one scene, while seeking Lionel behind the rebel lines, the Loyalist heroine encounters a general who appears to be genuinely and thoroughly mad. Though the insane commander is probably meant by Cooper to be Charles Lee, the girl instantly assumes from his lunatic behavior that he is George Washington.

15. Bewley, *Eccentric Design*, especially pp. 48–64, and Donald A. Ringe, *James Fenimore Cooper* (New Haven: Twayne's United States Authors, 1962), especially pp. 58–68.

16. James Fenimore Cooper, *The Heidenmauer, or The Benedictines* (New York: Co-operative Publication Society, n.d.), Chapter XI, p. 175.

17. As Bewley and Ringe have indicated, the resemblance of *The Bravo* to the modern novel of totalitarianism is strong, and this may account for some of its appeal.

18. Cooper, *Heidenmauer*, Chapter XXX, p. 413.

19. Bewley, *Eccentric Design*, is rather uncritical in his acceptance of Brooks Adams as an authority on the Reformation, and while correctly pointing out the meanness of Heinrich's motives, fails to recognize that Emich and Benedictus work from an equally selfish and narrowly interested position.

20. See, for example, Twain's account of "the abandoned villain" Abelard, Chapter XV.

21. Cooper, *The Heidenmauer*, Chapter XXX, p. 413.

22. Henry Nash Smith, *Virgin Land* (New York: Vintage, 1959), first published in 1950; Chapter VI.

23. Ringe, *James Fenimore Cooper*, p. 52.

24. The splendid savage's-eye-view of the battle of Bunker Hill as related by Saucy Nick reveals—especially when compared to Cooper's masterly but traditional account of the battle in *Lionel Lincoln*—how ambiguous all Cooper's attitudes towards the Revolution had become in the intervening fifteen years.

25. D. H. Lawrence, *Studies in Classic American Literature* (Garden City, N.Y.: Doubleday, n.d.), first published in 1922; Chapter V, p. 59.
26. James Fenimore Cooper, *The Last of the Mohicans* (New York: New American Library, 1962), Chapter I, p. 11.
27. *Ibid.*, p. 13.
28. *Ibid.*, Chapter X, p. 110.
29. *Ibid.*, Chapter XVIII, p. 212.
30. *Ibid.*, Chapter XIX, p. 233.
31. For a full discussion of this ambivalent attitude towards the blessings of civilization, see Roy Harvey Pearce, *Savagism and Civilization* (Baltimore: Johns Hopkins University Press, 1953). Cf. the discussion of the sexual implications of the holistic barrier between savage and civilized in Leslie Fiedler, *Love and Death in the American Novel* (New York: Stein and Day, 1966), second edition revised. See especially discussion of *The Last of the Mohicans*, pp. 200–209.
32. Based, as A. N. Kaul has pointed out, on the labor theory of value and other strong but "progressive" foundations, in *The American Vision: Actual and Ideal Society in Nineteenth-Century Fiction* (New Haven and London: Yale University Press, 1963), Chapter III, p. 109.
33. George Dekker, *James Fenimore Cooper the Novelist* (London: Routledge & Kegan Paul, 1967), p. 227.
34. Donald Davie, *The Hey-Day of Walter Scott* (New York: Barnes and Noble, 1961), p. 9.
35. Welsh, *Hero of the Waverley Novels*.
36. James Fenimore Cooper, *Satanstoe; or, The Littlepage Manuscripts* (Garden City, N.Y.: Doubleday, n.d., Dolphin reprint of edition published by Burgess, Stringer & Co., 1845), Vol. II, Chapter V, pp. 310–11.

Chapter Four
HAWTHORNE

1. Nathaniel Hawthorne, "Alice Doane's Appeal," *The Complete Short Stories* (Garden City, N.Y.: Hanover House, 1959), p. 557.
2. *Ibid.*
3. *Ibid.*, p. 558.
4. Frederick C. Crews has a fine Freudian analysis of the tale in *The Sins of the Fathers* (New York: Oxford University Press, 1966), Chapter III.
5. Hawthorne, "Alice Doane's Appeal," p. 561.
6. *Ibid.*, p. 563. David Levin provides some valuable insights into the way in which Hawthorne uses the "specter evidence" of the Puritans in "Young Goodman Brown" in *In Defense of Historical Literature* (New York: Hill and Wang, 1967), pp. 77–87.
7. Hawthorne, "Alice Doane's Appeal," p. 563.

8. *Ibid.*

9. *Ibid.*

10. *Ibid.*, p. 564.

11. Nathaniel Hawthorne, "The Custom-House," *The Scarlet Letter*, ed. by Sculley Bradley, Richard Croom Beatty, and E. Hudson Long (New York: Norton, 1961), p. 18.

12. Nathaniel Hawthorne, "Mrs. Hutchinson," *Works*, with Introductory Notes by George Parsons Lathrop (Boston and New York: Houghton, Mifflin and Co., The Riverside Press, Cambridge, Mass., 1883), XII, p. 220.

13. *Ibid.*, p. 226.

14. *Ibid.*, p. 223.

15. *Ibid.*, p. 222.

16. *Ibid.*

17. Hawthorne, "Life of Franklin Pierce," *Complete Short Stories*, p. 415.

18. Lawrence Sargent Hall, *Hawthorne, Critic of Society* (New Haven: Yale University Press, 1944), Chapter III, "The Decade between Theory and Practice."

19. Hawthorne, "Chiefly About War Matters," *Works*, XII, p. 332.

20. Hawthorne, "Main Street," *Works*, III, p. 449.

21. The publication dates of the more important tales and sketches are: "Roger Malvin," "Gentle Boy," "Molineux" (1832); "Young Goodman Brown," "Alice Doane," "Old News," "The Gray Champion" (1835); "The Minister's Black Veil," "Merrymount," "Endicott and the Red Cross," "Old Ticonderoga" (1836); "Randolph's Portrait," "Howe's Masquerade," "Lady Eleanore's Mantle," "Old Esther Dudley" (1838); "Drowne's Wooden Image" (1844); "Main Street" (1849); "Feather-top" (1852).

22. Hawthorne, "Dr. Bullivant," *Works*, XII, p. 81.

23. Hawthorne, "The Gentle Boy," *Complete Short Stories*, p. 48.

24. *Ibid.*, p. 61.

25. I have greatly profited from the exploration of this problem in Kai T. Erikson, *Wayward Puritans: A Study in the Sociology of Deviance* (New York: John Wiley, 1966).

26. See Seymour Gross, "Hawthorne's Revision of 'The Gentle Boy,'" *American Literature*, XXVI (May, 1954), pp. 196–208, for an analysis of this schematization in Hawthorne's revision for *Twice-Told Tales*.

27. Edward Gibbon, "A Vindication of Some Passages, etc.," *Miscellaneous Works* (London: Murray, 1814), p. 599. See also pp. 599–602.

28. An economic motive is also imputed to Tobias' removal to New England, but by "bigoted Puritans," not by the narrator.

29. Hawthorne, "The Gentle Boy," *Complete Short Stories*, p. 52.

30. *Ibid.*, p. 56.

31. *Ibid.*

32. *Ibid.*, p. 61.

33. Cf. Crews, *Sins of Fathers*, and Simon Lesser, *Fiction and the Unconscious* (New York: Random House, 1957), esp. pp. 212–24.

34. Cf. Crews, *Sins of Fathers*, Chapter V.

35. See Lesser, *Fiction and the Unconscious*; Daniel G. Hoffman, *Form and Fable in American Fiction* (New York: Oxford University Press, 1961), Chapter VI. Also, Q. D. Leavis, "Hawthorne as Poet": Part I, *The Sewanee Review*, LIX (Spring, 1951), pp. 179–205, Part II, *The Sewanee Review*, LIX (Summer, 1951), pp. 426–58; and Roy Harvey Pearce, "Hawthorne and the Sense of the Past, or the Immortality of Major Molineux," *English Literary History*, XXI (December, 1954), pp. 327–49.

36. Hawthorne, "My Kinsman, Major Molineux," *Complete Short Stories*, pp. 519 and 521.

37. *Ibid.*, p. 526.

38. *Ibid.*, p. 529.

39. Cf. Hawthorne, "Edward Randolph's Portrait," *Complete Short Stories*, pp. 129–36.

40. Cf. Hawthorne, "The Gray Champion," *Complete Short Stories*, pp. 21–25.

41. Hawthorne, "Major Molineux," *Complete Short Stories*, p. 524.

42. *Ibid.*, p. 528.

43. *Ibid.*, p. 529.

44. Quoted in Randall Stewart, "Hawthorne's Contributions to *The Salem Advertiser*," *American Literature*, V (January, 1934), pp. 331–32.

45. Hawthorne, *The Scarlet Letter*, Chapter II, p. 44.

46. *Ibid.*, p. 40.

47. *Ibid.*, p. 46.

48. *Ibid.*, Chapter III, p. 50.

49. *Ibid.*, Chapter XII, p. 109.

50. *Ibid.*, p. 110.

51. *Ibid.*, Chapter XIII, pp. 117–18.

52. *Ibid.*, Chapter VIII, pp. 79–80.

53. *Ibid.*, Chapter IX, p. 87.

54. For a very extensive analysis of the references to the Overbury affair see Alfred S. Reid, *The Yellow Ruff and The Scarlet Letter* (Gainesville: University of Florida Press, 1955), and Reid, ed., *Sir Thomas Overbury's Vision and Other English Sources of The Scarlet Letter* (Gainesville: Scholars' Facsimiles, 1957). The "sources" of *The Scarlet Letter* in English and American annals and documents have received considerable attention from scholars, and these "sources" illuminate the genesis of the tale in many ways. It is important, in analyzing such "sources," to remember that they are not "history" upon which the author draws for "fiction"

but that they are merely primary documents that must be recreated by the author's imagination in the same way that the author's other reading and experience of life is recreated in fiction. When he draws our attention to the "historical sources," however, as Hawthorne certainly does with Chillingworth and the Overbury affair, it is because the resonance gained by opening a window on the Actual has some special meaning in the novel. See Charles Boewe and Murray G. Murphey, "Hester Prynne in History," *American Literature*, XXXII (May, 1960), pp. 202–4.

55. Hawthorne, *The Scarlet Letter*, Chapter XIV, p. 126. The priest Claude Frollo in Hugo's *Nôtre-Dame de Paris* (1834) might very well be a melodramatic model for Chillingworth, especially in his explicit fatalism. There are other indications of possible influence or shared direction in the development of the holist historical novel by Hugo and Hawthorne. The presentation of a whole culture which was *not* in overt conflict with outsiders, but rather was struggling with deviant behavior, is one such. The spatial terms—scaffolds and towers as points of vantage—are also an element shared by *The Scarlet Letter* and *Nôtre-Dame de Paris*.

56. D. H. Lawrence, *Studies in Classic American Literature* (Garden City, N.Y.: Doubleday, n.d.), Chapter VII, p. 110.

57. Hawthorne, *The Scarlet Letter*, Chapter IX, p. 90.

58. *Ibid.*, Chapter X, p. 97.

59. *Ibid.*, Chapter XI, p. 104.

60. *Ibid.*, Chapter XIII, p. 118.

61. *Ibid.*, p. 119.

62. *Ibid.*

63. Hawthorne, "Chiefly About War Matters," *Works*, XII, p. 328.

64. Hawthorne, *The Scarlet Letter*, Chapter XIII, p. 120. The meaning of Mistress Hibbens' interest in Hester (and later in Dimmesdale) would seem to have great relevance to an interpretation of Hester's character emphasizing *The Scarlet Letter* as an historical novel. After Hester's vociferous defense of her right to keep her child from Bellingham and Wilson, "it is averred" that she is accosted by Mistress Hibbens (Chapter VII). Hester then swears that if her child had been taken from her, "I would willingly have gone with thee into the forest, and signed my name in the Black Man's book, and that with my own blood!" Those critics who make much of Mistress Hibbens ignore the fact that it is only "averred" that the interview took place and that Hawthorne says we may only draw definite conclusions "if we suppose this interview betwixt Mistress Hibbens to be authentic and not a parable." We are faced by a predominantly social, not supernatural or theological, problem in the chapter surrounding Hester's visit to the Governor's mansion. The meaning of the "parable" of the conversation is surely (unless not only the Puritans, but Hawthorne and his audience, *believe* in witches and "the

Black Man") that Hester was saved from the fate of an "enthusiast"—
a fanatic deviant—by being allowed to retain her child, and was thus
preserved from the career of a Mistress Hibbens, an Anne Hutchinson, or
a Catherine.
65. *Ibid.*, Chapter VI, p. 67.
66. *Ibid.*, Chapter XXI, p. 165.
67. Hawthorne, "Mrs. Hutchinson," *Works*, XII, p. 223.
68. Hawthorne, *The Scarlet Letter*, Chapter XXIII, p. 176.
69. *Ibid.*, Chapter XXI, p. 163.
70. *Ibid.*, Chapter II, p. 45.

Chapter Five
MELVILLE

1. Howard Doughty, *Francis Parkman* (New York: Macmillan, 1962), has a
   brilliant analysis of the similarities of *Typee* and *The Oregon Trail*, p. 158.
2. Herman Melville, *Typee: A Peep at Polynesian Life* (New York: Avon
   Publications, n.d.), originally published in 1846, p. 197.
3. Herman Melville, *Moby Dick or The Whale* (Indianapolis, New York,
   Kansas City: Bobbs-Merrill Company, 1964), originally published in
   1851, p. 96.
4. See A. N. Kaul, *The American Vision: Actual and Ideal Society in Nineteenth-Century Fiction* (New Haven and London: Yale University Press,
   1963), for a thoughtful discussion of the theme of escape from history
   in American literature.
5. Merrell R. Davis, *Mardi: A Chartless Voyage* (New Haven: Yale University Press, 1960), pp. 45–59, 77–99, 142–59.
6. Herman Melville, *Mardi—And A Voyage Thither* (London: Constable,
   1922), p. 242.
7. *Ibid.*, pp. 242–43.
8. F. O. Matthiessen, *American Renaissance* (New York: Oxford University
   Press, 1941), p. 396.
9. Perry Miller, *The Raven and the Whale* (New York: Harcourt Brace &
   World, 1956), and John Stafford, *The Literary Criticism of Young America* (Berkeley: University of California Press, 1952), are the fullest studies
   of this group of writers and their associates.
10. See William H. Gilman, *Melville's Early Life and "Redburn"* (New
    York: New York University Press, 1951), pp. 136–39, for a description
    of Duyckinck on the Grand Tour in Liverpool at the same time Melville
    was exploring the low life of the city as a common sailor.
11. Richard Moody, *Edwin Forrest* (New York: Knopf, 1960), p. 281.
12. An American Citizen, *A Rejoinder to the Replies from England,
    Etc!* . . . (New York: Stringer and Townsend, 1849), p. 112.

13. I discuss the effects of the riot on the other Young Americans and go into other aspects of the affair more fully in my "Young America and the Astor Place Riot" (unpublished Master's essay, Columbia University, 1963).

14. *Ibid.*, especially pp. 126–34.

15. Melville composed both novels between April and September, 1849.

16. William Wordsworth, *Selected Poems and Preludes* (Boston: Houghton Mifflin Co., 1965), *The Prelude*, Book XI, lines 142–44, p. 333.

17. Herman Melville, *White Jacket* (New York: Grove Press, n.d.), originally published in 1850, Chapters XLVI, p. 193, and XLIX, p. 203.

18. *Ibid.*, Chapter XXXVI, p. 151.

19. Herman Melville, *Pierre, or The Ambiguities* (New York: Grove Press, 1957), pp. 293–300.

20. Melville, *Moby Dick*, Chapter LIV.

21. *Ibid.*, p. 322.

22. *Ibid.*, Chapter CXXIII.

23. *Ibid.*, Chapter XLI, p. 239.

24. *Ibid.*, Chapter XXXIII, p. 198.

25. *Ibid.*, Chapter XCIX.

26. *Ibid.*, Chapter XXXVIII, p. 228.

27. *Ibid.*, Chapter XXXVI, pp. 220–21.

28. Herman Melville, *His Fifty Years of Exile (Israel Potter)* (New York: Sagamore, 1957), Dedication, p. v. The original narrative is Israel R. Potter, *The Life and Remarkable Adventures of . . .* (Henry Trumbull, 1824).

29. *Ibid.*, Chapter V, p. 38.

30. *Ibid.*, p. 42.

31. *Ibid.*, Chapter IX, p. 72.

32. *Ibid.*, p. 74.

33. Ethan Allen, *The Narrative of Colonel Ethan Allen* (New York: Corinth, 1961), first published in 1779; John S. Barnes, ed., *Fanning's Narrative: Being the Memoirs of Nathaniel Fanning, an Officer of the Revolutionary Navy 1778–1783* (New York: Naval History Society, 1912).

34. Melville, *Israel Potter*, Chapter XXV, p. 227.

35. *Ibid.*, Chapter XXVII, p. 239.

36. *Ibid.*, p. 241, and Dedication, p. v.

37. See Kenneth Burke, *Attitudes Toward History* (2d ed. rev.; Boston: Beacon Press, 1961), originally published 1937, especially Part I.

38. Melville, *Israel Potter*, Chapter XIX, p. 170.

39. *Ibid.*, p. 186.

40. Cf. Cooper: "Civilization means a condition of society that is the *opposite* of the savage, or barbarous state" (my italics). James Fenimore Cooper, *The American Democrat* (New York: Vintage, 1956), p. 160.

41. Melville, *Israel Potter*, Chapter VIII, p. 66, and Chapter VII, p. 62.

42. Ralph Waldo Emerson, *Representative Men* (Garden City, N.Y.: Doubleday, n.d.), p. 273.
43. One must resolutely resist the temptation to read the attitudes of D. H. Lawrence or William Carlos Williams back into Melville.
44. Melville, *Israel Potter*, Chapter XV, p. 135.
45. *Ibid.*, Chapter XVIII, p. 169.
46. The mystifying and contradictory in Jones' nature had earlier been exploited by both Fanning and Cooper.
47. Melville, *Israel Potter*, Chapter XI, p. 88.
48. Emerson, *Representative Men*, p. 369.
49. Richard Chase, *Herman Melville: A Critical Study* (New York: Macmillan, 1949).
50. Herman Melville, *Great Short Works of* . . . (New York: Harper and Row, 1969), p. 242.
51. *Ibid.*, p. 272.
52. Amasa Delano, *A Narrative of Voyages and Travels, in the Northern and Southern Hemispheres: Comprising Three Voyages Round the World, Together with a Voyage of Survey and Discovery in the Pacific Ocean and Oriental Islands* (Boston: printed by E. G. House, for the author, 1817), p. 279.
53. *Ibid.*, pp. 80–81.
54. *Ibid.*, p. 325.
55. *Ibid.*, p. 320.
56. Melville, *Great Short Works of* . . . , p. 295.
57. *Ibid.*, p. 314.
58. Karl Mannheim, *Ideology and Utopia: An Introduction to the Sociology of Knowledge*, trans. by Louis Wirth and Edward Shils (New York: Harcourt, Brace and Co., 1936), pp. 94–97.
59. Herman Melville, *Collected Poems*, edited by Howard P. Vincent (Chicago: Packard and Company, 1947), p. 57.
60. Herman Melville, *White Jacket*, Chapter XXXIV, p. 143.
61. Herman Melville, "Supplement" to *Battle-Pieces* in *The Collected Poems*, p. 467.
62. The evidence presented by Hayford and Sealts to show that the historical "Preface" of *Billy Budd* may not properly be considered part of the "text" at all in no way affects the validity of my reading, though one could never claim in its absence that the French Revolution is what *Billy Budd* is "about." More significantly, the fact that Melville did *not* include it in his last draft shows at least that he was not wedded to the historical gradualism of the "Preface."
63. Herman Melville, *Billy Budd, Sailor*, edited by Harrison Hayford and Merton M. Sealts, Jr. (Chicago: University of Chicago Press, 1962), p. 54.

64. K. Burke, *Attitudes Toward History*, Part I, Chapter I.

65. Melville, *Billy Budd*, p. 54.

66. *Ibid.*, p. 55.

67. *Ibid.*

68. Edmund Burke, *Reflections on the Revolution in France* (Garden City, N.Y.: Doubleday, n.d.), originally published 1790, p. 155.

69. Thomas Paine, *Rights of Man* (Garden City, N.Y.: Doubleday, n.d.), originally published 1791, 1792, p. 445.

70. See, for example, Wendell Glick, "Expediency and Absolute Morality in *Billy Budd*," *Publications of the Modern Language Association*, LXVIII (March, 1953), pp. 103–10, for a confusion of the value of historical example to artist and to agent.

71. Melville, *Billy Budd*, p. 66.

72. "Sequel" to "At the Hostelry" in Melville, *Collected Poems*, p. 337.

73. Cf. *ibid.*, p. 58: "If thus to have adorned himself for the altar and the sacrifice were indeed vainglory, then affectation and fustian is each more heroic line in the great epics and dramas, since in such lines the poet but embodies in verse those exaltations of sentiment that a nature like Nelson, the opportunity being given, vitalizes into acts."

74. Robert Southey, *The Life of Horatio Nelson* (New York: Dutton, 1906), pp. 90–91.

75. Jay Leyda, *The Melville Log; a documentary life of Herman Melville 1819–1891* (New York: Harcourt, Brace, 1951).

76. Melville, *Billy Budd*, p. 57.

77. Another work which conforms to this formula is Hugo's 1793 (1874), and it is quite possible that the trial of Gauvain by Cimourdain at the end was a major influence on *Billy Budd*. In Hugo's novel the three main characters represent the ideas of family, humanity, and country. A comparison might well be drawn between Lantenac and Claggart, Gauvain and Billy, Vere and Cimourdain.

78. Cf. Mark Twain, *A Connecticut Yankee in King Arthur's Court* (New York: Random House, The Modern Library, n.d.), first published in 1889; Chapter XIII.

79. For a creative use of the "historical image cluster" in cultural criticism, see Jonah Raskin, "Henry James and the French Revolution," *American Quarterly* (Winter, 1965).

80. Melville, *Billy Budd*, p. 63.

81. *Ibid.*, p. 104.

82. The best modern account of this event is James Dugan, *The Great Mutiny* (New York: Putnam's, 1965).

83. Melville, *Billy Budd*, p. 76.

84. *Ibid.*, p. 115.

85. E. Burke, *Reflections*, p. 94.

86. Melville, *Billy Budd*, p. 128. Cf. p. 59: "Discontent foreran the Two Mutinies, and more or less it lurkingly survived them."
87. Melville, *Collected Poems*, p. 6.

Chapter Six
TWAIN

1. See Philip S. Foner, *Mark Twain: Social Critic* (New York: International Publishers, 1958); Roger B. Salomon, *Twain and the Image of History* (New Haven: Yale University Press, 1961); James M. Cox, "A Connecticut Yankee in King Arthur's Court: The Machinery of Self-Preservation," *Yale Review* (Autumn, 1960) and *Mark Twain: The Fate of Humor* (Princeton: Princeton University Press, 1966); and especially Henry Nash Smith, *Mark Twain's Fable of Progress: Political and Economic Ideas in "A Connecticut Yankee"* (New Brunswick, N.J.: Rutgers University Press, 1964) and *Mark Twain: The Development of a Writer* (New York: Atheneum, Reprint of edition published by Harvard University Press, 1962).
2. One of the more interesting phenomena in recent criticism of nineteenth-century fiction has been the steady effort to show Hawthorne as psychologically "normal" and Twain as unbearably fraught with conflict. I would submit that critical respect for formal perfection, not the respective behavior patterns of the two authors, has been the criterion of "normality."
3. See, respectively, Cox, "Yankee," Robert A. Wiggins, *Mark Twain: Jackleg Novelist* (Seattle: University of Washington Press, 1964), and Smith, *Fable*.
4. Salomon, *Twain and the Image of History*, p. 94.
5. See Sydney J. Krause, *Mark Twain as Critic* (Baltimore: Johns Hopkins Press, 1967), Chapters VIII and IX, for extended analyses of Twain's critiques.
6. Mark Twain, *Life on the Mississippi* (New York: Bantam Pathfinder Edition, 1963), Chapter XXXV, p. 176.
7. *Ibid.*, Chapter I, p. 3.
8. Cf. Mark Twain, "The Czar's Soliloquy," *North American Review* (March, 1905).
9. See Georg Lukács, *The Historical Novel* (Boston: Beacon, 1963), first published in the U.S.S.R. in 1937, especially pp. 86–88. Also, Isaiah Berlin, *The Hedgehog and the Fox* (New York: Mentor, 1957), and James T. Farrell, *Selected Essays* (New York: McGraw-Hill, 1964), pp. 37–118.
10. Cf. the footnotes written in the "twenty-seventh century" to Jack London's *The Iron Heel*. See Chapter VII below.
11. For an interesting variation on this theme, using an anthropological ob-

server rather than a time-traveller, see the story by George P. Elliot, "Among the Dangs" (1958).

12. Mark Twain, *Mark Twain in Eruption*, ed. Bernard De Voto (New York and London: Harper and Brothers, 1940), p. 211.

13. Mark Twain, *Personal Recollections of Joan of Arc* (New York: Harper, 1896), Preface.

14. Mark Twain, *A Connecticut Yankee in King Arthur's Court* (New York: Random House, The Modern Library, n.d.), "A Word of Explanation," p. 5.

15. Mark Twain, *Adventures of Huckleberry Finn* (New York: Norton, 1961), Chapter XXIII, p. 124.

16. *Ibid.*, p. 123.

17. At one point in the composition, Twain even promised Mrs. Fairbanks that he would not debunk the "great and beautiful *characters*" of Malory and Tennyson. One of the novel's ironies is that he kept his promise. See Justin Kaplan, *Mr. Clemens and Mark Twain* (New York: Simon & Schuster, 1966), pp. 347–48.

18. Twain, *Yankee*, Chapter I, p. 12.

19. *Ibid.*, Chapter III, p. 24.

20. *Ibid.*, Chapter II, p. 19.

21. See Robert H. Wilson, "Malory in the *Connecticut Yankee*," *University of Texas Studies in English*, XXVII (1948), pp. 185–206.

22. Twain, *Yankee*, Chapter XV, p. 122.

23. *Ibid.*, p. 121.

24. *Ibid.*, p. 119.

25. *Ibid.*, Chapter XXVIII, p. 277.

26. Erich Auerbach, *Mimesis*, trans. by Willard R. Trask (Princeton, N.J.: Princeton University Press, 1968), first published in 1946; see Chapter VI, p. 138.

27. See Kaplan, *Mr. Clemens*.

28. Cf. William Edward Hartpole Lecky, *The History of European Morals from Augustus to Charlemagne* (New York: Appleton, 1877).

29. Twain, *Yankee*, Chapter XVIII, p. 234 and ff.

30. *Ibid.*, Chapter XIII, p. 103.

31. *Ibid.*, p. 108.

32. *Ibid.*, Chapter XX, p. 171.

33. *Ibid.*, Chapter XXI, p. 189.

34. *Ibid.*, Chapter XXXI, p. 303.

35. *Ibid.*, Chapter XXXIX, p. 386.

36. *Ibid.*, Chapter XLII, p. 420.

37. Smith, *Fable*, p. 36.

Chapter Seven
BELLAMY, CABLE, JAMES, ADAMS, CRANE

1. See Erich Fromm, "Introduction," Edward Bellamy, *Looking Backward: 2000–1887* (New York: New American Library, 1960), and Daniel Aaron, *Men of Good Hope* (New York: Oxford University Press, 1951), Chapter IV.
2. Review of *Looking Backward* in *The Commonweal*, June 24, 1889.
3. Bellamy, *Looking Backward*, Chapter XVIII, p. 137.
4. See David Bleich, "Eros and Bellamy," *American Quarterly* (Fall, 1964), for this analysis based on Herbert Marcuse.
5. The novel was originally published serially in the *Berkshire Courier* in 1879, and later re-issued in bowdlerized volume form in 1901. It is presently available in an excellent edition edited by Joseph Schiffman (Cambridge: Harvard University Press, 1962).
6. Bellamy, *Looking Backward*, Chapter XXIV, p. 170.
7. Martin Buber, *Paths in Utopia* (Boston: Beacon, 1958), p. 10. On the apocalyptic strain in modern American fiction see R. W. B. Lewis, *Trials of the Word* (New Haven: Yale University Press, 1965), Chapter IX.
8. Cf. Arlin Turner, *George W. Cable* (Baton Rouge: Louisiana State University Press, 1966), pp. 47, 68, and *passim*.
9. Cf. George W. Cable, *The Grandissimes* (New York: Sagamore Press, American Century Series, 1957), p. 108. In referring to the betrayal of Negro relatives of one of the Grandissimes, Cable intends an obvious satire on the Republican Party's abandonment of the freedmen in the Compromise of 1877: "It was necessary to save the party—nay, that was a slip; we should say, to save the family; this is not a parable."
10. *Ibid.*, Chapter IV, p. 19.
11. *Ibid.*, Chapter XVIII, p. 103.
12. *Ibid.*, Chapter XXX, p. 196.
13. Richard Poirier, *A World Elsewhere: The Place of Style in American Literature* (New York: Oxford University Press, 1966), pp. 93–106. Poirier has an excellent formal analysis of *The Europeans* in his *The Comic Sense of Henry James* (New York: Oxford University Press, 1960).
14. Henry James, *Hawthorne* (Garden City, N.Y.: Doubleday), Chapter V, pp. 121–22.
15. T. S. Eliot, "Henry James," *The Shock of Recognition*, ed. Edmund Wilson (New York: Random House, The Modern Library, 1955), p. 861.
16. Henry James, *The Sense of the Past* (New York: Scribner's, 1917), pp. 48–49.
17. Henry James, *The Europeans* (New York: The New American Library, 1964), Chapter III, p. 33.
18. *Ibid.*, Chapter XII, p. 383.

19. Henry Adams, *Democracy* (Garden City, N.Y.: Doubleday, 1961), first published in 1880; Chapter I, p. 8.
20. *Ibid.*, p. 5.
21. *Ibid.*, pp. 8–9.
22. *Ibid.*, Chapter XIII, p. 203.
23. Henry Adams, *The Education of Henry Adams* (New York: Random House, The Modern Library, 1931), Chapter XVIII.
24. H. Adams, *Democracy*, Chapter IV, p. 45.
25. *Ibid.*, p. 43.
26. *Ibid.*, Chapter VI, pp. 75–76.
27. Brooks Adams, in Introduction to Henry Adams, *The Degradation of the Democratic Dogma* (New York: Macmillan, 1919), p. 35.
28. H. G. Wells, "Stephen Crane from an English Standpoint," *North American Review* (August, 1900), reprinted in Wilson, *Shock*, p. 671.
29. All Frederic's Civil War stories have been collected by Thomas F. O'Donnell, *Harold Frederic's Stories of York State* (Syracuse: Syracuse University Press, 1966).
30. See Arthur O. Lovejoy, "On the Discrimination of Romanticisms," in *Essays in the History of Ideas* (Baltimore: Johns Hopkins, 1948).
31. From an 1898 review, quoted in Edward Garnett, *Friday Nights* (New York: Knopf, 1922), p. 205.
32. Wells, "Stephen Crane," *Shock*, p. 663.
33. Stephen Crane, *The Red Badge of Courage*, ed. Richard Chase (Cambridge, Mass.: Riverside, 1960), Chapter XXIV, p. 118. This edition is based on the first edition text.
34. See Thomas A. Gullason, ed., *The Complete Novels of Stephen Crane* (Garden City, N.Y.: Doubleday, 1967), Appendix 3, p. 805. This is an uncanceled passage in the manuscript which did not appear in the first edition.
35. Mark Twain, *A Connecticut Yankee in King Arthur's Court* (New York: Random House, The Modern Library, n.d.), Chapter XXX, p. 301.
36. Crane, *Red Badge*, Chapter XIX, p. 94.
37. *Ibid.*, p. 95.
38. *Ibid.*, Chapter XXII, p. 110.
39. *Ibid.*, Chapter I, p. 5.
40. *Ibid.*, Chapter III, p. 22.
41. *Ibid.*, p. 23.
42. *Ibid.*, p. 24.
43. See E. R. Hagemann, "Crane's 'Real' War in His Short Stories," *American Quarterly*, VIII (Winter, 1956), pp. 356–67.
44. Stephen Crane, "God Rest Ye, Merry Gentlemen," *The Complete Short Stories and Sketches*, p. 542.
45. An interesting interpretation of Henry Fleming's attempt for self-defini-

tion by another standard than that of History is Gerald W. Johnson, "Stephen Crane's Metaphor of Decorum," *Publications of the Modern Language Association*, LXXVIII (June, 1963), pp. 250–56.

46. Crane, *Red Badge*, Chapter V, p. 32.

47. *Ibid.*, Chapter XI, p. 61.

48. For an interpretation which emphasizes the non-aggressive courage of Fleming's new role, see Kermit Vanderbilt and Daniel Weiss, "From Rifleman to Flagbearer: Henry Fleming's Separate Peace in *The Red Badge of Courage*," *Modern Fiction Studies*, XI (Winter, 1965–66), pp. 371–80.

49. Crane, *Red Badge*, Chapter XIX, p. 96.

Chapter Eight
THE HISTORICAL IMAGINATION IN THE
TWENTIETH CENTURY

1. Bouck White, *The Book of Daniel Drew* (New York: Frontier Press, 1969).

2. Robert Penn Warren, *Homage to Theodore Dreiser* (New York: Random House, 1971), p. 62.

3. Theodore Dreiser, *The Titan* (New York: Dell Publishing Co., 1959), p. 28. Originally published by John Lane Co. in 1914.

4. Warren, *Homage*, p. 76.

5. Edith Wharton, *The Age of Innocence* (New York: New American Library, 1962), p. 114. Originally published by D. Appleton & Co. in 1920.

6. Henry James, *The Europeans* (New York: The New American Library, 1964), Chapter XII, p. 178.

7. F. R. Leavis, "The Europeans," *Anna Karenina and Other Essays* (New York: Clarion Book, 1969), originally published in 1933; and Richard Poirier, *The Comic Sense of Henry James: A Study of the Early Novels* (New York: Oxford University Press, 1960).

8. Percy Lubbock, *The Craft of Fiction* (New York: J. Cape and H. Smith, 1929).

9. Northrop Frye, *Anatomy of Criticism* (New York: Atheneum, 1966), p. 223.

10. David Mizener, in *Twelve Great American Novels* (New York: New America Library, 1967), points to a Swiftian side to Dos Passos' use of types. This further suggests a moral stance which is closely related to the progressive position.

11. John Dos Passos, *U.S.A.* (Boston: Houghton Mifflin Company, 1960), *The Big Money*, p. 413. Originally published in three parts: *The 42nd*

Parallel (1930), *1919* (1932), and *The Big Money* (1936) and collected 1938.

12. Jean-Paul Sartre, "John Dos Passos and *1919*," *Literary and Philosophical Essays* (New York: Macmillan, 1970), p. 95. Originally published in France in 1938.

13. *Ibid.*, p. 96.

14. Henry Adams, *The Degradation of the Democratic Dogma* (New York: Macmillan, 1919). Ed. with Introduction by Brooks Adams.

15. John Dos Passos, *The Best Times: An Informal Memoir* (New York: New American Library, 1966), pp. 86–87.

16. Henry Adams, *Democracy* (Garden City, N.Y.: Doubleday, 1961).

17. John Dos Passos, "Satire as a Way of Seeing," *Occasions and Protests* (Chicago: Henry Regnery Co., 1964), p. 30.

18. Edith Wharton, *The Custom of the Country* (New York: Charles Scribner's Sons, 1913).

19. Thorstein Veblen, "The Intellectual Pre-Eminence of Jews in Modern Europe," *Essays in Our Changing Order* (New York: Viking Press, 1934), p. 227.

20. R. G. Collingwood, *The Idea of History* (London: Oxford University Press, 1969), originally published in 1946, and *Essays in the Philosophy of History* (University of Texas Press, McGraw-Hill, 1965), discuss Croce's concepts of history as well as F. H. Bradley's 1874 *Presuppositions of Critical History* (Chicago: Quadrangle Books, 1968), and his later work, *Principles of Logic* and *Appearance and Reality*.

21. Hart Crane, *The Complete Poems and Selected Letters and Prose of Hart Crane* (Garden City, N.Y.: Doubleday & Co., 1966).

22. Ralph Waldo Emerson, "History," *The Complete Essays and Other Writings of Ralph Waldo Emerson* (New York: Random House, The Modern Library, 1940), pp. 126–27.

23. In his own notes on *The Waste Land*, Eliot quoted Bradley in reference to the lines: "We think of the key, each in his prison/ Thinking of the key, each confirms a prison" as follows: "My external sensations are no less private to myself than are my thoughts or my feelings. In either case my experience falls within my own circle, a circle closed on the outside; and, with all its elements alike, every sphere is opaque to the others which surround it. . . . In brief, regarded as an existence which appears in a soul, the whole world for each is peculiar and private to that soul." (*Appearance and Reality*, p. 346.) T. S. Eliot, *The Complete Poems and Plays* (New York: Harcourt, Brace and World, Inc., 1971), p. 49 and note on p. 54.

24. As quoted by Collingwood in *The Idea of History*, p. 199; from Benedetto Croce, *Theory and History of Historiography* (London, n.p., 1921), pp. 134–35.

25. *The Letters of Hart Crane*, edited by Brom Weber (Berkeley and Los Angeles: University of California Press, 1965), pp. 124 (from a letter to Gorham Munson, Feb. 18th, 1923) and 305 (from a letter to Otto H. Kahn, Sept. 12th, 1927).

26. Crane, *Poems*, p. 94.

27. Hart Crane mentions reading Ouspensky in a letter to Allen Tate, Feb. 15, 1923: "I have also enjoyed reading Ouspensky's *Tertium Organum* lately. Its corroboration of several experiences in consciousness that I have had gave it particular interest." *Letters*, p. 124. In *Tertium Organum*, Ouspensky argues against the limitations of the positivist view that holds that material phenomena are the only knowable reality: "Gradually convinced by reason of the unreality of phenomena, or inwardly sensing this unreality and the reality which lies behind, we free ourselves from the mirage of phenomena, we begin to understand that all the phenomenal world is in substance subjective also, that the great realities lie deeper down. Then a complete change takes place in consciousness in all its concepts *about reality*. That which before was regarded as real becomes unreal, and that which was regarded as unreal becomes real.

"This transition into the absolute state of consciousness is 'UNION WITH DIVINITY,' 'VISION OF GOD,' EXPERIENCING THE 'KINGDOM OF HEAVEN,' 'ENTERING NIRVANA.'" P. D. Ouspensky, *Tertium Organum* (New York: Random House, 1970), pp. 215–16.

The place of poetry in Ouspensky's scheme would have appealed to Crane with his passion for bridging: "Poetry endeavors to express both music and thought together. The combination of feeling and thought of high tension leads to a higher form of psychic life. Thus in art we have already the first experiments in *a language of the future*. Art anticipates a psychic evolution and divines its future forms" (p. 73).

28. Crane, *Poems*, p. 193.

29. Crane, *Letters*, p. 241.

30. Willa Cather, *Not Under Forty* (New York: Alfred A. Knopf, 1936), in Prefatory Note.

31. Henry Adams, *The Education of Henry Adams* (New York: Random House, The Modern Library, 1931), Chapter XV, p. 379.

32. Georg Lukács, *The Historical Novel* (Boston: Beacon, 1963), p. 182. First published in Moscow, translated from the German, 1937.

33. Willa Cather, *Death Comes for the Archbishop* (New York: Alfred A. Knopf, 1959), pp. 289–90. Originally published in 1927.

34. *Ibid.*, p. 282.

35. William Faulkner, *Absalom, Absalom!* (New York: Random House, The Modern Library, 1951), Chapter II, p. 46. Originally published in 1936.

36. David Minter, *The Interpreted Design as a Structural Principle in American Prose* (New Haven: Yale University Press, 1969).

37. Faulkner, *Absalom, Absalom!*, Chapter VII, p. 263.
38. *Ibid.*, p. 274.
39. *Ibid.*, p. 273.
40. *Ibid.*, p. 260.
41. *Ibid.*, Chapter I, p. 11.
42. *Ibid.*, Chapter VII, p. 251.
43. Ilse Dusoir Lind, "The Design and Meaning of *Absalom, Absalom!*," *PMLA*, 60 (December, 1955).
44. Faulkner, *Absalom, Absalom!*, Chapter VII, p. 269.
45. Cleanth Brooks, *William Faulkner: The Yoknapatawpha Country* (New Haven and London: Yale University Press, 1963), pp. 314–17. The "Chronology" appended to *Absalom, Absalom!* states it as a "fact," but this was an addition Faulkner made many years later. In a lecture at Yale University in 1965, Jay H. Martin suggested that the "Chronology," like the documents at the end of Melville's *Benito Cereno*, functions as a source of ironic resonance with the text of the novel. The final narrator of the tale is farthest away from its events, academic, "objective," and unreliable.
46. In the "Epilegomena" to *The Idea of History*, R. G. Collingwood recounts a murder mystery and its solution by an inspector of Scotland Yard. He apologizes for bringing in a sample of a literary genre "beneath the dignity" of the reader, but justifies doing so because the analogy "between legal methods and historical methods is of some value for the understanding of history," or, rather, the accumulation of historical evidence (p. 268).
47. Faulkner himself practiced the form in his novel *Knight's Gambit* (1949) and in his scenario for the Hollywood film *The Big Sleep*.
48. Faulkner, *Absalom, Absalom!*, Chapter IX, p. 378.
49. *Ibid.*, Chapter VIII, p. 356.
50. *Ibid.*, Chapter VII, p. 280.
51. *Ibid.*, Chapter IX, p. 378.

Chapter Nine
LIBERAL CONSCIENCE AND APOCALYPTIC PARODY

1. R. W. B. Lewis, *Trials of the Word: Essays in American Literature and the Humanistic Tradition* (New Haven and London: Yale University Press, 1965), Chapter IX.
2. Robert Penn Warren, *All the King's Men* (New York: Bantam Books, 1955), Chapter VIII, p. 326.
3. *Ibid.*, Chapter V, p. 228.
4. *Ibid.*, Chapter X, p. 438.
5. See Richard Hofstadter, *The Paranoid Style in American Politics and Other Essays* (New York: Knopf, 1965).

6. Bernard Malamud, *The Fixer* (New York: Farrar, Straus and Giroux, 1966), Chapter VIII, p. 274.

7. See the collection of essays by ten black writers, *William Styron's Nat Turner*, edited by John Henrik Clarke (Boston: Beacon Press, 1968).

8. John Barth, *The Sot-Weed Factor* (New York: Grosset & Dunlap, Universal Library, 1964), originally published in 1960; Part III, Chapter XVIII, p. 725.

9. Henry Adams, *The Degradation of the Democratic Dogma* (New York: Macmillan, 1919).

10. Barth, *Sot-Weed Factor*, Part III, Chapter V, p. 572.

11. Henry Adams, *The Education of Henry Adams* (New York: Random House, The Modern Library, 1931), p. 382.

12. Eric Ambler, *A Coffin for Dimitrios* (New York: Bantam, 1972), Chapter II, pp. 19–20. Originally published in 1939.

13. Barth, *Sot-Weed Factor*, Part III, Chapter XIII, p. 670.

14. *Ibid.*, Chapter IX, p. 617.

15. Thomas Pynchon, V. (New York: Bantam Books, 1964), originally published in 1963; Chapter II, p. 317.

16. Mircea Eliade, *Cosmos and History: The Myth of the Eternal Return*, trans. by Willard R. Trask (New York: Harper and Row, 1959).

17. Lewis, *Trials of the Word*, Chapter IX.

18. Barth, *Sot-Weed Factor*, Part III, Chapter XVI, p. 707.

19. Pynchon, V., Chapter XIII, p. 345.

20. André Malraux, *Man's Fate* (New York: Random House, The Modern Library, 1961), p. 65.

21. Ralph Ellison, *Invisible Man* (New York: Random House, The Modern Library, 1952), Prologue, p. 3, and Epilogue, p. 439.

22. Homer, *The Odyssey*. Translated by Robert Fitzgerald (Garden City, N.Y.: Doubleday & Co., 1963), p. 156.

23. Ezra Pound, *The Cantos* (New York: A New Directions Book, 1948), originally published 1934; "Canto I," p. 4, originally published in 1917.

24. Ellison, *Invisible Man*, Prologue, p. 11.

25. *Ibid.*, Epilogue, p. 433.

26. *Ibid.*, Chapter I, p. 13.

27. *Ibid.*

28. T. S. Eliot, *The Complete Poems and Plays* (New York: Harcourt, Brace & World, 1971), p. 123.

29. Ellison, *Invisible Man*, Chapter VI, p. 107.

30. *Ibid.*, p. 110.

31. *Ibid.*, Chapter X, p. 165.

32. *Ibid.*, p. 166.

33. *Ibid.*, p. 165.

34. *Ibid.*, p. 172.

35. *Ibid.*, Chapter XI, p. 185.

36. *Ibid.*, p. 180.
37. *Ibid.*, p. 185.
38. *Ibid.*, Chapter XVII, p. 282.
39. *Ibid.*, p. 283.
40. *Ibid.*, Chapter XVI, pp. 261–62.
41. *Ibid.*, p. 268.
42. *Ibid.*, Chapter XXII, p. 359.
43. *Ibid.*, Chapter XXIII, p. 379.
44. *Ibid.*, p. 383.
45. *Ibid.*
46. *Ibid.*
47. *Ibid.*, Chapter XIII, p. 202.
48. *Ibid.*, p. 207.
49. *Ibid.*, Epilogue, p. 434.
50. *Ibid.*, p. 437.
51. *Ibid.*, pp. 437–38.
52. *Ibid.*, p. 433.
53. *Ibid.*, p. 435.
54. Warren, *All the King's Men*, p. 438.
55. Ellison, *Invisible Man*, Epilogue, p. 439.
56. *Ibid.*
57. Norman Mailer, *The Armies of the Night* (New York: New American Library, 1968), p. 64.
58. *Ibid.*, p. 241.
59. *Ibid.*, p. 284.
60. *Ibid.*
61. *Ibid.*, p. 53.
62. *Ibid.*, pp. 254–56.
63. Norman Mailer, *Why Are We in Vietnam?* (New York: G. P. Putnam's Sons, 1967).
64. Mailer, *Armies*, p. 105.
65. *Ibid.*, p. 157.

INDEX